STRATEGIC HOSPITALITY MANAGEMENT

before the last

Strategic Hospitality Management

Theory and Practice for the 1990s

Edited by

Richard Teare

and

Andrew Boer

CASSELL

First published 1991 by **Cassell Educational Limited**
Villiers House, 41–47 Strand, London WC2N 5JE, England
387 Park Avenue South, New York, NY 10016-8810, USA.

British Library Cataloguing in Publication Data
Strategic hospitality management.
 1. Hotels. Management   2. Restaurants. Management
 I. Teare, Richard   II. Boer, Andrew
 647.94068

ISBN 0-304-32535-X
ISBN 0-304-32285-7 pbk

Phototypeset by Litho Link Ltd, Welshpool, Powys, Wales
Printed and bound in Great Britain by Dotesios Ltd, Trowbridge, Wiltshire

Contents

Contributors

EDITORS

Richard Teare BSc (Hons), Ph.D., MHCIMA, Cert.Ed.
Richard Teare is Associate Head of the Department of Food and Hospitality Management at Bournemouth Polytechnic, UK, and editor of the *International Journal of Contemporary Hospitality Management*. He is also editor of a recent textbook on services management. A graduate of the University of Surrey, he has held management positions with both national and international hotel companies. He gained his Ph.D. in Business Administration from the City University Business School, London, and has undertaken a variety of research and consultancy projects for hospitality firms.

Andrew Boer BA, MBA, MHCIMA
Andrew Boer is Senior Lecturer in the Department of Food and Hospitality Management at Bournemouth Polytechnic. He is a graduate of Huddersfield Polytechnic and obtained his MBA from Brunel University. He has contributed to several case studies and articles on strategic management, and has most recently undertaken research on 'Small firms' failure in the hospitality industry'.

CONTRIBUTORS

Bob Brotherton is Senior Lecturer in Hospitality Management at Blackpool and The Fylde College. He is currently involved in a range of hospitality management education and training development projects in Turkey. His main research interests are in the area of operations management.

Simon Crawford-Welch is Assistant Professor of Marketing and Research at the William F. Harrah College of Hotel Administration, University of Las Vegas, USA, and editor of the *Journal of Restaurant and Foodservice Marketing*. He received his Ph.D. with a major in strategic management from Virginia Polytechnic Institute and State University.

The Hon. Rocco Forte is a graduate of Oxford University and is Chief Executive of Trusthouse Forte plc, one of the world's most successful multinational hospitality firms.

Paul R. Gamble is Professor and Dean of the Faculty of Human Studies and Director of the Surrey European Management School at the University of Surrey, where he also obtained his Ph.D. He has published several books and many papers on aspects of hospitality and tourism planning, development and operations.

Evert Gummesson obtained his Ph.D. at the University of Stockholm and is Professor of Service Management and Marketing at the Service Research Center (CTF). He also works for the Scandinavian consulting firm Cicero Executive and is a member of the Faculties of the University of Stockholm, the Gothenburg School of Economics, Sweden, and the Swedish School of Economics and Business Administration, Helsinki, Finland.

Terry Hudson is Assistant Dean, Programme of Consumer and Leisure Studies at Leeds Polytechnic. He has extensive management experience in both the public and private sectors of industry, and his research interests are in the areas of financial management, strategic management and franchising.

Stephanie M. Jameson is Senior Lecturer in the Department of Hotel and Catering Studies at Huddersfield Polytechnic, where she obtained her M.Phil. degree for research in industrial relations. She also works for the Commission for Racial Equality. Her main research interest is graduate recruitment in the hospitality industry.

Nick Johns is Reader in Hospitality Studies at the Norwich Hotel School. A graduate of the University of Surrey, he obtained his Ph.D. at Loughborough University and has written widely on scientific, educational and management topics including a book on food hygiene management. His research interests include systems planning and design, productivity management and quality management.

Peter A. Jones is Head of the Department of Food and Hospitality Management at Bournemouth Polytechnic and was formerly a Lieutenant-Colonel in the Army Catering Corps. A graduate of the University of Surrey, he obtained his M.Phil. degree for researching and developing a catering information system which is used in both Army and Royal Air Force units worldwide. His areas of research interest are information systems, quality systems, strategic planning and management development in the hospitality industry.

David Leslie is Senior Lecturer in the Department of Hospitality Management at Leeds Polytechnic. Prior to his present position he worked for many years as an operations manager in the hospitality industry before taking up a lectureship at the University of Ulster. His main area of research interest is the application of information technology to aid managerial planning and decision making.

David Litteljohn lectures in Hospitality Management at Napier Polytechnic of Edinburgh. His main research interests are in the strategic and marketing aspects of internationalization, and he has authored many reports, articles and book chapters which provide management and economic interpretations of the hospitality industry.

J. John Lennon is Lecturer at the Scottish Hotel School, University of Strathclyde, and formerly held several management posts in the hospitality industry. He has a range of research and writing interests, including the application of retailing techniques to the management of hospitality operations.

Michael D. Olsen is Professor and Head of the Department of Hotel, Restaurant and Institutional Management at Virginia Polytechnic Institute and State University, USA, where he also obtained his Ph.D. He is the Founding President of the International Academy of Hospitality Research and has served as Chairman of the Board and President of the Council on Hotel, Restaurant and Institutional Education (CHRIE). In his thirty years of industrial and academic experience, he has published extensively and served as a visiting professor in the UK, France, the Netherlands, China, Australia and Hong Kong.

Angela J. Roper is Market Analyst at Gillies Melville Associates, Hotel and Leisure Division, London. She was previously a lecturer at Huddersfield Polytechnic, where she established the Hotel Groups Database and Hotel Groups Directory. She is presently completing a Ph.D. entitled 'Hotel consortia: their structures and strategies'.

Paul Slattery is Research Director at Kleinwort Benson Securities, London. A graduate of Strathclyde University, he was previously a Principal Lecturer at Huddersfield Polytechnic. He has published widely in the area of strategic management.

Eliza C. Tse is Assistant Professor in the Department of Hotel, Restaurant and Institutional Management at Virginia Polytechnic Institute and State University, USA, where she also obtained her Ph.D. Her research interests lie in the areas of strategic management, mergers and acquisitions, entrepreneurship, cost control and market analysis.

Michele M. Webster is a graduate of Huddersfield Polytechnic and is undertaking research in the field of strategic management for an M.Phil. degree at Leeds Polytechnic. She has also held several management posts in the hospitality industry.

Kenneth Wheeler is a graduate of the University of Surrey, where he subsequently obtained an MSc degree in international hotel management. He also holds the Chartered Association of Certified Accountants' Diploma in Accounting and Finance, and he is Principal Lecturer in Financial Management at the Norwich Hotel School. His research interests are in the areas of operations management and productivity in the hospitality industry.

Philip Worsfold holds degrees in management, psychology and occupational psychology and currently lectures in organizational psychology and human resource management at the University of Wales, Cardiff. His recent research and publications have focused on human resource management and behaviour in the hospitality industry.

Preface

During the period of industrial and economic change which lies ahead, the hospitality industry, with its rich diversity of catering, accommodation and leisure services, will need to be more forward thinking than ever before. Indeed, there are plenty of examples of this already happening in the areas of product innovation and new market development among others. Viewed in this context, strategic decision making is the management process responsible for co-ordinating a company's business activity. It embraces every area and function of business from information gathering and performance monitoring to the formulation of strategies for international markets. Consequently, the emerging discipline of strategic management is of considerable interest to industrialists, academics and students seeking to discover how to achieve and maintain competitive edge in the 1990s.

The aim of this book is to examine the theory and practice of strategic management in the hospitality industry, and to incorporate research findings and informed analysis. Four parts provide the framework for the thirteen chapters.

Part 1 describes the strategic planning process used by Trusthouse Forte and reviews the literature on strategic management and the relevance of theoretical frameworks to managerial practice in the hospitality industry.

Part 2 focuses on strategic business systems by reviewing current approaches to environmental scanning, information systems management, techniques and methods used in monitoring productivity and business monitoring. The application of quality and retailing concepts to the management of hospitality concludes the review of operational influences on strategic management.

Part 3 concentrates on human aspects of strategy by examining human resource issues for the 1990s and consumer expectations of service delivery. Effective marketing communication is essential in order to anticipate consumer needs and develop competitive strategies which relate closely to consumer needs. Part 3 concludes by looking at the requirements for integrated marketing organization in hospitality firms.

Part 4 is concerned with strategy for international markets, beginning with an overview of the structural theory of business travel developed at Kleinwort Benson. The following three chapters provide a detailed account of international marketing in the hospitality industry, the changing strategies of international hotel companies and, in conclusion, a future perspective on the global hospitality industry of the 1990s.

I would like to thank all of the contributors, some of whom also presented material contained in the book at the second International Journal of Contemporary Hospitality Management conference on 'Strategic developments for the 1990s' held in May 1990. I am especially grateful to my colleague Andrew Boer, to David Royle and Peter Harrison at Cassell, and to Chris Bessant, Diana Russell and my wife Rachel.

Richard Teare
May 1991

PART 1
INTRODUCTION

1

Strategic planning in action: the Trusthouse Forte approach

Rocco Forte with Richard Teare

INTRODUCTION

Entering the 1990s Trusthouse Forte plc continues to build on its position as market leader in the hotel, public catering and contract catering sectors of the UK hospitality industry. The company's success is reflected in its performance during 1989/90, reporting an increase in sales of 21 per cent and in profit before tax of 12 per cent compared with 1988 results.

The size and diversity of Trusthouse Forte has enabled the company to support and develop its core businesses. These operate in national and international markets which offer excellent growth prospects for the 1990s. The desire to invest in growth and in maintaining and improving its existing portfolio means that the company needs to undertake detailed strategic planning. Although development can be funded internally from trading cash flows and divestments, the increasing number of options for development means that strategic planning assumes greater significance. How does a large and highly successful organization approach the complex process of strategic planning? This chapter explains the Trusthouse Forte approach from the chief executive's perspective.

THE ROLE OF THE CHIEF EXECUTIVE IN STRATEGIC PLANNING

Strategic planning is not a static process; it evolves as the size and structure of the company changes. Fifteen or twenty years ago the process was different, and strategy was formulated almost exclusively at the centre. The chief executive made investment decisions and then delegated responsibility for integrating new acquisitions into the company. A different approach is needed today because the company is much larger and operates in a number of sectors. Consequently, it is no longer possible for one individual at the centre to focus in sufficient detail on every aspect of the business. The strategic thrust of the company therefore comes from a dialogue between the centre and the operating divisions, which prepare their own strategic plans. The plans then form the basis of a discussion from which a corporate plan is constructed.

The chief executive's role is a multi-faceted one. Assuming that the various operating divisions are being managed effectively, the expectation is that they will generate their own drive. In order to encourage and channel this activity, the chief executive must provide direction from the centre and stimulate the debate which will enable the divisions to focus their strategic thinking and planning. There are a number of functional specialists at the centre who are responsible for sustaining the debate. Their task is to review market developments and the wide range of information which must be collected, reduced and disseminated for use at every organizational level in the company.

Information gathering is primarily a task for the marketing function, and each major sector of the business has its own marketing team which collects information. The categories include in-company research data, commissioned research and publicly available research reports. Information from these sources is summarized and circulated for decision-making purposes. It thereby informs the debate between the chief executive and the divisional managing directors and, critically, the decisions which are taken about future developments.

Priorities must also be established as it is becoming increasingly difficult to develop every sector of the company simultaneously. Looking ahead, this may mean that it will become necessary to undertake consolidation in some areas of the business in order to finance expansion in others. A decision to consolidate will be difficult to take, especially if it affects a long-established part of the company. Decision support is provided by the divisional reporting procedure, which constitutes a formal mechanism for strategic planning. This is supplemented by informal meetings which take place throughout the organization: in particular, the informal meetings between the chief executive and divisional managing directors, which provide a flexible and effective way of reviewing strategic issues.

THE IMPACT OF GROWTH ON THE ORGANIZATIONAL STRUCTURE

Inevitably as the company grows the role of the chief executive changes. In practice this means less involvement in the day-to-day operations and more time devoted to the key strategic issues affecting future plans and prospects. To stay in touch with divisional affairs, it is necessary to review the monthly results and spend time visiting the various sectors of the business. In this way it is possible to identify potential problems and take corrective action: for example, changes in the economic outlook may make it necessary to review development plans or refocus certain operational procedures. As a service business, it is essential to act quickly and decisively because public confidence is vital. Consequently, the interface between the operating divisions, the media and the marketplace is given priority status.

A process of decentralization has taken place in order to devolve more authority and responsibility for decision making. This action has helped to create strong divisional teams and to channel the energy and enthusiasm that exists within the company in a very productive way. To balance the move towards greater divisional autonomy, management development courses, especially at a senior level, are interdivisional. The advantages are that managers and functional specialists can meet each other, benefit from the diversity of experience and knowledge that is available to them.

Although Trusthouse Forte has an identifiable corporate culture, there is a slight difference of approach in each division which relates to the managing director's particular interests and priorities. The need for a degree of flexibility is related to the issue of ownership of ideas and business methods. Managers who are committed to the businesses they run need the freedom to make decisions, and when they achieve success it is important that they gain the recognition that they deserve.

THE ROLE OF OPERATING DIVISIONS IN THE PLANNING PROCESS

In planning for new and developing markets it is important to adopt an appropriate strategy, a task which is often more difficult than it may seem. For example, in Western Europe the political influences on business development vary considerably. Additionally there are differences in labour laws, culture and the way in which business is conducted which may result in the need for a certain degree of product customization. The principal consideration is whether it is more appropriate to extend the existing operation or to acquire an established business which would provide a base for further development. In this respect it is necessary to take a balanced view, assessing opportunity costs in relation to their likely impact on the company as a whole.

Assessing the performance of key competitors in the marketplace assists with strategy formulation and clarifies, where appropriate, acquisition priorities. For example, it is possible to identify a business which is not operating at optimum efficiency. This may signify an acquisition opportunity if the evidence suggests that performance could be improved. However, the potential for improving margins is less today than it was fifteen years ago because businesses are generally run much more efficiently. The acquisition of Crest Hotels, for example, was perceived to be a good fit with the existing UK hotels portfolio. During the mid-1970s it may have been possible to improve trading margins by up to 10 per cent, whereas the potential for improvement in the 1990s may only be 1 or 2 per cent.

When the company was smaller, the issue of financing new development was less contentious, but as strategic planning is now a divisional responsibility, more ambitious development plans are emerging. The need to debate options and priorities has therefore become central to the strategic planning process. As a direct consequence of this, corporate aims and objectives are continually monitored to determine where the company should be heading and what the emphasis for the future should be. These considerations determine when and how changes to the product portfolio are made. All of these issues will influence the direction and structure of the company during the 1990s because it cannot sustain growth in every division at the same time and at the same pace.

The Trusthouse Forte approach to development in the 1990s is to look at a wide range of options for every sector of the business. To maximize growth in the shortest possible time, it is necessary to examine the potential for growth. For example, in the diverse range of restaurant businesses such as Little Chef, Harvester and the motorway service areas, it is important to ask a number of key questions such as:

What is the maximum potential of each operation?
How do we reach the point where we are realizing this potential if we decide to support development?
How much will the development cost?
How quickly can we penetrate the market to achieve market leadership?

These are the balances that we set in order to examine development decisions. Once these issues have been dealt with, a corporate plan begins to take shape and priorities can be established. This is necessary because, without issuing shares, financial resources are finite. There is also a limit to the amount of borrowed money which can be utilized without overgearing the business.

MAINTAINING QUALITY IN SERVICE DELIVERY

In setting an agenda for the development and maintenance of service quality within a large company, it is essential for the chief executive to establish priorities. Difficulties arise because there are numerous priority issues, and objectives can be misconstrued. Profit orientation, for instance, can be misunderstood unless it is set in the context of clearly defined operating standards. Service quality and profitability are not mutually exclusive, and managers require guidance which will enable them to establish realistic targets for achieving objectives in both areas.

Training and communication play a central role in the maintenance of service quality. Each operating division undertakes a process of succession planning for human resource needs, which takes into consideration new posts as well as replacement projections. Forecasts are then included in the annual corporate manpower plan. This is reviewed by the chief executive in conjunction with a review of development plans for the coming year.

Regardless of how large and sophisticated a hospitality company becomes, attention to detail in each individual establishment requires management in perpetuity. To facilitate progress and support change, it is necessary to keep under constant review the effectiveness of organizational structures, the flow of ideas and information, and the impact of training on employees and the business. Good communication is also essential, and the people and parts of the company enjoying the most success are those that communicate well by giving careful consideration to the way in which they present information both within the organization and to the outside world. As encouragement to others, an effort is made to cross-fertilize methods and ideas on good communication and training policy and practice.

Systems development is an ongoing process and it is easy to be diverted by technical innovations which may or may not prove useful in managing operations more efficiently. The criteria should therefore be to concentrate on what is needed, what will help to improve margins and provide a competitive edge.

A number of experiences were instrumental in helping to formulate a systems development policy. Computerization was initially designed and managed by independent experts. The disadvantages were that the computing expertise was not being developed within the organization and the potential to generate management information was not being fully exploited. To resolve the situation it was necessary to reverse this approach, and today systems development is operator driven. In practice this means that suggestions for improvements to computerized systems are implemented by specialists working within the organization, which is much more effective.

Operations and systems design are co-ordinated from the centre by a design department which also undertakes a limited amount of experimental work. Due to the diversity of products in the company portfolio, the focus of activity is on improving design specifications in facility construction, equipment specification and systems implementation rather than on devising new design concepts. By concentrating on improving or updating aspects of design, it is also possible to make progress in achieving higher quality standards and greater operational efficiency. The evolution of the Little Chef menu over the last fifteen years provides an example of how continuous monitoring and adjustment has been used to maintain a contemporary image. In addition to changes in the menu in response to customer needs, the appearance of the unit, its décor, equipment and layout have also been modernized to reflect market tastes, trends and expectations.

Although the strategic direction of the company is well defined and understood, it is important to maintain an informal and flexible review procedure. It is especially helpful when looking ahead and for ensuring that corporate strengths are fully exploited. For example, it would be pointless to try to run hotels in the same way as independent owner/operators. It is more sensible to ensure that the various divisions develop a unique form of competitive advantage derived from the company's size and specialist expertise. In this way the business can be geared towards performance standards which it can replicate easily and effectively. In turn this helps to create and retain loyal customers who will visit new outlets because they know the product and feel comfortable and happy with it.

PLANNING FOR CHANGE: A PROACTIVE APPROACH

It is not possible to run a business effectively today without the aid of key performance indicators and ratios. The management statistics used by Trusthouse Forte have been continually refined as information technology has developed, so that relatively sophisticated measures of business performance are now available. Additionally, there is a greater emphasis today on short-term forecasting at an operational level, so that costs can be adjusted in relation to expected demand two or three weeks beforehand. This is an important initiative because simultaneous adjustments or even retrogressive cost-cutting to offset the effects of an unexpected shortfall in demand are relatively unhelpful options. As far as operational costs are concerned, Trusthouse Forte is much more responsive in the short term than many other similarly sized companies. However, in planning capital expenditure it is necessary to take a longer-term view, as the decisions which are made today will affect the future direction of the business.

Computer-based real-time analysis of detailed management information has largely replaced manual methods, so that at the touch of a button it is possible to review the contribution made by different customer types in every unit of a division. This level of sophistication is able to support a variety of strategic decisions, such as where, when and whom to sell to, and the most effective way of reaching particular target market segments.

A KEY CHALLENGE FOR THE 1990s

Consistent performance regardless of the trading conditions is the key measure of a very well-run business, an objective which Trusthouse Forte aspires to achieve during the 1990s. If you examine the performance of companies like Sainsbury's and Marks & Spencer during the 1980s, they were just as successful in terms of profit growth during the recessionary period of the early 1980s as they were during the boom years of the late 1980s. In contrast, many other companies suffered or prospered according to the economic changes throughout the decade.

A related task is the need to stimulate a realignment of thinking and practice at the operational level, given that competition is increasing and growth in demand is likely to take place at a slower rate over the next few years. The present economic climate is a challenging one, as it follows five years of strong demand. Inevitably, this will require more emphasis on cost control than during the boom years of the 1980s, but also more creative thinking about ways of maintaining a competitive edge in the years ahead.

Note
On 3 June 1991 shareholders voted overwhelmingly in favour of a change of name for Trusthouse Forte. The company is now known as Forte plc.

2

Strategic Management: a theoretical overview and its application to the hospitality industry

Michele Webster and Terry Hudson

INTRODUCTION

Strategic management has been developed by various authors both to explain what makes some companies particularly successful and to describe the 'ideal' managerial processes for a proactive company. It requires a holistic view and the term 'strategic management' in outline entails a stream of decisions and actions which lead to the development and implementation of effective strategy.

Figure 2.1 shows the formal strategic planning process as outlined by Armstrong.[1] This model shows the *explicit* process for determining an organization's objectives, procedures for generating and evaluating alternative strategies, and a system for monitoring the results of the implemented plan. Although it is a simple process model, it does indicate that commitment should be gained from all those who are affected.

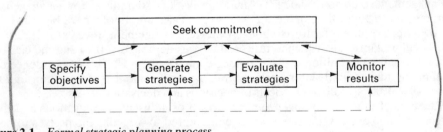

Figure 2.1 *Formal strategic planning process.*
Source: Armstrong, J.S., 'The value of formal planning for strategic decisions: review of empirical decisions', *Strategic Management Journal*, vol. 3, 1982, pp. 197–211.

Strategy formulation is recognized as a continuous process, each element being interactive and often interdependent: 'The best strategic plan is not linear; it is continuously evaluated and revised as it is carried out.'[2] Strategic decisions are those which have a fundamental effect on an organization and which are of major importance to it. Strategies such as growth, consolidation and diversification are general programmes of action which have an implied commitment of emphasis and resources.

From a managerial point of view it is difficult to make decisions concerning the long-term direction of an organization without an understanding of both the external environment and the internal resources of that organization. An understanding of an organization's distinctive competence is important because this knowledge enables managers to obtain and make best use of the necessary physical, financial and human resources:

> a critical aspect of top management's work today involves matching operational competencies with the opportunities and risks created by environmental change in ways that will be both effective and efficient over the time such resources will be deployed. The basic characteristics of the match an organization achieves with its environment is [*sic*] called its strategy.[3]

The business environment has become more uncertain and changeable in recent years, and in this dynamic environment an ability to anticipate problems is of considerable value: 'The successful business of the future will be those [*sic*] which learn to live with uncertainty and incorporate it within their decision-making processes.'[4] Strategic planning has been developed as a tool to help organizations to plan for uncertainty more effectively than simply extrapolating from current information. Mechanistic planning is unlikely to anticipate opportunities or threats which come from unexpected sources, and it is within a strategic management framework that this critical aspect can be discussed.

However, it is misleading to assume that only *some* organizations make decisions which are of major consequence to their long-term well-being: 'all organizations make strategic decisions and have done so since the dawn of history . . . strategic decisions can be taken carefully or negligently, deliberately or haphazardly or systematically'.[5]

In attempting to understand strategic management it is important to be able to recognize which decisions are, or have been, of strategic significance and to identify whether the decisions were made haphazardly or systematically. This is not always as obvious as it may superficially appear; written evidence of long-range planning is not the only indicator of successful strategic management.

Management theory has devised many ways of examining how management operates, and many influential and persuasive articles and books have been written. An overview of the literature about strategic management reveals a variety of theoretical backgrounds, which in turn lead to considerable diversity and the lack of a commonly agreed definition of what strategic management is. There is evidence of a widening of interest in the later work on strategic management as authors consider the psychological and sociological aspects of decisions and decision-makers.

A feature of this century has been the growth of industrial corporations and their increasing complexity. Organizations have attempted to organize themselves to be as efficient and effective as possible. Growth has been a source of competitive advantage, but it has also caused some great difficulties. Internal diversity causes a managerial gap

> between the corporate level, which has the power to commit resources but often only a superficial knowledge of each business, and the business level, where managers have the substantive knowledge required to make resource allocation decisions but lack the 'big corporate picture'.[6]

Strategic management has been developed as an attempt to fill this gap. Bridging the gap has been a significant reason why attempts have been made to formalize and justify the decision-making process and why strategic management process models have been devised.

Glossary of terms

It is necessary to untangle the semantic problems as many different terms have been used to describe the emergent subject area of business policy of which strategic management is a part: 'Language is very important in comprehending a subject as complex as business policy. Unfortunately, the lack of a widely shared and understood language is a liability that business policy has yet to overcome.'[7] This statement still holds true, and it has therefore been considered necessary to provide a glossary of the most widely used terms to facilitate understanding. The definitions have been drawn from many sources, but are substantially the authors' own.

> *Strategy:* a general programme of action of major importance with an implied commitment of emphasis and resources to achieve a basic mission.
> *Strategic management:* a stream of decisions and actions which lead to the development and implementation of effective strategy within the culture and context of an organization.
> *Business policy:* the term traditionally associated with educational courses which deal with strategy and strategic management.
> *Corporate planning:* the formalized process within an organization, usually evidenced by written long-range plans devised by senior management.

WHAT IS STRATEGIC MANAGEMENT?

Put simply, 'Strategic management is concerned with deciding on strategy and planning how that strategy is to be put into effect.'[8] Strategy is formally evolved through the managerial processes within an organization, although ideas concerning changes of a strategic nature could originate anywhere within the organization.

Strategies will exist at a number of levels in an organization, and depending upon the size and type at least three different levels may emerge:

- corporate level: strategy concerned with what types of business the company as a whole should be in, and therefore concerned with decisions of scope;

- competitive or business level: strategy concerned with how to compete in a particular market;

- operational level: strategies concerned with tactics or how the different functions of the enterprise contribute to the other levels of strategy.

These levels are interdependent because strategy at one level should be consistent with that at other levels.

Management has been described in many ways, but in this context it is sufficient to accept one definition by Ansoff, who is credited with popularizing the term 'strategic management': 'the active process of determining and guiding the course of a firm towards its objectives'.[9] It is therefore necessary to have an understanding of what the organization's objectives are. The formulation of objectives is often cited as the first stage of strategic management. Unless top management knows where the organization is going, how can it be expected either to plan strategically or to recognize when the goals have been achieved? It can be difficult to measure success, and it would appear essential to have goals in order to be able to recognize when they have been achieved. Many companies produce a mission statement which outlines major financial and non-financial goals, and the creation of this statement is usually a top management function:

> 'The role of top management is thus to determine the strategic objectives of the enterprise, to decide what the organization is, or is to become, based on its distinctive competencies and then to determine progress toward the firm's objectives by measured criteria.'[10]

Thus having understood the objectives and possibly conceived of them in terms of a mission statement, managers then have to make progress towards achieving the objectives through a strategic plan: 'It is widely agreed that the development and communication of strategy is the most important single activity of top managers.'[11] The responsibility for strategy formulation, implementation and control is at the top level of management, and its decisions are critical because they determine 'whether a firm excels, survives or dies. This decision process is called strategic management.'[12]

After strategy has been formulated, implemented and controlled, the objectives may be re-evaluated as a consequence of unpredicted events and in the light of experience, and so the circular process continues. Strategic management can be seen to encompass more than strategy planning, for it can be seen to be 'linking the vigour of formal planning to rigorous, operational execution'.[13] Thus strategic management is not just a theoretical planning tool but also a practical ongoing process.

There are many suggested techniques of evaluation. These can be broken into three main areas:

- financial and quantitative models, examples being gap analysis, sensitivity analysis, simulation modelling, profitability analysis and investment appraisal techniques;

- matrices evaluation: decision matrices, growth vectors,[14] nine-cell GE matrix, BCG matrix;

- perceptive judgements: competitive analysis,[15] heuristic models, scenarios, scoring methods, decision trees.

The changing nature of the business environment has been examined by Channon in his influential work *The Strategy and Structure of British Enterprise*.[16] He describes the change from owners or individual entrepreneurs to managers and the 'techno-structure' of group decisions. It is therefore logical to assume that as a consequence the decision-making process has fragmented and become more rational than intuitive.

There has also been a trend toward professional managers, particularly those who develop through functional specialisms such as finance, marketing, production and personnel. As a consequence of this there may be competition for resources and a lack of unified direction for the organization. Strategic management developed as a method of reunifying the organization: 'Strategic management can be described as an ongoing, proactive, future-result oriented process of managing organizations and their environments through utilising knowledge derived from various disciplines.'[17] Strategic management is concerned not with functional or specialist management but with the full scope of an organization's activities. It provides in effect an overview to ensure a co-ordinated and effective approach.

STRATEGIC MANAGEMENT FOR THE HOSPITALITY INDUSTRY

Some material has been written about strategy and strategic management for the hospitality industry, although the volume is not very great. Of particular note is Reichel,[18] who describes how to use a simple process planning model with examples from the US hospitality industry. Schaffer[19] is interested in strategy and structure in the US lodging industry, and describes the preliminary research findings which support his strategic choice model. Tse and Olsen have individually and jointly published the results of empirical work on US restaurants.[20]

A plausible explanation has been put forward for the lack of work about the service sector: 'Because manufacturing has been the dominant economic force of the last century, most managers have been educated through experience and/or formal education to think about strategic management in product-oriented terms.'[21] Strategic management has much to offer the service sector, which faces many similar problems to manufacturing or indeed other industries. However, it is logical that the emphasis service sector managers place in some areas of their planning may be different: 'Many managers of service businesses are aware that the strategic management of service businesses is different from that in manufacturing businesses.'[22]

There is little conclusive evidence about the suitability of strategic management for the hotel and catering industry. Nanus and Lundberg point to a formalization of the strategic planning process: 'Many hospitality companies have recognized the need to review strategies and have installed formal strategic-planning processes.'[23] Their view that management has become more progressive is shared by Reichel: 'It has become clear to top management that survival and profit making are increasingly contingent upon proactive, aggressive actions and very speedy reactions to change, as opposed to slow, reactive organizational practices towards environmental threats and opportunities.'[24]

Recent work by Slattery and Clark indicated that members of top management may have worked their way up through the hospitality industry but that significantly more moved across from other industries: 'it is clear that there are few corporate jobs for hotel and catering professionals, their careers remain within the hotels'.[25] What determined whether a person was in a top management job was therefore professional qualifications and knowledge of a specialist area (accountancy, marketing, personnel) rather than 'hotelkeeping' experience. Thus their research indicated that unit managers and corporate managers often came from different backgrounds. This indicates a clear need for strategic planning to bridge the gap and for strategic management in its broadest sense to create a greater strategic awareness throughout the organization.

In effect, strategic management is appropriate for the same reasons as it is appropriate for any other industry and is being adopted by hospitality organizations. This may partly be as a result of reaching a stage in the life-cycle where decisions of a strategic nature become increasingly important: 'For firms in the maturing hospitality industry to survive and grow, they will have to depend upon their ability to strategically align themselves with the turbulent environment and select appropriate strategies to create defendable competitive positions.'[26] There is certainly evidence of interest in strategy: 'Strategy has become a byword for the hospitality industry.'[27] This is reinforced in the 1989 Dairy Crest *Catering Report*, which was explicit that it was 'using this report as a forum to explore elements of strategy as it relates to caterers. We are attempting to stimulate interest and discussion and to encourage the industry to discuss its strategic approaches.'[28]

Thomas[29] lists six questions about strategic management, related to the service sector but not specifically the hospitality industry, that he recommends top managers should ask, and he comments that the answers are often unique.

- Do we fully understand the specific type of service business we are in?
- How can we defend our business from competitors?
- How can we obtain the most cost-effective operations?
- What is the rationale for our pricing strategy?
- What process are we using to develop and test new services?
- What acquisitions, if any, would make sense for our company?

He concludes that:

> One of the best ways to change managers' thinking patterns and thus avoid the trap of force-fitting product-oriented management techniques into a service-oriented business is to change the language system in the company. If managers talk about services instead of products, they also think about services and those characteristics that make services unique.[30]

Although the questions are relevant, in many respects the arguments against product-oriented techniques sound rather facile. Managers who run service organizations understand that they are dealing with complexity and are likely to talk about an amalgam of products and services. Thomas's list of questions simply substitute the word 'service' for 'product', and it would therefore seem counterproductive to argue that service management is significantly different from any other type of management.

An interesting development has been the realization by non-pure-service businesses that the service element of their output has major strategic implications which may be underestimated. In effect a customer orientation is being rediscovered.

Peters and Waterman in their influential book *In Search of Excellence*[31] describe how excellence is recognizable across industry barriers and is achieved in similar ways. The very successful US businesses which they identify defined themselves as *service businesses* and emphasized quality and service as the keystone of their excellence. These companies had a strongly developed corporate culture which sustained an innovative outlook and commitment to customers and staff members.

The fundamental question therefore relates to *belief* rather than to facts about whether managing service industries is unique. There is a strong case that the management function is *not* significantly different from, for example, that in manufacturing where much research work has been undertaken. If it is accepted that good management practices are relevant to any type of business, then strategic management *is* appropriate for service sector businesses and hence the hospitality industry. Indeed one of the major strengths of the concept is that it is flexible and allows for a wide analysis of all aspects of a business.

The complex nature of the product–service amalgam which hospitality organizations provide indicates a *greater* need for tools and techniques designed to help their management. However, it could be argued that the hospitality industry is generally slow to adopt good management practices.

VALUE OF STRATEGY MANAGEMENT

There are certain fundamental questions to address about whether it is of value to a company to formalize strategy management, and unfortunately there are no definitive answers. Most authors are vague about the value of strategy to specific sizes of organization, but Tiles[32] comments that explicit strategy is required to reconcile co-ordinated action and entrepreneurial effort as a company grows, and this is the tacit implication of most writers.

If strategy is important then its formulation should not be left to chance but should be managed. Some reasons are given for the use of procedures by Hofer and Schendel.[33] These are interesting because, along with rational–economic reasons (the development of objectives, the allocation of resources, to co-ordinate and integrate complex business organizations and to forecast future performance), there is also a focus on human resource issues and in particular the value of management development.

Research has failed to prove that formal planning is directly associated with superior financial performance. However, despite this, a claim has been made (which has widespread agreement) that formal planning is 'of much less value as a device for dramatically improving results than as a defence against the rising penalty for error'.[34] As strategic management has progressed as an area of interest, the reasons for strategy management have broadened. Some of the most significant advantages and disadvantages are listed below.

Advantages and disadvantages of strategic management

Advantages

- An overall view or perspective can be formed of the organization, spanning the past, present and future.[35]
- Clear direction is provided via a framework for decision making which can assist in choice.[36]
- A greater ability to anticipate and manage change is attained.[37]
- A dual approach to problem solving is created:
    Exploration of the most effective means to overcome difficulties and subdue competition;
    Development, conservation and deployment of limited resources to maximize returns.[38]
- The co-ordination of plans and improved communication result. This is especially noticeable in large corporations.[39]
- Businesses which perform strategic management are more effective.[40]
- It is a complete way of running a business, and therefore indicative of better management.[41]

Disadvantages

- Flair and intuition are restricted, and objectives limit the field of search. Therefore potential objectives are left unconsidered.[42]
- The benefits of strategic management may be oversold, ignoring such issues as the divisions caused between those who implement the plan and those who do the planning.[43]
- The process oversimplifies the variables involved, and is therefore only a partial approach to ensuring business success.[44]
- Flexibility is decreased, and therefore strategic management is unable to cope with today's rapidly changing environment.[45]
- Time, money and executive talent would be saved if extensive analysis did not take place. It is also questionable how much notice managers take of research anyway.[46]
- One cannot take advantage of the delay principle as, by delaying commitment until an opportunity is confirmed, it may be lost.[47]
- The information needed for analysis is very rarely available to create a full picture.[48]
- Fewer than one in ten American companies produce a corporate strategy that is achieving its goals.[49]

Given the above, the question remains as to whether the advantages outweigh the disadvantages. It is difficult to judge the cost-effectiveness of strategy management, but the belief is widely expressed that even if benefits are largely intangible they are worthwhile.

INCREMENTAL ADOPTION OF FORMAL STRATEGIC MANAGEMENT

An organization sometimes make a decision to introduce strategic planning which 'means that it will in future clarify its objectives, and make its strategic decisions in a more deliberately systematic manner'.[50] Some research has been carried out to try to establish whether there is any pattern to the adoption of formal strategic management. Research was done in America to understand why some giant US companies were 'nimbly leapfrogging smaller competitors with technical or market innovations in true entrepreneurial style'.[51] Their work identified four sequential phases: basic financial planning, forecast-based planning, externally oriented planning and strategic management. Each stage was marked by clear advances over its predecessor in terms of explicit formulation of issues and alternatives, quality of preparatory staffwork, readiness of top management to participate in and guide the strategic decision process, and effectiveness of implementation.

This research is particularly interesting because it recognizes that the tools and techniques which have been developed may not be appropriate for all organizations. Strategic management is a complex phenomena which develops over time, and there is an incremental adoption of techniques as previous techniques become insufficiently detailed for the organization's needs. This makes logical sense because it can explain why some of the more costly and elaborate tools and techniques are appropriate for large organizations when decision making becomes too complex for one individual. This is interesting because there is a lack of attention to the question of size related to strategy, and what there is tends to focus on the structure–strategy debate.

STRATEGIC MANAGEMENT: THE THEORY OF THE PLANNING PROCESS

Much of the written work about strategy identifies a process which enables important decisions to be made concerning an organization. Several authors have constructed models to describe the process, but at this stage one model by Glueck is presented by way of example (Figure 2.2).

In this analysis there are four major elements in the strategic management process: analysis and diagnosis; choice; implementation; and evaluation. At the start are the strategic management elements, the enterprise objectives and the enterprise strategists, which are interlinked. Once the process is in operation the elements are revised after the evaluation of strategy is complete.

In Glueck's model the descriptions of the contingent parts are self-explanatory, and other process models are very similar. The environment is scanned for external opportunities and threats, and the internal strengths and weaknesses are considered. The two are matched to provide a coherent idea of the distinctive competencies and unique competitive advantages the organization possesses. Following this analysis, appropriate alternative strategies can be considered and one chosen. The chosen strategy is implemented by leaders (usually management), and the strategy is broken down into more manageable parts. The resulting policies and action plans may have targets to enable monitoring and control to be effective. Any structural change which is necessary is instigated and the strategy is implemented. After implementation the strategy is evaluated to see if the objectives have been realized, and any revision or corrective action which is necessary is undertaken.

It is quite simple to examine strategic management in this way, as it is possible to visualize the steps which must be gone through to achieve strategic plans. As a starting point this simplicity is extremely useful.

As a practical tool the process models are of limited use. The simplicity which is a great benefit when starting to understand strategy masks a great deal of complexity when trying to understand the wider implications of strategic management. However, following the process model can be a valuable technique for practising managers who feel the need for a more structured method of making important decisions which will affect their organizations far into the future.

Unfortunately, the deficiencies in this type of model were exposed quite quickly when attempting to put the process into practice. Objections have been voiced to the basic premises of the formal process:

- Strategy formulation can be intuitive and opportunistic.
- Successful strategy implementation is not guaranteed even if the chief executive is committed, and the impetus for change can come from any part of the organization, or indeed from outside agents.
- The resulting strategy may be flexible and can only be a partial statement of corporate intent because of conflicting and competing individual perceptions and motives.
- Strategy may not be made explicit and in writing, especially if there is a strong, entrepreneurial leader whose vision is guiding the organization, or where secrecy is considered desirable.
- Implementation often fails to be successful or complete.

It is possible to argue that calling the process models strategic management is inappropriate. They do go some way towards providing a checklist of areas to consider

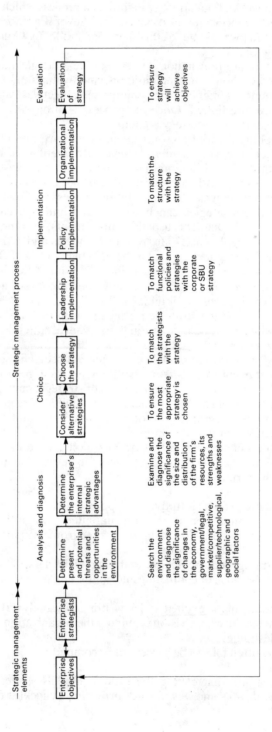

Figure 2.2 *A model of strategic management.*
Source: Glueck, W.F. and Jauch, L.R., *Business Policy and Strategic Management* (4th edn),
McGraw-Hill, New York, 1984.

when formulating and implementing strategy, but they are inadequate to encompass the wider issues which separate strategy planning from strategic management. There are broader issues of strategic management, and it is necessary to understand the behavioural issues which complicate rational–economic decision making. This is now reflected in recent work, particularly the more comprehensive texts.[52]

STRATEGIC MANAGEMENT: THE BROADER IMPLICATIONS

As well as identifying a formal process of how to draw up, implement and control strategic plans, it is possible to explore strategic management in a wider sense. The more recent approaches to strategic management demonstrate this broadening of interest. This requires an examination of the organizational and cultural context managers work in, as well as their individual personal characteristics. Taken together these militate against strategic management being a thoroughly rational process; indeed strategic management has been described as 'more to do with vision and involvement than it does with analytical technique'.[53]

Henry Mintzberg has made some interesting comments on strategic management. He made his international reputation fifteen years ago by revealing (as a result of observation) how managers actually worked, as opposed to how they had been assumed to work by classical theorists. His more recent work covered power within organizations, which led to an analysis of strategy. Again his interest was the discrepancy between theory and practice. In the early 1970s strategy was very topical and many companies were investing much management time and energy in formulating strategic plans. However, Mintzberg noticed that plans were not always implemented and followed through. This was not always because of a lack of management commitment, but was often because of outside events which were not foreseen. There were also internal reasons why strategic plans were not fully implemented: for example, insufficient understanding of the plans by other members of the organization. Some practitioners became disillusioned with the concept, possibly because they overestimated the benefits.

It is therefore pertinent to examine some of the human variabilities which will affect strategy.

STRATEGIC MANAGEMENT: THE FIT WITH THE CORPORATE CULTURE

However convenient it might be to imagine strategic management as a totally rational and logical, almost scientific process, it is certainly misleading. Strategy texts can read as if effective strategic management depends on assembling facts about an organization and its environment, analysing them and writing and implementing a plan. However:

> a strategy based upon facts plus logic alone, no matter how important the challenge is, or how persuasively the strategy is pursued, will degenerate into mere words unless it fits with and is sustained by the behavioural fabric of the business and the society in which the business operates.[54]

To understand how an organization functions it is necessary to consider the corporate culture. The corporate culture is the shared beliefs, assumptions and values of all members of an organization: 'culture, that difficult to define set of norms and attitudes that help shape an organization, has come to be viewed as an important element of a successful firm'.[55] Johnson and Scholes discuss the set of beliefs and assumptions which form the culture of an organization (described as 'recipes') as the symbols, power structures, organizational structures, control systems, routines, rituals and myths.

Corporate culture is an element of strategic importance because if the prevailing beliefs, values and assumptions do not fit with the strategies, they are unlikely to be successful. A supportive corporate culture can have many benefits. Research into the success of Japanese companies has emphasized the importance of shared values of management and workers. Their shared values resulted in behavioural norms that demonstrated a commitment to quality, problem solving and co-operative effort.[56]

> There is now a growing understanding that the strategy of an enterprise, its structure, the sorts of people who hold power, its control systems and the way it operates, tend to reflect the culture of that organization. [57]

The influence of the corporate culture can operate unconsciously, yet it may define the organization's basic rules and routines: 'the way we do things around here'.[58] Of course, there is no such thing as an 'ideal' culture: 'culture can powerfully reinforce the comparative advantage a generic strategy seeks to achieve, if the culture is an appropriate one. There is no such thing as a good or bad culture *per se.*'[59]

Managers should try to analyse the prevailing corporate culture because they need to understand how their perception limits their decision-making abilities and affects the effectiveness of strategy implementation. The principal benefit of undertaking a culture audit is that 'the executive who will take steps to better understand his own and other men's values can gain an important advantage in developing workable and well-supported policies'.[60]

Culture is a limiting factor on what is seen and therefore on the acceptable responses. Lorsch[61] contends that the beliefs top management holds can inhibit strategic change in two ways:

- Beliefs can produce strategic myopia, leading them to see events with tunnel vision, and this leads them to overlook the significance of changing external conditions.
- When top management recognizes the need for strategic change, it responds within its existing culture, using responses that have worked in the past. In this way, yesterday's solution may become today's problems.

Understanding the culture of an organization may lead to a further dilemma: 'It is important to know one's culture before one thinks about change. It may be more appropriate to tailor one's strategy to one's culture rather than the other way round.'[62]

Strategy is a broad concept which according to Mintzberg[63] may be concerned with position or perspective. A company's position is judged relative to its competitors in an industry (for example, a dominant market share). Perspective covers the purpose and self-image of an organization, and as such underpins other decisions. Again the quality of perception and judgement is crucial, and because it derives from the prevailing corporate culture, perspective may well be more difficult to change than position.

The corporate culture is not fixed and it may develop naturally over time as well as be manipulated by top management or power groups within an organization. It is important to remember that the political processes at work in an organization do not always fit the hierarchical structure shown on the organization chart. Power has a major influence on the strategic behaviour of an organization, and any strategy which does not appeal to powerful groups or influential individuals is unlikely to succeed. Workers with scarce skills or knowledge may be in an extremely powerful position if they are essential for the organization's operation and success. However, a key figure is usually the chief executive or whoever heads the organization: 'It is quite clear, on the basis both of observation and of systematic studies of top managers in business organizations that personal values are important determinants in the choice of corporate strategy.'[64]

The chief executive should be able to identify and reward behaviour which is consistent with his or her expressed strategy: 'one of the key tasks of the chief executive is so to create or change a subculture that executive behaviour is appropriate to the organization's objectives and strategy'.[65] This influence on the culture is seen in the formal and informal patterns of reward and punishment, and the acceptable and unacceptable patterns of behaviour and status. The chief executive is certainly influential because he or she can initiate structural change, choose senior executives and determine the formal systems of reward and punishment. These must be related to the organization's strategy.

The corporate culture will have a far-reaching effect on the attitude towards risk, the desired amount of centralized control, acceptable performance levels and many other factors. It is possible, therefore, to distinguish practical strategic management as being quite all-encompassing: 'the reality of strategic management as a social, political and cultural phenomenon'.[66]

STRATEGIC BEHAVIOUR

The question needs to be addressed as to whether it is possible to identify strategic behaviour. With this question in mind we shall discuss the work of several authors. Taking an external viewpoint, they examine organizations for patterns in their behaviour. Miles and Snow[67] characterize organizations in terms of how they behave strategically and describe some basic types. Campbell and Gould[68] identify commonly used management styles. Drawing on these sources, Hassard[69] constructs a model of strategic decision making. These are particularly interesting because they allow an overview of an organization from an outside viewpoint. They draw on historical data that is more commonly available than current internal information, which may be confidential, and they can also prescribe indications of future strategic direction.

Miles and Snow 1978

Miles and Snow characterize organizations into three basic types in terms of how they behave strategically: 'When understanding a strategic analysis this provides a means of assessing the dominant culture of the organization.'[70] They look at alternative ways in which organizations define their product-market domains (strategy) and how they construct mechanisms (structures and processes) to pursue these strategies. The framework has two major elements:

(a) a general model of the process of adaptation which specifies the major decisions needed by the organization to maintain an effective alignment with its environment, and (b) an organizational typography which portrays different patterns of adaptive behaviour used by organizations within a given industry or other grouping.[71]

Miles and Snow identify three broad problems which all organizations face: entrepreneurial, engineering and administrative. The ways these problems are perceived and resolved are reflected in some basic strategic types which they call 'Defenders', 'analysers' and 'prospectors' (see Table 2.1).

A fourth basic type is a 'reactor', which is a form of strategic 'failure'. There are inconsistencies among its strategy, technology, structure and process. The first three categories can all be proactive to an extent, whereas reactors are basically unstable. A reactor can come about for many reasons: top management may not have clearly articulated the organization's strategy or may not fully shape the organization's structure and processes to fit a chosen strategy. There may also be a tendency for management to maintain the organization's strategy and structure relationship despite overwhelming changes in the environmental conditions.

Table 2.1   *Type of organization*

Organization type	Dominant objectives	Strategies	Internal structure	Risk
Defender	Protect current market share	Retrenchment; specialization; vertical integration; cost-efficient production; advertise to hold customers	Centralized; mechanistic; bureaucratic	Ineffective; unable to respond to major shift in environment
Analyser	Protect current market share and locate new opportunities	Market penetration; steady growth; market followers	Tight control over existing activities; looser control for growing lines and new activities	Ineffective and inefficient if cannot maintain balance
Prospector	Locate and exploit new product and market opportunities	Growth; product and market development; multiple technologies; constant environmental scanning	Decentralized; organic; flexible	Inefficient; low profitability; over-extension of resources

Sources: Adapted from Miles, R. and Snow, C., *Organization Strategy, Structure and Process*, McGraw-Hill, New York, 1978; with reference to Johnson, G. and Scholes, K., *Exploring Corporate Strategy* (2nd edn), Prentice-Hall, Englewood Cliffs, NJ, 1988; Hassard, J., 'A matrix model of corporate decision-making', *Management Decision*, vol. 26, no. 6, 1988, pp. 47–55.

'The proposed theoretical framework deals with alternative ways in which organizations define their product-market domains (strategy) and construct mechanisms (structures and processes) to pursue these strategies.'[72] Miles and Snow have therefore created a model which shows that the performance of an organization is largely the outcome of a series of choices made by the creators or top echelons of the organization. The focus is on business-level strategy and the attempt to identify the correct strategies to adopt within a given business or product line. Thus the main areas of concern are the demand for the product from the environment, the organization's internal structure and the firm's methods of resource allocation: 'This process of matching structure, strategy and environment is the basis of the "strategic choice" model of organizations.'[73]

These concepts have been subjected to empirical validation, and Hall in 1980 discussed a study of 64 American firms in eight different industries. He described how the top performers shared common strategic characteristics regardless of the nature of their industry:

> This study found that high performers generally moved toward and vigorously defended a winning strategic position, whether it be lowest cost (defenders), differentiation (prospectors) or a focused approach combining parts of the first two (analysers). The results of the study left little doubt that consistency, and clarity of purpose help to mobilise and co-ordinate internal resources in gaining and defending a leadership position.[74]

Campbell and Gould 1986

Campbell and Gould concentrate on strategic management styles and identify the three most commonly used styles of management: strategic planning, strategic control and financial control. They argue that the key relationship in a multi-business company is that between centre and business unit managers, and that the two mechanisms through which the centre affects strategic decision making are planning influence and control influence.

Figure 2.3 shows 'a typology of eight ways in which the centre can relate to its business units . . . Of these, however, they feel the most significant styles are those of strategic planning, strategic control and financial control.'[75] Thus the scope and range of the relationship between the centre and the unit is analysed in terms of the amount of influence exerted.

- *Financial control* companies generally have no formal strategic planning system. The responsibility for strategy is on the business unit managers. The centre is involved with capital approval and the annual budgeting process, and is therefore involved in controlling and monitoring results.
- *Strategic control* companies devolve more strategy responsibilities to divisional management and devote more attention to annual financial performance. They have extensive planning systems used to raise the quality of strategic thinking of business unit managers and to indicate weaknesses or problems. The headquarters tend to be small as senior line managers are responsible for their own business area.
- *Strategic planning* companies are those where the centre takes the lead in developing strategy and they therefore have sophisticated strategic planning

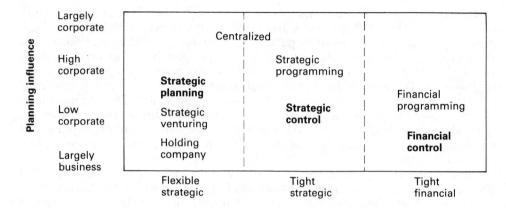

Figure 2.3 *Strategic management styles.*
Source: Campbell, A. and Gould, M., *Strategic Management Styles*, 3 vols, London Business School, 1968, as adapted by Hassard, J., 'A matrix model of corporate decision-making', *Managament Decision*, vol. 26, no. 6, 1988, pp. 47–55.

systems. Strategies are co-ordinated from the centre, and business units are actively supported. This structure limits the influence of the business unit relative to the centre.

Hassard 1988

Hassard draws on the Boston Consulting Group, Miles and Snow, and Campbell and Gould to construct a model for strategic decision making (see Figure 2.4). 'The idea is to develop a "map" for strategic decision-making – a way of documenting the analytical terrain of corporate strategy; a method for situating the main approaches to strategic decision-making in the multi-divisional firm.'[76]

Two dimensions are plotted: development strategy and control strategy. Development strategy considers the extent to which policy making is centralized or decentralized, whilst control strategies involve the timescale that the centre imposes for realizing profit at the business unit level. The intersections on the model produce four major strategic styles as described:

- *Navigator.* This style navigates the business by taking frequent readings of business positions from the centre. The approach to strategy formulation tends to be conservative and centralized.
- *Banker.* This style monitors the company's financial results but is not very concerned with expenditure strategies. It may hold diverse portfolios and press for short-term results.
- *Gambler.* This style will take calculated risks because it is a longer-term interest. It often operates in sectors whose product markets are in the early stages of development.
- *Strategist.* The centre takes a lead in strategic planning and is able to take a long-term view. Business unit managers may have some autonomy, but will ultimately be subject to central control.

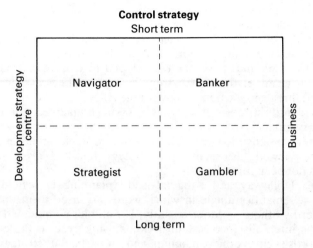

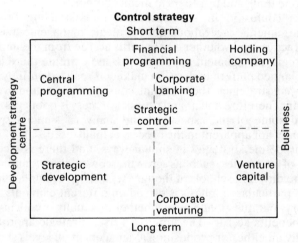

Figure 2.4   *A model of strategic decision making.*
Source: Hassard, J., 'A matrix model of corporate decision making', *Management Decision*, vol. 26, no. 6, 1988, pp. 47–55.

Hassard then goes on to interpret different approaches to corporate strategy and to plot major decision-making styles. From there he also plots individual companies and draws speculative trends.

This analysis is largely unsupported by detailed research, but does show an increasing interest in sophisticated tools for analysts to use in undertaking industry reviews.

CONCLUSIONS

A great deal has been and continues to be written about strategic management, whether it be called strategic management, business policy, business strategy, strategic planning or corporate planning. There is a prodigious amount of research being undertaken under the strategic management umbrella.

In identifying the process of strategic management a largely microeconomic viewpoint is assumed by some authors in that the starting point is an individual company. Various techniques have been developed to help managers analyse their own companies in terms of their own strengths and weaknesses and in relation to opportunities and threats in the outside environment.

Other authors identify strategic archetypes by taking a macroeconomic view and by assuming that all companies follow strategies whether they are formalized or not. This leads to a further complication in understanding strategic management: business decisions can be viewed historically and strategy imputed even when strategic management has not been formalized.

Ten years ago Holloway and King advised: 'planning is a field that can be characterised as a semantics jungle in which words are used to mean one thing by some and another by others'.[77] More recently, Leontiades commented that 'business policies lexicon is internally inconsistent and confusing even to the cognoscente'.[78] Nevertheless, words such as policy, planning and, in particular, strategy are still used by some to mean one thing and by others to mean another.

To add to this confusion in semantics and understanding of what strategic management is, arguments rage about how strategic management is or should be implemented in practice, and whether any benefits accrue from the implementation of a formulated strategic management approach. At one extreme there is the *deliberate* strategy where a planned pattern in decision making is realized entirely as intended; at the other, in *emergent* strategies, there is some consistency in action over time without prior intention of it. Therefore a neat and rational process is not necessarily employed by managers, and some of the aspects of the many (if similar) strategic models outlined are normally not apparent in the process actually used.

Writers basically define strategies in similar ways, and there is a consensus about the implications of strategies such as growth, consolidation and diversification. However, there are different schools of thought regarding the application of strategies management, and particular emphasis is placed on different elements. The concept is supported in theory, but questioned as to whether it actually occurs in practice and, if so, whether any benefits accrue. The intuitive versus strategic approach to decision making is not really an either/or proposition. Managers at all levels should inject their intuition and judgement into the strategic management process. One could argue that a strategic management approach is a problem-solving vehicle which disciplines and duplicates what goes on in the mind of a brilliant intuitive planner.

Paradoxically, the scope of the subject lends itself to a focus on one of the many elements. However, before one can concentrate on a part, one has to understand the whole. Indeed some argue that strategy concerns the nature of the forest, not of the trees. Therefore initially the strategic management process can best be understood, prior to application, by using a strategic management model encompassing all elements. There are, however, key factors for a basic introduction to a subject which is more complex than any one area of functional management. Those who seek to develop their skills in this area must be aware of the following:

- A comprehensive understanding of strategic management requires a knowledge of the firm, its environment and all the functional areas of business. It is necessary to develop a holistic view.

- Strategic management can be used effectively by all types and sizes of organization in both the public and private sectors.
- The decision-making process is not solely a senior management function and should always involve valid perceptions of many individuals at all levels of the organization.
- Strategic decisions occur at a number of different levels in an organization. They are concerned with the scope of activities and matching those activities with both the environment and the resource capability. As such they will have major operational implications.
- Strategy is about not just deciding on the future direction but also the actual implementation at operational level. This is often quoted as the most difficult part of the process.
- There is no consensus about whether the process of strategic management is necessary for business success. Some texts (mainly American) claim empirical evidence that those organizations with formal strategic management systems significantly outperformed the others on earnings per share, return on equity and return on total capital employed. Other texts, mainly British, advise that no such empirical evidence exists in the UK and are understandably sceptical.
- Irrespective of opinion regarding relevance, application and success rate, all texts extol the virtue of a proactive management style in what is agreed is a volatile business environment.
- All texts discuss the subject within a model of elements in a decision-making process. The process includes strategic analysis, strategic choice and strategic implementation.
- There has to be a synthesis of a formal prescriptive approach with a knowledge of behavioural factors. Many firms manage strategically without being aware of it. In this way, intuitive strategy can play a significant role. This is particularly relevant to a number of privately owned and entrepreneurially run businesses.
- It is necessary to be aware of the corporate culture and its role in shaping and affecting strategy. To be effective a strategy must fit with and be sustained by the behavioural fabric of the organization and society.
- Functional specialists may need to bridge the gap and acquire a broader span of knowledge as they move into top management where they are required to provide strategic direction for the organization as a whole.
- Effective strategic planning may require an understanding of the organization's strategic style and that of competitors. There are tools and techniques available which are designed to make this possible.

It has not been possible to identify whether hospitality organizations view their business in explicitly strategic ways. There is, however, an indication that the terminology is in the managerial vocabulary. This is evidenced by some articles and the inclusion of the subject on business studies and hospitality management undergraduate and postgraduate courses. The tools and techniques can therefore be expected to become more prominent as they are used and developed by hospitality organizations.

Strategic management, it could be argued, is as much an art as a science and is not a panacea or a prescription for success. It is rather a synthesis of past and present management theory and practice, packaged and presented in a new way. It is frequently described in a mechanistic manner, but more recently the influence of corporate culture and the value of intuition is acknowledged. It seems likely that strategic management will continue to be relevant to managers and therefore also to academics and students for a long time to come.

NOTES

1. Armstrong, J.S., 'The value of formal planning for strategic decisions: review of empirical decisions', *Strategic Management Journal*, vol. 3, 1982, pp. 197–211.
2. McConkey, D., 'Planning in a changing environment', *Business Horizons'*, Sep./Oct. 1988, p. 66.
3. Hofer, C. W. and Schendel, D., *Strategy Formulation: Analytical Concepts*, West Publishing, St Paul, Minn., 1978, p. 4.
4. Twiss, B., *Managing Technological Innovation* (2nd edn), Longman, London, 1980, p. xxi.
5. Argenti, J., *Systematic Corporate Planning*, Nelson, Walton-on-Thames, 1974, p. 18.
6. Haspeslagh, P., 'Portfolio planning: uses and limits', *Harvard Business Review*, Jan./Feb. 1982, p. 58.
7. Leontiadies, M., 'The confusing words of business policy', *Academy of Management Review*, vol. 7, no. 1, 1982, p. 45.
8. Johnson, G. and Scholes, K., *Exploring Corporate Strategy* (2nd edn), Prentice-Hall International, Hemel Hempstead, 1988, p. 10.
9. Ansoff, H. I., Author's preface to *Corporate Strategy: An Analytic Approach to Corporate Strategy*, McGraw-Hill, New York, 1965.
10. Channon, D. F., *The Strategy and Structure of British Enterprise*, Macmillan, London, 1973, p. 241.
11. Koontz, H., 'Making strategic planning work', *Business Horizons*, vol.19, no. 2, 1976, p. 35.
12. Glueck, W. F. and Jauch, L.R., *Business Policy and Strategic Management* (4th edn), McGraw-Hill, New York, 1984, p. 1.
13. Gluck, F.W., Kaufman, S.P. and Walleck, S., 'Strategic management for competitive advantage', *Harvard Business Review*, Jul./Aug. 1980, p. 161.
14. Ansoff, op. cit.
15. Porter, M.E., *Competitive Advantage: Creating and Sustaining Superior Performance*, Free Press, New York, 1985.
16. Channon, op. cit.
17. Reichel, A., 'Strategic management: how to apply it to firms in the hospitality industry', *Service Industries Journal*, no. 3, 1983, p. 333.
18. Ibid.
19. Schaffer, J. D., 'Strategy, organisation structure and success in the lodging industry', *International Journal of Hospitality Management*, vol. 3, no. 4, 1984, pp. 159–65; Schaffer, J. D., 'Structure and strategy: two sides of success', *Cornell HRA Quarterly*, Feb. 1986, pp. 76–81.
20. Tse, E., 'Defining corporate strengths and weaknesses: is it essential for successful strategy implementation?', *Hospitality Education and Research Journal*, vol. 12, no. 2, 1988, pp. 57–72; Tse, E. and Olsen, M.D., 'The impact of strategy and structure on the organisational performance of restaurant firms', *Hospitality Education and Research Journal*, vol. 12, no. 2, 1988, pp. 265–76; Tse, E. and Olsen, M.D., 'Relating Porter's business strategy to organisation structure: a case of US restaurant firms', *Proceedings of the Launch Conference of the Journal of*

Contemporary Hospitality Management, Dorset Institute, 1989, pp. 87–105.
21. Thomas, D. R. E., 'Strategy is different in service businesses', *Harvard Business Review*, Jul./Aug. 1978, pp. 158–9.
22. Ibid., p. 158.
23. Nanus, B. and Lundberg, C., 'In QUEST of strategic planning', *Cornell HRA Quarterly*, Aug. 1988, p. 18.
24. Reichel, op. cit., p. 331.
25. Slattery, P. and Clark, A., 'Major variables in the corporate structure of hotel groups', *International Journal of Hospitality Management*, vol. 7, no. 2, 1988, p. 120.
26. Tse and Olsen, 'Relating Porter's business strategy', op. cit., p. 89.
27. Nanus and Lundberg, op. cit., p. 18.
28. Dairy Crest, *Catering Report*, 1989, p. 9.
29. Thomas, op. cit., pp. 158–9.
30. Ibid., p. 165.
31. Peters, T. J. and Waterman, R. H., *In Search of Excellence: Lessons from America's Best Run Companies*, Harper & Row, New York, 1982.
32. Tiles, S., 'Making strategy explicit', in Ansoff, H. I. (ed.), *Business Strategy*, Penguin, Harmondsworth, 1969.
33. Hofer and Schendel, op. cit.
34. Argenti, op. cit., p. 35.
35. Chang, Y. N., and Campo-Flores, F.C., *Business Policy and Strategy: Text and Cases*, Goodyear, Santa Monica, 1980; Howe, W.S., *Corporate Strategy*, Macmillan Education, Basingstoke, 1986; Grieve-Smith, J., *Business Strategy: An Introduction*, Basil Blackwell, Oxford, 1985.
36. Ansoff, op. cit.; Glueck, op. cit.; Chang and Campo-Flores, op. cit.; Bowman, C. and Asch, D., *Strategic Management*, Macmillan Education, Basingstoke, 1987.
37. Ibid.
38. Chang and Campo-Flores, op. cit.
39. Goold, M. and Campbell, A., 'Many best ways to make strategy', *Harvard Business Review*, Nov./Dec. 1987, pp. 70–6; Glueck and Jauch, op. cit.
40. Ansoff, op., cit.; Glueck and Jauch, op. cit.
41. Glueck and Jauch, op. cit.; Hussey, D. E., *Introducing Corporate Planning* (3rd edn), Pergamon, Oxford, 1985.
42. Ansoff, op. cit.; Howe, op. cit.; Bowman and Asch, op. cit.
43. Howe, op. cit.; Bowman and Asch, op. cit.
44. Ibid.
45. Ibid.; Glueck and Jauch, op. cit.
46. Ansoff, op. cit.; Glueck and Jauch, op. cit.
47. Ansoff, op. cit.
48. Bowman and Asch, op. cit.
49. Peters and Waterman, op. cit.
50. Argenti, op. cit., p. 18.
51. Gluck, Kaufman and Walleck, op. cit., p. 155.
52. See, for example, Johnson and Scholes, op. cit.
53. Mintzberg, H., 'Crafting strategy', *Harvard Business Review*, Jul./Aug. 1987, p. 74.
54. McNamee, P., *Tools and Techniques for Strategic Management*, Pergamon, Oxford, 1985, p. 11.
55. Ibid., p. 24.

56. Gorman, L., 'Corporate culture', *Management Decision*, vol. 27, no. 1, 1989, pp. 14–19.
57. Johnson and Scholes, op. cit., p. 38.
58. Deal, T. and Kennedy, A., *Corporate Cultures: The Rites and Rituals of Corporate Life*, Addison-Wesley, Wokingham, 1982.
59. Porter, op. cit., p. 24.
60. Guth, W. D. and Taguiri, R., 'Personal values and corporate strategy', *Harvard Business Review*, Sep. 1965, p. 123.
61. Lorsch, J.W. 'Strategic myopia: culture as an invisible barrier to change', in Kilmann, R.H., Saxton, M.J., Serpa, R. *et al.*, *Gaining Control of the Corporate Culture*, Jossey-Bass, San Francisco, 1985.
62. Gorman, op. cit., p. 15.
63. Mintzberg, H., 'Crafting strategy', *Harvard Business Review*, vol. 65, no. 4, Jul./Aug. 1987, pp. 67–74.
64. Guth and Taguiri, op. cit., p. 123.
65. Denning, B. W., 'The integration of business studies at the conceptual level', *Journal of Management Studies*, no. 5, Feb. 1968, p. 11.
66. Johnson and Scholes, op. cit., p. 46.
67. Miles, R. and Snow, C., *Organization Strategy, Structure and Process*, McGraw-Hill, New York, 1978.
68. Campbell, A. and Gould, M., *Strategic Management Styles*, 3 vols, London Business School, 1968.
69. Hassard, J., 'A matrix model of corporate decision-making', *Management Decision*, vol. 26, no. 6, 1988, pp. 47–55.
70. Johnson and Scholes, op. cit., p. 121.
71. Miles and Snow, op. cit., p. 547.
72. Ibid., p. 546.
73. Schaffer, 'Structure and strategy', op. cit., p. 76.
74. Ibid., p. 81.
75. Hassard, op. cit., p. 50.
76. Ibid., p. 51.
77. Holloway, C. and King, W.R., 'Evaluating alternative approaches to strategic planning', *Long Range Planning*, vol. 12, Aug. 1979, p. 74.
78. Leontiadies, op. cit., p. 45.

PART 2
STRATEGIC BUSINESS SYSTEMS

3

Critical information needs for achieving strategic goals

Robert Brotherton and David Leslie

INTRODUCTION

The 'life blood' of any organization is information. Within organizations information abounds, and this may be contained within, and transferred through, a variety of formal procedures and systems, many of which are directly or indirectly concerned with performance. Information will also flow through information communication channels and may or may not relate to the operations of the organization. In addition, the organization may have a separate department or departmental subsection which is primarily oriented to environmental change.

Undoubtedly there are companies in the hospitality industry adopting such an approach to environmental scanning. However, the majority probably operate on an ad-hoc and informal basis, perhaps attending to relevant publications, published research and 'policy centres', and scanning the financial press. This approach may be supported by a network of 'contacts' in various professional fields. In total (and taking account of both internal and external sources of information), any organization has a potentially large and diverse quantity of data available to aid senior management's decision making.

The quantity of information available for such purposes frequently creates an information overload and quality problems. In many situations it is not feasible, let alone desirable, for strategic decision-makers to cope with the available information and make optimal decisions. Under these circumstances it is unlikely that the decision-makers will be able to respond quickly and accurately.

Successful planning to secure competitive advantage depends on three aspects: speed, originality and control.[1] Thus, it is imperative that the right information is available at the right time and in the right place. To achieve this it is necessary to identify the information needs of senior management and to exploit key information sources as a first step towards the design of an information-processing system. This is particularly true in the need to develop a careful, critical analysis of the potential opportunities and threats arising from changes in the external environment.

A potential problem in this proposal, however, is an over-abundance of information, available from both internal and external sources, which could lead to information overload and/or loss of focus. A major function of a strategic business information system is the focus it brings and its ability to assess the degree to which strategies, and through them corporate objectives, are being achieved.

Crucial to the attainment of such objectives are *critical success factors*.[2] By identifying the company's critical success factors a framework can be established to aid the definition of the company's information needs. These information requirements provide the basis for fundamental performance data to be generated from the strategic business information survey to assess the degree of congruence between strategic objectives and outcomes. Such needs may be termed *critical information needs*. The benefit of this approach lies not only in the positive contribution it makes to the company's strategy, but also in its emphasis upon the strategic roles and functions of the company's information sub-systems. Hitherto managerial perceptions may have primarily viewed the latter in terms of the operational reporting output they generate rather than as an integral part of the strategic planning process.

Through a development of the 'critical' focus embodied in the critical success factor and critical information needs concepts we contend that it is possible to overcome potential obstacles facing the integration of externally and internally focused information systems and to establish a *strategic business information system*. Accordingly, we now turn our attention to the development of a framework to achieve this objective.

THE CRITICAL INFORMATION SYSTEMS MODEL

Any attempt merely to merge the existing *environmental scanning and management information system* components of a company's information system is fraught with difficulties in the absence of an appropiate conceptual framework. This is likely to create a range of problems concerning the ability of the system to provide appropriate strategic and operational information in a systematic and coherent format. The Critical Information Systems model (see Figure 3.1) provides a framework to avoid these problems through its focus upon the 'critical' elements of the information system. Taking the support for managerial decision making as the central rationale for an information system, the Critical Information Systems model demonstrates how integration can be achieved between the environmental scanning and management information systems.

The key to this model is its focus on the 'critical' aspects of the strategic and operational decision-making process. To ensure effective integration between the environmental scanning and management information components of the information system it is necessary to identify and analyse the critical aspects of interaction between the system and the management decision-making component. This analysis will allow priorities to be assigned to the design, operation and output of the system factors which come initially from the company's strategic and operational plans, the essential link between these plans and the information system being the company's critical success factors and critical information needs.

Critical success factors have been defined as 'the few key areas in which things must go right if a business's goals are to be achieved'.[3] They may vary on an inter-company (see Figure 3.2) and inter-industry basis, and between management levels within companies (see Figure 3.3). However, they are the factors requiring constant management attention. Critical success factors are thus priority areas for on-going information provision and constitute the basis for a company's information system and its management decision making. The translation of criticial success factors into critical information needs provides the mechanism for operationalizing the critical success factor/management decision making relationship. Given a company's goals,

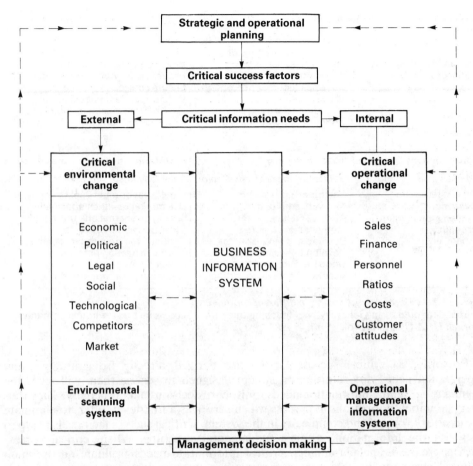

Figure 3.1   *The Critical Information Systems (CIS) model.*

critical information needs are essentially measures of performance or 'triggers' which indicate a necessity for management action.

Critical information needs may be defined as: the key information required by managers to effectively discharge their decision-making functions. These may be either internal or external. The internal critical information needs will be strongly influenced by the company's particular *critical performance measures* and can be used to monitor the effectiveness of operational decision making. These in turn may be defined as: the key indicators which enable managers to monitor the achievement of the company's critical success factors. The external critical information needs are a function of the external environment of the company and are closely related to *critical events* in this environment. These may be defined as: the separate factors which signify substantial and enduring changes in environmental sub-domains and impinge upon the company's ability to achieve its critical success factors.

The importance of the critical success factor/critical information need framework to a company's information system lies in the discipline it brings to the design, operation and output of the system. This is evident in a number of ways.

Hotel Company A: a centralized company		Hotel Company C: a young firm
Goals	*Selected critical success factors*	*Selected critical success factors*
Build repeat visitor loyalty Profitability matched with quality of service	Develop best accommodation Develop best service Reduce complaints Develop customer perception of price/value Good financial image Good investment policy	Identify and purchase good sites Develop pool of management talent Ensure clean, well-maintained rooms Ensure courteous service Obtain sufficient financing Have current design for hotel product Develop cost controls
Hotel Company B: a decentralized company		**Hotel Company D: a mature company**
Goals	*Selected critical success factors*	*Selected critical success factors*
Highest return on investment Deepen management strength Expansion	Customer satisfaction Motivate employees Attract and hire people motivated to careers Develop human resources Develop policy manual Good product mix Accurate financial reporting	Provide favourable guest experience Use market research effectively Pricing policy that ensures a high guest perception of value Continue to reinvest in properties Tough inspection programmes Develop new properties Weed out poor properties

Figure 3.2 *Critical success factors in different companies.*
Source: Adapted from Geller, A.N., 'Tracking the critical success factors for hotel companies', *Cornell HRA Quarterly*, vol. 25 no. 4, 1985, p. 79.

Primarily, as critical success factors are derived directly from strategic and operational plans, any information system designed to service them will meet the company's essential information needs for its core decision-making activity. They thus form an initial 'prioritization' process which serves as a first-level 'filter' to eliminate unnecessary volume and complexity in the system. Critical success factors also help to establish the information system's fundamental structure. Where critical success factors create design parameters, critical information needs facilitate an optimum internal structure by determining the number, type and content of the system's data bases, as well as the relative balance between 'hard' and 'soft' data held in the system.

Critical events and critical performance measures govern the system's output and the nature of the system/user interface. The monitoring or tracking components of the system therefore should be constructed to 'trigger' the attention of management when a significant change occurs in critical event performance measures. This will enable the system to provide an 'early warning' function for significant external/internal threats and opportunities and to facilitate appropriate and timely responses by management.

An important element of an information system is its 'usability'. The system's output should be limited to that necessary and desirable, through the provision of timely, accurate, relevant and systematic information in appropriate formats to support management decision making.

The dimensions of the Critical Information Systems model therefore demonstrate a need for the development of an overall strategic business information system. This would effectively link the company's internal management information system and external environmental scanning components and focus them toward the harmonization of current operational performance and strategic direction within the planning

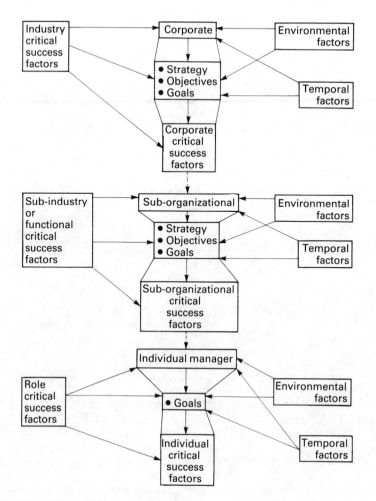

Figure 3.3   *The critical success factor hierarchy.*
Source: Bullen, C.V. and Rockart, J.F., *A Primer on Critical Success Factors.* Center for
Systems Research. Sloan Management Center, MIT, Cambridge, Mass.

framework. To achieve this it is necessary to break down the strategic business
information system and consider the individual aspects of its environmental scanning
and management information system components prior to the presentation of the final
SBIS framework.

THE ENVIRONMENTAL SCANNING SYSTEM

The environmental scanning design characteristics implied by the critical success
factors and critical information needs are illustrated in Figure 3.4. To establish a
progressive, multi-layered and selective filtering system, a logical and systematic
process of external information identification, analysis and diagnosis must be
implemented. We can consider the development of this system as a series of stages.

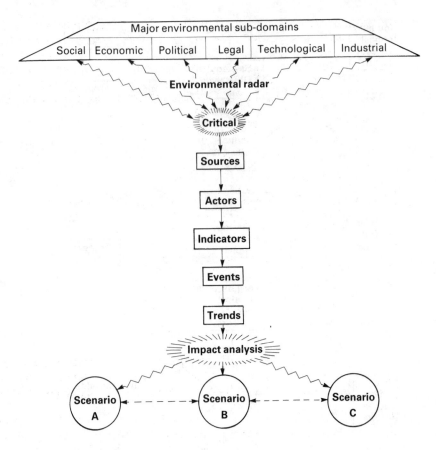

Figure 3.4   *The Critical Environmental Scanning model.*

In the first stage, *critical sources* serve the function of allowing key information sources to be identified and accessed in each environmental sub-domain. Critical sources identification and selection is thus a vital first step in designing the company's environmental scanning system and helps to avoid the collection of unnecessary and unusable information.[4] Critical sources can thus be defined as the most reliable, consistent, accurate, valid and valuable sources of information in relation to the company's critical success factors. Considerable time and effort should be devoted to the establishment of an appropriate portfolio of critical sources which reflect the desired balance of qualitative and quantitative information required.

In the second stage of the construction of the environmental scanning system, the *environmental radar system* is used to monitor systematically the critical sources. The exact form of the environmental radar system will depend on the scale, complexity and instability of the environment faced by the company, as well as the organizational structures and procedures embodied in the environmental radar system. It may incorporate the use of *environmental agents* (see Figure 3.5), which are essentially designated individuals, institutions or organizations contracted to filter defined elements of a given environment. At appropriate time intervals, the environmental agents may be required to produce status reports for the company. The use of internal and external environment agents can help to reduce the number of critical sources that the environmental radar system has to scan and also introduces the potential for a first-line analysis function to be incorporated in the system. As both of these alternatives have advantages and disadvantages for a company,[5] the final pattern of agents will tend to reflect the company's attitude toward its economy, its efficiency, its effectiveness and the risk inherent in its environmental information-gathering activities.

Internal sources	External sources
• Sales staff	• Customers
• General managers	• Consultants
• Purchasing	• Market research agencies
• Finance	• Business information services
• Personnel	• Media personnel
• The workforce	• Politicians
	• Trade associations
	• Government employees
	• Educational institutions
	• Suppliers
	• Financial institutions

Figure 3.5 *Potential sources for environmental agents.*

The *critical actors* are the major sources of change in the external environment. These may be viewed as the individuals, institutions and organizations which are frequently the leading generators and promoters of change within each environmental sub-domain.

Any change in their behaviour and relationships with other critical actors is likely to provide an early indication of possible new trends. The development of a *capability profile*[6] for critical actors helps to establish their relative strengths and weaknesses, their power, reliability and influence. This can be a powerful tool to assist in the assessment of their potential effect on the company's strategy. Any change in the behaviour and activities of a critical actor will create new conditions and states within their domain of operation and will alter established relationships and alignments.

Changes in the state, status, behaviour or activity of critical actors which hold significant implications for a company's critical success factors are called *critical indicators*. These should be identified and monitored at an early stage of development as they constitute evidence of potential threats or opportunities. To achieve this, the environmental radar system should incorporate not only an array of appropriate sensors to locate the occurrence of critical indicators, but also a series of *sensitivity thresholds* to initiate varying degrees of action related to the perceived significance and strength of the critical indicators.[7]

By systematically tracking the critical indicators, the critical events will begin to emerge. These are the factors which signify substantial and enduring changes in the environmental sub-domains and which impinge upon a company's ability to achieve its critical success factors. The accumulation and aggregation of critical indicators over time will facilitate predictions of the types of critical event these may generate.

The *critical trends* may be defined as the distinct and related total of the critical events over time which pose significant threats to, or present significant opportunities for, a company's critical success factors. Though environmental trends are frequently viewed as a starting point for environmental scanning activities, this is an inappropriate focus for such activity as trends are essentially the cumulative effects of prior actions and events. To identify causal factors underlying environmental change, the scanning process should concentrate on the initiating, not the confirming, factors: the critical trends.

The final component of the environment radar system, and the point of contact between it and the internal management information system, is *scenario impact analysis*. At this point, the strategic planning process, emanating from scenario analysis, is supported by the external and internal components of the company's information system and becomes dynamic.

THE MANAGEMENT INFORMATION SYSTEM

In the Critical Information Systems model the central role of critical success factors is clearly defined. The establishment of a company's criticial success factors facilitates a more accurate focusing of the information for strategic purposes. It also isolates the points within the company from which the information is required and helps to assess the degree to which the defined strategies and plans are actioned and achieved. In the absence of a clear critical success factor framework, a company's management information system may well be oriented towards specific monitoring and planning functions but is unlikely to be optimally arranged to meet the managers' critical information needs. Frequently, management information systems have been developed independently and are function specific or do not readily interface. Interfacing existing management information system components is the key to the successful translation of the Critical Information Systems model into practice.

This process can be clarified by reference to Figure 3.6. Here the main operational and associated functions are identified, i.e. the company's sub-domains. In each sub-domain various systems will exist to service the information requirements of management. Some of the output measures from these systems may be seen as critical performance measures – occupancy levels, profit percentages, payroll costs, sales revenue, etc.– and should be derived from the company's critical success factor/critical information need framework.

The *critical information providers* within the system act as a first-level filter through their role as identifiers and transmitters of critical performance measures and other information pertinent to critical success factor achievement. In the absence of interfaced systems across the company's operational sub-domains, critical performance measuring information would require manual transmissions between the systems. The critical information needs would this be diverted from their decision-support functions to routine information transfer and processing activities.

However, collectively, the systems constitute the company's *internal information radar* (see Figure 3.6), which, through the function of *internal information analysis*, is the linchpin connecting managerial decision making and the company's sub-domains.

Such systems, with their primary emphasis on internal information support and their recognition of the value of the critical success factor/critical information need framework, are perhaps the exception rather than the rule. There is frequently a lack of attention given to sub-system integration and the use of software capable of utilizing information already contained in the system's data bases. Where information systems already exist, the problems of system reassessment, modification and integration are significant.

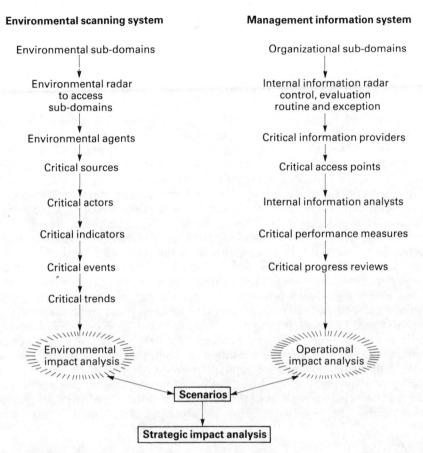

Figure 3.6 *Critical elements of the strategic business information system: comparison of the two components.*

One key problem encountered in the development, or redevelopment, of a strategic business information system is design: not only in terms of hard or software, but because of a division resulting from the design architect on the one hand and the user on the other. At a simplistic level this problem can be addressed by designing the strategic business information system of critical information needs for strategic decision-making support. However, in the same way that the people designing, operating and using the strategic business information system will be the key to its success, they are also likely to pose a number of key problems to its successful introduction and operation.

The organizational size is one such problem as this raises the issue of the transfer and communication of information and the active involvement of different parties.[8] Similarly, managerial decision making is not always conducted through rational procedures, and personal perceptions and relationships will affect the operation of a strategic business information system. A lack of communication between the system designers and users may also result in the system's failure to meet the company's critical information needs.[9]

Finally, the awareness of, and commitment to, the use of information technology in the planning process by senior management may be absent.[10] A careful consideration of such issues will greatly enhance the success of a strategic business information system.

THE STRATEGIC BUSINESS INFORMATION SYSTEM

To integrate and fuse the environmental scanning and management information system components of a company's strategic business information system is not without its problems. However, this fusion must be achieved for long-term competitive success. The key to its successful achievement lies in the design of a strategic business information system on the basis of the prior definition of strategic and operational critical success factors and an identification of the consequent external and internal critical information needs required to support the managerial decision-making process. At the heart of this process lie the company's strategic objectives and plans. This is the link between the environmental scanning and management information system components. At this point, the effects of environmental change and operational activity will be communicated to, and analysed by, the strategic decision-makers. Similarly, strategic decisions will be communicated to the external environment and operational units via the return channels within the environmental scanning and management information system components.

The Strategic Business Information System model in Figure 3.7 illustrates the nature of this two-way process. Through attention in the design stage to the development of a two-way communication channel, potential problems arising from individual dissatisfaction will be limited or resolved. Following the definition of critical success factors, and the identification of critical information needs, progress can be made toward an analysis of the various sub-systems' potential for meeting the defined needs. The key to the Strategic Business Information System model is

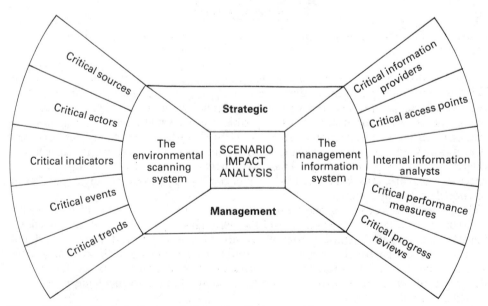

Figure 3.7   *The Strategic Business Information System model.*

therefore an accurate definition of needs and the targeting of sources from which the required information may be accessed and processed as succinctly as possible. It is not necessary to link with each component of every sub-system to achieve this goal. To realize the full potential of the Strategic Business Information System model, all critical data bases must be readily accessible.

SUMMARY

As a consequence of designing the strategic business information system to allow the utilization of information sub-systems, the benefits of reducing the volume of information transferred should be achieved. This becomes possible through the enhanced opportunities it creates for the integration of sub-system information at operational level.[11] It is both necessary and desirable to reduce the managerial time and attention it requires and to increase the speed and quality of the decision/action response.[12]

Finally, as we have commented earlier, the problems caused by disaffection and resistance to the introduction of a strategic business information system are not easily resolved. However, by attending to the crucial role people play in the system, resistance can be overcome and converted into support. In essence the aim is to dispel threats, such as displacement of people, fear of change and lack of user confidence.[13] An approach of this type will facilitate the success of the system at operational level, but it will not necessarily address the crucial issues at senior management level, where understanding, support and encouragement is vital.[14] In this case a process of strategic business information system education may need to be implemented to secure the active involvement and support of senior management.

NOTES

1. Tyrell, R., *Planning for Social Changes*, The Henley Centre, 1988.
2. Geller, A.N., 'Tracking the critical success factors for hotel companies', *Cornell HRA Quarterly*, vol. 25, no. 4, 1985; pp. 76–82.
3. Ibid.
4. Boshoff, H., 'Testing plans against alternative futures', *Long Range Planning*, vol. 22, no. 5, 1989, pp. 69–75.
5. Zentner, R.D., 'How to evaluate the present and the future corporate environment', *Journal of Business Strategy*, Spring 1981, pp. 42–51; Gilad, B. and Gilad, T., *The Business Intelligence System*, Amacom, New York, 1988; Glueck, W.F., and Jauch, R., *Business Policy and Strategic Management* (4th edn), McGraw-Hill, Singapore, 1984; Yavitz, B. and Newman, W.H., *Strategy In Action*, Free Press, New York, 1982.
6. Child, J., 'Organisational structure, environment and performance: the role of strategic choice', *Sociology*, vol. 6, 1972, pp. 2–21.
7. Linnerman, R.E., and Kennell, F.D., 'Shirt-sleeve approach to long range plans', *Harvard Business Review*, Mar./Apr. 1977, pp. 141–50.
8. Radley, G.W. *Management Information Systems*, International Textbook Co., Glasgow, 1973; Verziji, J.J., *Planning and Information Systems for Jobs Allocation*, Macmillan, London, 1981.

9. Burn, J., and O'Neil, M., *Information Analysis*, Paradigm, London, 1987; Gamble, P.R. and Smith, G., 'Expert front office management by computer', *International Journal of Hospitality Management*, vol. 5, no. 3, 1986, pp. 109–14.
10. West, J.J. and Olson, M.D., 'Environmental scanning, industry structure and strategy making: concepts and research in the hospitality industry', *International Journal of Hospitality Management*, vol. 8, no. 4, 1989, pp. 282–98.
11. Kiechal, W, 'To compute or not to compute', *Cornell HRA Quarterly*, vol. 24, no. 4, 1984, pp. 9–11.
12. Geller, A.N., 'How to improve your information system', *Cornell HRA Quarterly*, vol. 26, no. 2, 1985, pp. 19–27.
13. Leslie, D., McDowell, D.A. and Gummer, H., 'The application of computers to the control function', *Journal of Contemporary Hospitality Management*, vol. 1, no. 1, 1990, pp. 23–6.
14. Wack, P., 'Scenarios: uncharted waters ahead', *Harvard Business Review*, Sep./Oct. 1985, pp. 73–89.

4

Productivity and performance measurement and monitoring

Nick Johns and Ken Wheeler

INTRODUCTION

The objectives of this chapter are twofold:

- to define productivity, and to describe and explain the theory and practice underlying productivity measurement;
- to identify the relevance of productivity management to the future of the hospitality industry, and to examine possible strategies for increasing productivity within the industry.

Economic studies of service industries and of the hospitality subsector tend to reveal a poor track record in productivity. For example, Elfing[1] points out that productivity in the service sectors of British, US and European industry lags behind that of the manufacturing sector in these countries. Elfing and Medlik[2] also note that the rate of productivity growth within the hospitality industry is actually falling, whilst that in other service industries, such as transport, retail and banking, is slowly growing. These industries have improved their productivity performance as a matter of strategy during the past two decades. The implication is that a similar strategic emphasis is desirable within the hospitality industry. Johnston[3] identifies increasing productivity as one way for British service industries to become more competitive. The market for hospitality services is expected to mature during the 1990s, requiring a greater competitive thrust.[4] At the same time, supplies of labour in the UK, USA, Australia[5] and elsewhere are dwindling. A management focus on productivity can potentially offer increases in market share and at the same time make the industry somewhat less reliant on staff recruitment. For these reasons, productivity is likely to become a major concern of hospitality management during the 1990s and into the twenty-first century.

DEFINITIONS

Productivity is basically an economic concept. Sources such as the *Oxford English Dictionary* (*OED*) and *Encyclopaedia Britannica* (*EB*) define it variously as follows:

The rate of output per unit of input. (*OED*)

The arithmetical ratio between the amount produced and the amount of resources used in the course of production. (*OED*)

The ratio of what is produced over what is required to produce it. (*EB*)

Expressed arithmetically, this economists' definition is:

$$\text{Productivity} = \frac{\text{Wealth generated}}{\text{Resources used}}$$

Wealth is dependent on two factors: the quantity and quality of what is produced. If the quantity or the quality of goods increases, so does the wealth generated. If both quantity and quality are increased, the wealth generated increases arithmetically in proportion, so:

$$\text{Wealth generated} = \text{Quantity} \times \text{Quality}$$

Thus quantity, quality and resources all play a part in determining productivity:

$$\text{Productivity} = \frac{\text{Volume} \times \text{Quality}}{\text{Resources used}}$$

This model of production was originally developed from manufacturing industry, but is equally applicable to service subsectors such as hospitality. We can view the hospitality industry as improving the quality of life for its guests. 'Quantity' can then be regarded as the number of guests who receive this service.

Strategies for measuring and increasing productivity must take account of all these factors. For instance, a strategy which seeks to improve productivity by increasing quantity output must also make sure that quality is maintained or improved and that there is no accompanying increase in the resources used. Quantity measures such as room occupancy and number of covers sold tend to be poor estimates because increased output may strain resources so that quality falls.

'Quality' is at best a very difficult aspect to define. Its measurement tends to focus upon customer attitudes and 'satisfaction'. Thus the accuracy of quality measurement is often doubtful and the units in which it is measured are not comparable with those of quantity. Thus the expression: quantity × quality (e.g. no. of covers × attitude rating) is meaningless except as a comparison with other studies, conducted by the same methodology in the same hotel. However, the approach of separately measuring and comparing quantity and resource cost is recommended by Dittmer and Griffin[6] and may be useful as long as only one of the three factors changes at a time. An alternative approach is to base productivity measurement in 'hard' measures such as volume of sales. Selling price reflects economic value rather than true quality, but this approach nevertheless leads to a more useful and more widely comparable definition of productivity:

$$\text{Productivity} = \frac{\text{Sales revenue}}{\text{Costs}}$$

Defined in this way, productivity can be a practical measure of unit performance and management effectiveness.

Adam and Ebert[7] break down costs into labour, capital, materials and energy. UK practice generally involves identifying direct labour separately as a prime cost and including indirect labour with other costs as an overhead. Thus the definition of productivity becomes:

$$\text{Productivity} = \frac{\text{Sales revenue}}{\text{Labour} + \text{Overheads} + \text{Materials} + \text{Energy}}$$

Partial productivities are also used to monitor performance in the hospitality industry, i.e.:

$$\text{Material productivity} = \frac{\text{Sales revenue}}{\text{Material cost}}$$

$$\text{Labour productivity} = \frac{\text{Sales revenue}}{\text{Direct labour cost}}$$

and so on. These ratios may be reversed: for example, wage cost/sales revenue rather than sales revenue/wage cost.

Further useful management information can be derived from the original productivity equation of breaking down sales revenue and costs by department. The definition of productivity thus becomes:

$$\text{Productivity} = \frac{SR_1 + SR_2 + SR_3 + \ldots}{\text{costs}_1 + \text{costs}_2 + \text{costs}_3 + \ldots}$$

where: SR_1, SR_2, SR_3, etc. are the individual departmental sales revenues
costs_1, costs_2, costs_3, etc. are the individual departmental costs.

Another way of analysing productivity information is to break it down by product. In this case the items SR_1/costs_1, etc. refer to items sold: for example, banqueting, restaurant, coffee shop and bar sales. It is also possible to assess the sales revenues and costs of the different market segments. A spectrum of high- to low-price classifications can be used, i.e. SR_1, SR_2, SR_3, etc.

In summary, the concept 'productivity' always involves a ratio between generated wealth and resources. In strategic terms this implies three factors: volume, quality and resources. One approach to assessing productivity is through changes in these three factors, but since they are interdependent, results are almost meaningless unless only one factor varies at a time.

MEASURING PRODUCTIVITY

In the hospitality service industry the component parts of the productivity equation:

$$\text{Productivity} \quad = \quad \frac{\text{Wealth generated}}{\text{Resources used}}$$

are commonly measured in monetary terms. This infomration is derived by the accountant from the traditional cost-based revenue accounts. Productivity in its various forms is obtained from these data as a series of ratios, i.e. revenue/costs, etc.

Kotas[8] states that two things must be done to give accounting and control procedures the right orientation in the market-oriented (high-average-spend) sector of the industry. Firstly, we must develop new techniques. Secondly, we must adapt existing techniques to make them more purposeful and useful in the market-oriented business.

In a seller's market the traditional, cost-oriented accounting approach – with management focus on production and finance – may be appropriate. The hospitality industry, however, has been pushed by circumstances towards a consumer-oriented philosophy of provision. Such an orientation implies a high degree of dependence on market demand. Hence it is right to concentrate management attention on the revenue side of the business rather than the cost or production side. However, no company should ignore cost altogether. In terms of the productivity equation:

$$\frac{\text{Quantity} \times \text{Quality}}{\text{Costs}} \qquad \begin{array}{l}\text{(of output)}\\[4pt]\text{(of inputs)}\end{array}$$

market orientation relates to the top half of the equation (as represented by the organization's outputs) and cost control to the denominator (the system inputs).

Measures of quantity and quality

Quantitative sales-related outputs provide a yardstick against which an organization's effectiveness can be measured. They are primarily accounting and control procedures, concerned with optimizing product-based revenue. They imply a sales concept of market orientation, which Kotler sees as being 'a "product orientation" backed by selling promotion aimed at generating high sales as the key to achieving high profits'.[9]

On the other hand, the marketing concept is 'a consumer needs orientation backed by integrated marketing aimed at generating consumer satisfaction as the key to satisfying organizational goals'.[10]

Therefore, in addition to their responsibilities towards investors by the achievement of high profits, responsive organizations have a strong interest in how their publics see them and their products. It is the organization's image, not necessarily its reality, to which people respond.[11] The responsive organization has a vital interest in learning about its 'images' in the marketplace, and managers often want to know how customers view their company in terms of the quality of provision of the service product.

Although more difficult to quantify than the other performance indicators, methods have been proposed for measuring images. For example, survey methods have been proposed for measuring customers' perceptions. Kotler[12] sees a clear relationship between an organization's image and its delivery of consumer satisfaction. Others question whether this is the case. For instance, Bell says 'the measurement of satisfactions as an output of marketing is virtually impossible (because satisfactions are both physical and psychological, they are often extremely subjective)'.[13] Buckley notes that 'only indexes that are capable of objective measurement can be used as surrogates'.[14]

If there is any doubt about the correlation between a measured image and consumer satisfaction, a number of alternative, more objective measures are available. For instance, the rate of repeat purchasing may be used as a surrogate measure of satisfaction. Repeat sales are certainly a better measure than mere daily and weekly till receipts. The latter might include a high proportion of dissatisfied customers who subsequently abandon the product because of poor quality of service or food.[15]

Another type of measure is the audit of customer service standards. Questions which need to be asked usually fall into the following categories:

- *physical goods*: food and beverage quality; room size and maintenance; temperature and humidity control; swimming pool temperature; lift availability/efficiency; general cleanliness; furniture condition, etc.
- *physical environment*: site and situation; room location; atmosphere; ambience; noise; aspect; parking facilities, etc.
- *service and personnel*: interaction between service providers and guests, e.g. reservation handling; service level/speed; employee attitude, etc.

This information is often obtained by the use of self-completion questionnaires. However, the available evidence suggests that these are not a very good indicator of customer opinion. Nightingale[16] says that the response rate of room questionnaires is generally low and that they are probably unrepresentative. Research findings in the United States by Lewis[17] suggest that high-income groups are less likely to use questionnaires than others. Repeat customers are also less likely to use them, either to compliment or complain. Marris suggests that questionnaires should be

> given to selected customers personally, with a remark such as 'I would specially like you to go through this' or 'The Manager asked me specially to give this to you, sir' . . . Asked the right way, at the right time, people mostly take it as a compliment to be asked and it is likely to yield a higher response.[18]

This is certainly more friendly than the current practice of leaving the form in the guest bedroom. It increases the chance of completion and provides customer-relations desks with a specific task to undertake.

Ratios

A correct balance of the productivity equation is vital to the health of a business organization. Wilson[19] states that an organization must be able to make the link between the outputs and the inputs in the productivity equation referred to above. Only in this way can it 'learn' and adapt its behaviour to ensure that it is progressing along an acceptable path towards its objectives.

The link between outputs and inputs is termed a *feedback loop*. It is the essential mechanism for varying the system's inputs and ensuring that its behaviour (as represented by the system's outputs) is consistent with business objectives (see Figure 4.1).[20]

Productivity ratios may take two forms. They may concentrate on revenue by making this the numerator of the expression, i.e. revenue/costs. Alternatively they may concentrate on costs by inverting the expression, so that cost input becomes the numerator.

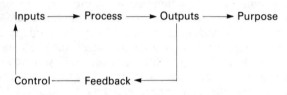

Figure 4.1   *Simple control loop.*

Ratios emphasizing sales revenue

The following measures are customarily used in the hospitality industry to gauge success in meeting efficiency targets.

Sales-related outputs (quantity and quality)

Parts of the management function is to specify quantitative targets. Relevant outputs from the system are the results of performance and target attainment. These include the base measures of sales (in units) and turnover or revenue (£). Many other techniques and tools are also available to the hospitality manager: for example, revenue-based ratios. Some of the more common ratios are discussed briefly below in the context of efficiency.[21]

Rooms division: quantitative measures

Occupancy percentage and/or *double occupancy* (on a daily, weekly, monthly or annual basis). This is calculated by dividing the rooms used during a period (a night, a week) by the rooms available during that period and multiplying by 100. High room occupancy and high double occupancy are both desirable in terms of efficiency. The proportion of 'doubles' let as 'singles' should be measured, as the latter normally generate lower room rates. Double occupancy is sometimes expressed as a room density index by dividing the total number of guests for a period by the total rooms occupied during that period.

Guest/bed/sleeper occupancy may be calculated on a daily, weekly, monthly or annual basis as:

$$\frac{\text{Beds sold}}{\text{Beds available}} \times 100$$

Bed occupancy is an indication of the utilization of sleeping accommodation. It is often regarded as a means of judging the efficiency of the front desk in filling the hotel. (It is quite possible to let every bedroom in the hotel – 100 per cent room occupancy – and yet not have sold every bed.)

Maximum apartment revenue (MAR) or room sales potential can be calculated on a daily, weekly, monthly or annual basis. This is the relationship between actual and potential room sales, the latter being calculated on the basis of published tariffs. The percentage MAR is especially significant when the hotel is discounting room rates to tour operators during periods of intense competition.

Average room rate per room occupied is calculated daily by dividing rooms revenue by the number of rooms occupied. The trend of this figure is important. When occupancy is low there may be a tendency for the lower-priced rooms to be more popular; the average room rate will fall. At times of low occupancy a high room rate can reflect the successful directing of sales effort into selling higher-priced rooms rather than lower-priced ones.

Average room rate per guest is calculated daily by dividing revenue from rooms by the number of guests. Again the trend of this figure is important and is affected greatly by the double occupancy rate.

Room sales per front-desk clerk per day, week or month is a productivity measure that can be compared against a standard.

Average spend of each guest is calculated by dividing the total revenue by the number of customers during a period. In the short term it may indicate the efficiency of staff in selling facilities which are not part of any inclusive tariff. It can also, of course, vary with changes in the overall price structure.

Room occupancy percentages by key segments, by business mix, etc. can also be calculated. This involves breaking down room occupancy percentages into business, conference, full rate and so on. Sales revenue can be broken down on a similar basis. This calculation is able to show which market segments predominate. This enables the manager to 'target' his or her promotion at particular groups.

Food and beverage operations: quantitative measures

Restaurant occupancy (by meal or by day) is the number of covers during a meal period divided by the restaurant seating capacity. In the high-average-spend sector the norm is 1; in fast-food outlets 7 or more is commonplace. An analysis of the restaurant occupancy trend may reveal poor service or low food quality. Alternatively it may indicate that high prices are keeping customers away.

Average spending power (US 'average check') is calculated by dividing food and beverage revenue by the number of meals served. The trend of this figure is important, but it may also be used to determine the revenue effect of a change in menu item(s).

Sales revenue per employee can be calculated per meal period, day, week or month. The measure is primarily used to assess the performance of employees against a standard, or to determine upward or downward trends in labour productivity. The number of guests served per waiter per meal period, day, week or month can be used for a similar purpose.

Percentage of beverage to food revenue can be used to direct the promotion of beverage items (wine with meals, for example). Separate sales mix figures are also often kept for food – starters, main dish, vegetables, sweets, etc.

Percentage of food/beverage to rooms revenue may also include revenue from minor operated departments. A change in the revenue mix among operated departments can be important because some are more profitable than others. Typical profit/volume ratios in the accommodation sectors of the industry are 90–95 per cent for rooms, 50–55 per cent for food and beverage and 10–20 per cent for minor operated departments such as telephone, garage/parking, rentals, etc. From a cost–benefit point of view, advertising is more beneficially spent on areas of higher profitability.

Ratios emphasizing costs

The revenue-oriented ratios discussed above emphasize a marketing approach to productivity accounting and measurement. Ratios can also emphasize cost orientation if they are inverted, so that costs are divided by revenue. Such ratios are instructive to management for evaluating operating success. They indicate areas of good or poor management and pinpoint reasons for differences in rates of growth of sales and profits. Ratios or percentages calculated from the current period's trading results may also be set against standards in order to measure performance. These should be considered alongside the management accounting system to judge departmental efficiency.

Harrington[22] suggests the calculation of standards in the form of ratios, the actual percentage varying according to the size of the unit, company policy and seasonal factors. For example, in the first item below (the ratio of rooms payroll to rooms sales) where rooms sales are represented as 100 per cent, wages should be between 20 and 25 per cent (UK hotels).

Performance standards ratios

Rooms division

Wages:	Rooms wages to rooms sales
Laundry:	Weekly cost to total rooms revenue
Cost of servicing:	Twin room to net room rate (includes wages, guest supplies and laundry)
Rooms trading profit:	Sales less wages and material cost to sales

Food and beverage division

Food department

Food department wages:	Restaurants
(% of departmental sales)	Coffee shop
	Breakfasts
	Banqueting
Materials cost:	Coffee shop or medium-sized restaurant
(% of food sales)	Luxury restaurant
'Cost per dollar sale':	Steak bars
Food trading profit:	'Cash gross profit' (sales less cost of materials, and wages to sales)

Food stock turnover per year

Beverage department

Similar ratios or percentages to those of food department, applied to bar operation and beverage sales.

Other departments

Administration and general wages/total sales
Advertising and sales promotion costs/total sales
Property operation, maintenance and energy costs/total sales

Fixed charges/total sales
Net profit/total sales
Net profit/capital employed (return on investment)
Monthly debts/total annual sales

Profitability and productivity

Two important ratios should be mentioned: namely, *gross profit* and *net margin*:

$$\text{Gross profit ratio} = \frac{\text{Gross profit}}{\text{Sales}} \times 100$$

$$\text{Net margin ratio} = \frac{\text{Net margin}}{\text{Sales}} \times 100$$

The gross profit ratio is useful as a measure of operating efficiency. It ensures that the business is earning sufficient revenue from trading to cover wages and other costs and to leave an adequate profit. Net margin is gross profit less wages and staff costs. These ratios tend to be calculated monthly or even weekly and are highly regarded in the industry as control indicators. The after-wage profit, or net margin, is seen as particularly important to ensure a correct adjustment of labour/sales. Depending upon variables such as size of unit, company policy and seasonal factors, this ratio may be as much as 30–35 per cent of total sales. Any unforeseen rise in labour costs could be critical to the sales/profit relationship. Because of the growing significance of labour as an element of cost (and a scarce resource), the UK hospitality industry has paid particular attention recently to developing standards of performance based on labour costs. The examples shown in Table 4.1 are based on standards developed by a major UK hotel company.

Similar production standards may be developed for other non-food and beverage staff. For example:

Dish washers:	110 covers per hour/per person
Room attendants:	12–15 occupied rooms per day per person
Front-desk clerks:	55 occupied rooms per shift per day

Each standard consists of a number of units (occupied rooms, covers, movements, etc.) that an employee is expected to achieve within a normal shift. The intention of such standards is to institutionalize efficiency and hence improve productivity. An essential preliminary step to preparing performance standards is to ensure that the establishment's quality standards are well understood. The link between

$$\frac{\text{Quantity} \times \text{Quality}}{\text{Costs}} \quad \text{(or productivity)}$$

Table 4.1   *Food and beverage performance standards*

Food service	Per waiter/waitress
Breakfast	
Full service	20 covers
Part self-service	24 covers
Lunch/dinner	
Restaurant	12 covers
Coffee shop	15 covers
Banquets	
Where basic charge under £14	12 covers
Where basic charge £14 and over	10 covers

Beverage service	Per waiter/waitress
Restaurant	
Drinks at table	40 covers
Coffee shop	
Drinks at table	50 covers
Banquets	
Cash or account orders	40 covers
Bar operation	40 covers

Payroll as % of departmental sales	
Food sales	
Restaurant	45%
Coffee shop	40%
Breakfasts	40%
Banqueting	35%
Beverage sales	
Restaurant	17.5%
Coffee shop	15%
Banqueting	15%
Bar operation	15%

Source: R. Kotas, *Management Accounting for Hotels and Restaurants* (2nd edn), Surrey University Press, 1986, pp. 299–300.

then becomes all too apparent. For example, the productivity of room attendants would be measured in terms of the number of rooms serviced in an eight-hour shift. This might be increased simply by reducing the amount of time spent on each room and could be one way to reduce costs and increase profitability. A national UK hotel company recently set a productivity standard of 20 minutes 7 seconds for cleaning a bedroom! One wonders whether such precise measures could ever be regarded as attainable standards by rooms staff. Such an approach may well prove counter-productive in terms of the quality of room cleanliness.

Controlling labour inputs

Peters and Waterman[23] suggest that treating people as the principal resource may be crucial to productivity. Attention to the care, feeding and unshackling of the average person is perhaps the key to success in the 1990s in an industry in which organization and people in the organization have to achieve greater synonymity. People orientation encourages respect for the product. This in turn results in the achievements of higher productivity: *productivity through people*.

However, the development of a staffing control system is more complicated than just deciding on performance standards. One of the main problems involves matching labour demand forecasts with the labour supply and with the sales forecast. This link involves productivity targets. If labour is going to be used to maximum efficiency, forecasts and targets must match. The demand for hospitality products, however, is constantly fluctuating. Management therefore has the problem of regulating labour supplies to meet demand. In addition, the proportion of fixed labour supply (i.e. minimum staffing levels) must be determined. So, how can management match labour supply to demand? What is the optimum level of employment in conditions of fluctuating business? What is the minimum staffing required?

There are no precise answers to these questions, but the following technique approaches the solution:

- forecast sales;
- classify jobs: identify jobs which vary with demand;
- establish a performance standard per employee, e.g. 15 rooms per 'person' day;
- translate sales forecast into a demand for labour;
- compare forecast demand for labour with forecast labour supply;
- adjust labour supply to match demand (the end process).

Example

Based on an employment level of 14 room attendants on a 5-day, 40-hour week, the labour supply per week would be:

$$14 \times 40 \; = \; 560 \text{ total hours per week}$$

This is adjusted for a 5-day, 40-hour week in each 7-day period, as follows:

$$\frac{560 \times 5}{40 \times 7} \; = \; \begin{array}{l} 10 \text{ room attendants} \\ \text{on duty per day} \end{array}$$

Given a performance standard of 15 rooms per shift, this would relate to forecast weekly sales as shown in Table 4.2.

Table 4.2   *Labour inputs: an example*

Day (1)	Room Sales (2)	Performance Standard (3)	Person days reqd[1] (4)	F/T staff[2] (5)	Staff diff.[3] (6)	Rooms diff.[4] (7)
1	180	15	12	10	−2	−30
2	210	15	14	10	−4	−60
3	240	15	16	10	−6	−90
4	105	15	7	10	+3	+45
5	240	15	16	10	−6	−90
6	180	15	12	10	−2	−30
7	150	15	10	10	0	0

[1]Col. (2) ÷ col. (3).
[2]Room attendants on duty each day based on an employment level of 14 room attendants.
[3]Differences in staff versus requirements: col. (4) − col. (5).
[4]Differences in rooms versus requirements: col. (3) × col. (6).

   In this example maximum efficiency is reached when columns (6) and (7) show zero (i.e. day 7). This is the only day on which maximum labour productivity is achieved. For the remainder of the week the existing employment level fluctuates, but in general is insufficient to match demand. The analysis gives the optimum staffing level (i.e. for this model between 16 and 18 room attendants). Additional staff could be employed to cope with the shortfall.
   Alternative tactics are available for adjusting the supply of labour. Overtime payments, bonuses for increased personal productivity or payments for casual or part-time staff are frequently used. Management should calculate the cost of increasing labour by these means, since control of cost inputs is essential for maximizing labour productivity.

Towards market-oriented measurement of outputs

This chapter has demonstrated the relationship between the two parts of the basic productivity equation: revenue (outputs) and costs (inputs). The two are linked by a conversion process (termed *management decision*) as shown in Figure 4.2. System

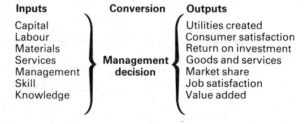

Figure 4.2   *Simple business system.*
Source: Based on Wilson, R.M.S., *Management Control and Marketing Planning*, Heinemann, London, 1982.

inputs and outputs must be monitored and controlled to ensure that business objectives are being achieved.

Revenue from hospitality outputs is easily measured. Like costs, it is commonly disaggregated on a *departmental* basis. Conventional accounts, however, normally only assess the function of departments. It would be useful to disaggregate in terms of *products*, i.e. the hotel's 'portfolio'. Figure 4.3 shows how this can be done for both departments (right-hand side) and market segments (left-hand side). The portfolio might include some of the following in its key segments:

- business (individual)
- groups (business)
- weekend and midweek break
- holiday (independent)
- coach tours

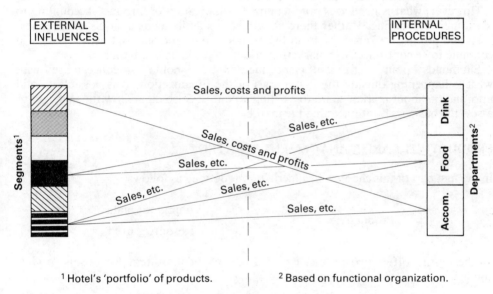

¹ Hotel's 'portfolio' of products.   ² Based on functional organization.

Table 4.3   *Disaggregation of an hotel's products to market segments.*

Traditional accounting systems, based on food, drink and accommodation, do not truly reflect market orientation. Instead they are *department oriented*, designed to emphasize responsibility and controllability. This way of breaking down the figures measures how well managers have performed. Arguably, more useful information could be gained by disaggregating accounting data into market segments. In this way a more *market-oriented* view of productivity could be obtained.

Traditional cost-based accounting is also subject to all the criticisms usually levelled at cost-control practices. For instance, there is an overemphasis on short-run results. This is in spite of the fact that output measures are oriented in the correct direction, i.e. towards the customer and the marketplace. Kaplan says there is a need to sensitize management to 'environmental dynamism'.[24] Accounting systems and the hospitality service industry exist in dynamic conditions. A focus on simple, aggregated, short-term financial measures is not sensitive enough. Performance indicators should be compatible with *proactive* management. Most of the productivity measures discussed in this section imply a *reactive* view.

Short-run measures are generally average indicators, which give no indication of the 'portfolio' of cost/profit centres. For example, departmental gross profit levels based on food, drink and accommodation are a function of multiple products and markets – some of which are growing, others falling. In these circumstances, aggregate gross profit levels disguise rather than reveal what is happening in productivity terms. The same criticism may be used against the single aggregate measure, return on investment (ROI). Optimization across multi-segments and multi-products produces few meaningful results. Hospitality accounting systems of the future must be able to assess the respective profitability/productivity of the diversified product portfolio. They must relate to the planning, decision-making and control needs of the marketing manager. No doubt departmental efficiency controls will continue to be important in the 1990s. However, it is important that accounting emphasis should change. The importance of the customer must become more evident.

However, what is needed is not a complete subjugation of 'product' accounting to 'customer' accounting. Rather there should be a simultaneous analysis of revenues, costs and profits, broken down by both customers and products. In this way costs will continue to be controlled, but marketing orientation will be strengthened.

Simmonds[25] points out that efficiency measurement should also concern itself with what is happening outside the boundaries of the organization. It is possible to add information about market share to existing accounts. Such data allow the manager to assess the business position within the market.

PRODUCTIVITY AND MANAGEMENT STRATEGY

In the first part of this chapter, productivity was defined as follows:

$$\text{Productivity} \quad = \quad \frac{\text{Volume} \times \text{Quality}}{\text{Resources used}}$$

In theory this offers two distinct types of management strategy for raising productivity:

- Volume and/or quality can be increased, while reducing, holding constant or only raising slightly the level of resources used. This strategy primarily involves aggressive marketing and improvements in product development, image, quality and market share. A number of techniques are available to achieve these goals without a proportional increase in resources. Such strategies may be called *expansive* productivity strategies.

- Resources can be decreased while the volume and/or quality are decreased slightly, held constant or increased. This is the type of strategy commonly associated with productivity management in the manufacturing sector. Typically it involves careful analysis of costs and profitability, with cutbacks in material, energy and labour wherever they can be made. Such strategies may be called *contractive* strategies.

Both types of strategy may be used together. However, the relative emphasis on expansive versus contractive tactics differs markedly between industries and organizations; it may also vary considerably as one particular industry or organization develops. Geller[26] lists the most important goals and critical success factors (CSFs) of 27 US hotel companies, as shown in Table 4.3.

From Geller's results it is clear that expansive strategies are readily accepted in the hospitality industry. They are particularly suited to the market-oriented outlook of managers. Geller's list contains no mention of productivity measurement, without which the effectiveness of expansive strategies cannot be controlled. The item 'cost control' is well down Geller's list and not related to productivity management *per se*. In fact contractive, cost-control tactics may offer the industry possibilities for progress in productivity, simply because they are not currently given priority.

Table 4.3   *Goals and critical success factors identified by 74 US hotel executives*

Goal	Rank	Critical success factor	Rank
Profitability/return on investment	1	Employee attitude	1
Growth	2	Guest satisfaction	2
Best management		Superior product	3
(including image)	3	Superior location	4
Greatest market share	4	Maximize revenue	5
Guest satisfaction	4	Cost control	5
Share value	5	Increase market share	6
Employee morale	5	Increase customer	
Maximize cash flow	6	price/value perception	7
Brand loyalty	6	Achieve market	
Financial stability	7	segmentation	8

Source: Geller, A. N., 'Tracking the critical success factors for hotel companies', *Cornell HRA Quarterly*, Feb. 1985, pp. 76–9.

Contractive strategies for productivity management

Costs may be reduced in six main areas: materials, physical plant, energy, general overheads, direct labour and indirect labour.

Controlling material costs

Materials contribute a substantial part of the cost of food and beverage operations. Therefore savings on materials may offer a worthwhile increase in productivity. Savings can be made by revising operational procedures to reduce quantities used, by controlling wastage and pilfering or by changing to cheaper materials. Merricks and Jones[27] give as an example of this the use of lumpfish roe as a garnish instead of caviare. These authors also mention renegotiating suppliers' contracts as a way of reducing material costs.

Although a large organization may achieve considerable economies in this way, for most units cost reductions are limited. Eventually there will come a point where customers perceive a fall in quality. Furthermore, acknowledging a substitution, for example by a menu description such as 'garnished with tinned lumpfish roe', may be destructive in marketing terms. On the other hand, failure to acknowledge such a substitution may contravene the Food or Trade Description Acts. Only food portions may be reduced in cost cutting; beverage measures are controlled by law.

Controlling costs incurred on physical plant

Physical plant mainly means room size and quality. Accommodation sales are a major contributor to hospitality revenue, so reductions in room costs are an attractive way to increase productivity. Possible tactics are to make rooms smaller by subdivision or redesign of the whole interior. Another area of potential savings is in maintenance, particularly redecoration.

Reduction of room size by lowering ceilings is often advantageous as it reduces energy costs. However, reducing floor area is inadvisable because it may be perceived as a lowering of quality. Once again there is a balance to be maintained between efficiency and customer expectations. Maintenance may be made more efficient: for example, by adopting planned, preventive maintenance strategies in place of corrective ones. However, reductions in maintenance expenditure may quickly be seen as a loss of quality.

Controlling energy costs

Energy costs do not make up a large part of a hotel's budget, but they are comparatively easily controlled. Many units are charged a high tariff, so savings can be considerable. Energy use can be controlled by thermal insulation, by staff awareness programmes and by automatic or customer-operated controls. Items of equipment or accommodation zones can be separately metered and budgeted. In energy-intensive operations such as cooking and laundry, more economical equipment such as induction hobs can be installed, or recovery devices such as heat pumps used. Capital outlay is high. Thermal insulation, on the other hand, usually needs little capital injection. It is almost always cost effective and frequently brings other benefits such as noise control. However, it is limited as a cost-cutting tactic.

Automatic electrical devices are now available which switch power on or off when a guest leaves a room, but these are of little use with double rooms where one guest wishes to remain in the room while the other goes out. Savings may also be made when guests can individually control the temperature of rooms. It is possible to meter energy use during food preparation and arrive at standard energy costs. These can be budgeted and analysed in the same way as food costs. By metering bedroom zones it is similarly possible to allocate accommodation energy costs. These can be used as budgetary goals for management and staff, in conjunction with an energy awareness programme.

It is common to contract laundry operations to outsiders, but to do the same with food preparation may fall short of customers' expectations. However, techniques such as *sous vide* now give a high-quality chilled product difficult to distinguish from the freshly prepared item. Schafheitle and Light[28] point out that the technique can be used to rationalize menu planning and extend choice as well as cutting energy and labour costs. Commercially produced *sous vide* items are currently available to the hospitality industry.

Controlling overheads

General overheads include such costs as advertising, printing, insurance and depreciation. They do not constitute a large part of the hospitality budget, and for the most part are not easily controlled. Advertising and printing costs offer potential savings, but these may jeopardize the marketing thrust. Sales revenue may fall, so that no actual increase in productivity is achieved.

Controlling direct labour costs

Direct labour is an attractive target for cost cutting. It is a significant expenditure in most departmental budgets. Reductions in direct labour costs can be made by reducing staffing levels and/or cutting rates of pay. The latter option is limited by market forces, but in any case is ill-advised. A fall in staff morale may result, eventually to be perceived as unfriendliness or inefficiency by guests. On the other hand, back-of-house staffing levels may be reduced by contracting food preparation, laundry, etc. to outsiders. It is now common practice for hotel and restaurant kitchens to buy ready-prepared vegetables. Reliable, high-quality cook-chill production heralds the possibility of purchasing completed menu items, with still further reductions in kitchen staff numbers.

Manufacturing industry has developed a number of tactics for improving the labour costs per unit produced. These include reorganization of facilities, scheduling, ergonomic analysis, work study and mechanization. Productivity improvement techniques of this kind can be applied to food production and are reviewed by Milson and Kirk.[29]

Reorganization of facilities. A typical development in food production is the centralized production of chilled or frozen meals. Labour savings are made by instituting production-line methods which reduce the labour time per item to a minimum. Much larger quantities can be produced at a time than in individual restaurant kitchens, and the need for expensive shift work is reduced. Savings may also be made in energy, wages, raw materials, transport and storage. If the centralized kitchen is large and versatile enough, there need be no loss of menu choice. Reorganization may also be applied to laundry, cleaning and maintenance services, particularly if a number of units are grouped closely together.

Reorganization can be applied to food service as well as to food production. Cafeteria-style operations, for example, improve productivity by replacing waiting staff with customer self-service at a counter. However, this tends to be perceived as a loss of service quality. More sophisticated models now allow the customer to find a seat, note the table number and make the order, which is brought from the kitchen by a waitress. There is probably scope for replacing porter and room service in hotels with customer self-service along these lines, though generally with a perceived loss of quality.

Scheduling. This involves identifying and matching the availability of equipment and staff with the required output. It is possible to estimate equipment and staff requirements with precision by investigating the menu cycle and the likely variations in demand. Scheduling techniques have been applied to detailed aspects such as tray assembly. Scheduling may also be useful as a means of saving energy. Coltman[30] describes the application of staff scheduling in the hospitality industry and its impact on labour costs.

Ergonomic analysis. Movements of personnel are analysed as they work using techniques such as 'string charts', cyclegraphs and stroboscopic pictures.[31] The analysis and subsequent workplace redesign are aimed at economy of motion. Hence labour is saved and labour productivity increases.

Work study. Tasks are timed in order to identify their labour content and cost.

Related techniques have been used in the USA, the UK and Sweden to set criteria for the labour content of individual dishes. Work study can aid scheduling or layout planning, and it can also be used to assess the potential value of mechanization or automation.

Mechanization. This involves replacing operations by mechanical ones. For example, machines are generally used to peel potatoes, and increasingly to chop foods. These operations were formerly done by hand, so there is a considerable labour saving and increase in productivity. Deskilling is an effect of mechanization. Usually it takes more skill to chop vegetables, etc. by hand than to operate a food-processing machine. When mechanical operations replace manual ones, a less skilled workforce is generally required. Thus mechanization reduces the labour cost in two ways. It reduces the number of person hours required on a job. By reducing the skill level it can also cut wage rates and training costs. However, there is a need for new, purpose-designed equipment for many catering operations.

Manufacturing industry has developed a number of quantitative, analytical techniques which can be used to assess the effectiveness of scheduling, reorganizing, mechanization, etc. These have a wider significance for productivity in the hospitality industry, as will be seen later in this chapter.

Controlling indirect labour costs

Indirect labour includes staff engaged in management, marketing, maintenance, the personnel function, security, etc. Many of these are involved in internal/external communication, record keeping and so on. Information technology can therefore replace certain functions. For example, Gamble and Kipps[32] describe a catering information system capable of greatly enhancing managerial performance by giving more rapid access to operational information. In theory similar systems could improve the flow of information concerned with maintenance, personnel, etc. Savings on staffing would always depend on unit size; technology may reduce the workable size of a department, but it is unlikely to replace departments altogether. However, the structure of many hospitality organizations is determined by tradition as much as by logic. Reorganization and in particular a review of staff function (see below) may pay dividends in terms of cost cutting.

Contractive strategies and the hospitality industry

Several researchers have examined the possibility of adapting productivity management techniques from manufacturing industry. Jones[33] identifies as a major difficulty the inherent diversity of most hospitality operations, compared with those found in manufacturing industry. He argues that the type of contractive strategies found in the manufacturing sector are only appropriate for back-of-house operations such as food production or laundry. Front-of-house management should be concerned with sales volume and quality: in other words, with expansive strategies.

Witt and Witt[34] present an impressive body of evidence that poor productivity in the hospitality industry is related to a lack of understanding and application of quantitative and analytical techniques. These authors quote findings by Martin and Clark,[35] which show operations management techniques to be seldom used by hotel companies. Only large groups, capable of supporting a management services department, admitted to using the techniques to a significant extent. Many respondents in the study indicated that they did not know of the techniques. Martin and Clark's list included statistical and quantitative methods: for example, critical path analysis, linear programming and queuing theory. All are commonly used in evaluating productivity tactics such as scheduling and reorganization. Martin and Clark's list also included value analysis and quality circles. Witt and Witt argue that many or all of these techniques are appropriate to hospitality operations. They discuss the impact on productivity monitoring and controlling inventory, labour and quality. They also discuss self-service techniques and the possible introduction of flexible working practices.

Various authors argue that contractive strategies are not appropriate for increasing productivity in the hospitality industry. Kotas,[36] for example, points out that the hospitality business is highly capital intensive and depends upon a highly perishable product. The industry therefore needs to adopt market-oriented operating strategies and above all to be responsive to market needs. According to Kotas, the higher the price and average spend within a sector, the more important marketing orientation becomes. On the other hand, hospitality operations certainly have high labour costs. One would therefore expect them to adopt strategies aimed at reducing labour expenditure. Kotas implies that time spent on making such reductions would be better employed on marketing. Pickworth warns that

> Cost cutting as a strategy can be successful as long as quality is not forgotten. Some organizations adopted this concept too zealously and quality was lost in the derive for efficiency . . . The sequence of declining quality leading to falling sales and in turn further cost cutting is termed the 'productivity trap'.[37]

The alternative is an *expansive* strategy which concentrates on the credit side of the profit and loss account. The aim is to increase sales revenue while holding costs down. This implies increasing both quantity and quality, as perceived by the customer.

Expansive strategies for productivity management

Increase in sales revenue can focus on two aspects: volume or quality. In the hospitality industry, volume is usually limited. For instance, room occupancy has a fixed ceiling at 100 per cent. In practice this figure is hardly ever actually reached. An increase in room occupancy from 75 to 95 per cent might be practically achievable, with a 27 per cent increase in sales revenue. That from 95 to 99 per cent might require much more marketing effort and the improvement in revenue would only be 4 per cent. A law of diminishing returns also operates in the food and beverage side of the operation.

However, individual hotels and groups can increase room availability by converting space currently used in other ways. For instance, an on-site laundry may be closed down in favour of an outside contract service. Alternatively a new wing can be built. This may be limited by site constraints or by planning permission. Eventually it may also increase the distances travelled by staff beyond practicable limits. Hotels and groups can also expand volume by building new units. However, this is not usually a productivity advantage in this, because the other costs also rise. Diminishing returns and diseconomies of scale may also operate in these cases as the group grows larger. Competitive strategies likely to improve productivity are improving quality, adding value, increasing prices, raising the star rating, etc. This can be done either by improving the quality of the tangible product or by improving the quality of service.

The tangible product

'Tangible products' include food and beverage items and rooms. The hospitality industry commonly sees upgrading quality solely in terms of increasing material costs or injecting capital. However, analytical techniques are available for identifying the most profitable menu items. Hayes and Huffman[38] review three of these techniques. All are broadly based on grids of high and low volume and high and low cost percentage. The grids allow items to be identified as 'ploughhorses', 'stars', 'dogs', etc. Hayes and Huffman offer a fourth technique, where individual profit and loss accounts are drawn up for menu items. The technique allows labour, energy and other costs to be taken into account. Lockwood and Jones[39] describe a similar approach for room tariff rates. Analysis of this kind offers the prospect of rationalizing tangible product offerings, while simultaneously increasing profitability and productivity.

The intangible product

Arguably more important than the quality of the product is the quality of the service itself. King[40] identifies service quality as having the following key aspects:

- intangible output;
- perishability: the product cannot be stockpiled and so must be produced on demand;
- a highly complex delivery system that requires integration of primary system and numerous support systems and is often very time sensitive;
- the presence of the customer in the system – an unknown, unpredictable factor;
- the customers' wants and standards are difficult to identify: they may be based on personal preference or mood rather than actual performance.

Martin[41] regards service quality as dependent on two factors: service procedures and staff conviviality. He describes ways of setting and evaluating service standards. Mill[42] suggests hiring flexible employees and building on their strengths as ways to achieve quality goals. Thompson[43] describes a model in which quality is enhanced by employee flexibility. Such a model is inherent in the THF 'hostess scheme'. Another similar approach, that of quality circles, has been used in the USA and UK but with limited success.[44] However, such approaches undoubtedly succeed in raising morale.

In the late 1980s quality circles largely gave way to 'internal marketing' approaches.[45] The departure point of internal marketing theory is that 'the personnel is the first market of the service company', and the main aims are teambuilding, improving internal communication and drawing individuals into line with company policy and standards. Price[46] describes a staff training programme aimed at service quality improvement in a large hospitality group. Outside consultants lead a team-building exercise for middle management, who then design and lead similar exercises for their own staff, in a cascade process.

Wyckoff[47] describes a quality circle approach aimed at improving productivity. This took place within a Californian restaurant chain, which hired a consultant to meet with small groups of employees. Discussion centred upon how productivity could be increased without reducing service quality. The groups paid particular attention to their communication skills in order that selling could be achieved quickly and efficiently without staff appearing rude, rushed or off-hand. The nub of Wyckoff's example is that sales efficiency is a part of service, as well as customer appeal, and that sales can be increased without loss of service quality and without extra staff. This approach seems to bring productivity within the scope of the intangible front-of-house 'product', rather than relegating it to a solely back-of-house concern. It points the way to a specifically 'service' view of and solution to the productivity question – an alternative to the contractive solutions of the manufacturing sector.

Although team-building methods are recommended for improving morale and service quality, some organizations have developed direct, 'carrot-and-stick' techniques. For example, front-office staff may be given a commission on the number of bookings they take. Tokens and certificates are also frequently awarded for good service. Some chains use techniques which identify poor service quality. 'Mystery shoppers' are an example: company employees who pose as guests and note the quality of their experience against agreed standard criteria. 'Quality assurance audits' may also be carried out by independent consultants or by the manager.[48] All of these techniques aim at improving productivity, since their intention is to improve quality with little increase in cost. However, productivity is unlikely to be improved in any measurable sense unless sales revenue increases.

Development of productivity in the 1990s

During the 1980s productivity management in the hospitality industry has become fragmented and two distinct productivity strategies have appeared: the application of operational management techniques derived from industry and the development of a 'hospitality-oriented' approach focusing on team building and sales skills. These two strategies have the following characteristics:

- *Operational techniques*. These are product oriented and treat staff as factors of production not as individuals. Operational techniques are most useful in mass production situations involving few product lines. Productivity improvements concentrate on reducing costs (contractive).
- *Team building*. These are marketing oriented. Staff individuality and inter-personal skill is emphasized. Team building aims to improve customer/staff interaction but also to increase sales, as the selling process is part of this interaction. Productivity improvements concentrate on increasing sales revenue, i.e. they are expansive.

Tension between these two strategies seems to be inevitable. It is possible (as Witt and Witt suggest) that some operational techniques may prove flexible enough for general application to hospitality management. However, the main thrust seems likely to be in back-of-house operations such as food production and laundry. Here gains in productivity will probably require the rationalizing and centralizing of operations. For instance, meals may be produced chilled, in a centralized plant. Large hotel groups may set up their own cook-chill units. In order to remain competitive, smaller units may be forced to buy chilled meals from independent suppliers: for instance, the *sous vide* items mentioned above. A number of firms currently supply the domestic chilled-food market and these could easily be adapted to satisfy the hospitality industry. Such a change in food production would mirror what has already largely occurred in terms of on-site, centralized and contract laundry services.

Such centralized services would be able to apply operational management techniques effectively to increase productivity. However, these techniques tend to work against team building. Their application tends to isolate the back-of-house functions from other aspects of hospitality in ways which may be physical or cultural or both. Physical isolation at another site may cause management problems. Cultural isolation may result from the difference in *modus operandi* between back- and front-of-house operations or from the psychological effects of merchandising, deskilling, etc. Managers will find themselves having to deal with an increasingly diverse workforce. Worse, isolation of one group of hospitality personnel will tend to work against team building in a unit as a whole. If productivity management continues to develop along the present, divergent lines, tension and frustration are likely to result.

Role redefinition

One potential way to reduce tension between these productivity management strategies is to review and redefine the roles of hospitality personnel. Sasser and Arbeit claim that 'people will remain services' essential ingredient for the relevant future'.[49] The one indispensable feature of the hospitality industry is probably face-to-face contact with the guest. Analysing the roles of staff is thus a matter of grouping them into the 'first line' (those who have direct contact with the customer) and the 'second line' (those who do not). The contractive view is then that productivity could be increased by removing as many 'second-line' personnel as possible, i.e. by servicing food production and other back-of-house functions using outside contractors. The need for office staff can be reduced by using new technology and so on. This is, of course, no different from strategies listed earlier in this chapter.

On the other hand, the expansive view might argue that personnel enagaged in 'second-line', back-of-house functions should be made into 'first-liners'. In other words, *all* staff should be engaged in selling the hotel to the customer. As Gummesson argues:

> all activities that influence customer relations and the generation of revenue are part of the marketing process. With this approach to marketing members of top management as well as of all other departments of the company become part-time marketers.[50]

The productivity challenge of the 1990s is to make everyone within the hospitality organization a 'part-time marketer'. In order to do this the industry will have to analyse carefully and in some cases redefine staff roles.

Front-of-house roles

A model already exists for reviewing staff roles in the front-of-house area. It is the internal marketing model mentioned above. Staff must be able to perceive selling as an important part of their service function. Training sessions should encourage them to identify ways to improve their sales output as well as the attentiveness or friendliness aspects of the service role. Contact with guests should be maximized, with staff attention focused clearly upon consumer needs. Tasks such as paperwork, which take staff away from the primary hospitality function, should be minimized: for example, by introducing electronic systems. Front-of-house staff should actively seek to make service encounters with guests and to sell food, beverages, accommodation, etc.

Back-of-house roles

Back-of-house roles require more scrutiny and present more of a challenge than front-of-house functions. However, there is obvious scope for role review in food production, housekeeping and maintenance, and no doubt in other areas too. For example, food production staff have virtually no 'part-time marketing' role in many hotels. Customers may never see the kitchen staff at all, so the only point of contact is the tangible quality of the food. Granted that this is important, the customer cannot know whether the food has in fact been prepared by hand on the premises or by machine elsewhere. From the productivity point of view an unseen chef is dispensable. Food freshly prepared on the premises is a selling point and should be given a marketing function. There are several ways to do this. One is the 'open kitchen' where customers may observe their food being prepared behind a glass screen. In Japanese sushi bars and also in some conventional Western kitchens the food production operation is the centrepiece of the restaurant. The approach adds an important marketing role to the chef's function. Being able to demonstrate his or her culinary skill tends to bond the chef with customers and to raise his or her morale. The requirements for an element of showmanship and the possibility of seeing the whole production cycle from initial order to empty plate enrich the chef's job.

Efficiency resulting solely from high morale is limited in scope. Activities within the 'open kitchen' should therefore be carefully analysed. All 'second-line' operations should be removed, i.e. vegetables should be bought peeled and chopped, fish filleted, etc. Only essential or spectacular operations should be allowed to remain.

Housekeeping staff generally have considerable contact with guests but no 'part-time marketing' role. Often they shun verbal encounters. Yet sometimes they appear to be the only staff available for human contact. Unofficial contact between housekeeping staff and guests should be formalized. Staff should be smartly attired and should be trained and encouraged to answer guests' enquiries, particularly those about hotel services. Maintenance and other personnel also have regular, unofficial contact with guests which represents a 'part-time marketing' opportunity. As with food production, efficiency will depend on removing 'second-line' functions as far as possible. Most back-of-house functions will be susceptible to role review and redefinition. These processes will make it possible to integrate front-and back-of-house staff into a coherent team. A single (expansive, internal marketing) strategy can then be employed for managing productivity throughout the hospitality operation.

TOWARDS A PRODUCTIVITY STRATEGY FOR THE HOSPITALITY INDUSTRY

Provided it is oriented towards sales volume rather than just service quality, the marketing approach will undoubtedly improve productivity. Its effectiveness will surely be enhanced by reorganization and role redefinition, as described above. It should not be forgotten, however, that for the marketing approach to work as a productivity strategy, costs must also be controlled. They must be either held constant or prevented from rising in proportion with revenue increases. In order to do this, two conditions are assumed:

- a buoyant market, so that increases in market share are relatively easy to make and marketing costs relatively low;
- a buoyant labour market, so that there is a constant, adequate supply of skilled staff.

During the 1980s both of these conditions were true. Most Western countries have experienced rising populations and a degree of unemployment. However, demographic predictions for the 1990s and beyond show that changes are coming. Olsen writes:

> Those individuals presently referred to as the 'Baby Boom' generation represent the largest proportion of the population in the economically developed nations of the western world. As such, total demand for the goods and services of the hospitality industry can be expected to experience no real growth in the decade ahead since there is no larger population segment following along behind this maturing age group. This implies that any new business for this industry will result from either taking it way from someone else or due to an influx of immigrants from other less-developed nations. While some immigration can be expected it will hardly be enough to shift the total industry demand curve further to the right.
> The context of the trend is further shaped by a mature and sophisticated consumer who has many more choices today for food and lodging services and expects the highest level of service possible. This is contrasted with a severe labor shortage across the western world horizon. Due to an aging workforce and solid economic recovery in many nations, the traditional labor pool for this industry – young people and females – is no longer available in the numbers necessary to meet the demands of the hospitality customer. These broad based environmental variables have contributed significantly to the maturing of the industry.[51]

In the maturing hospitality industry, marketing strategies will become less and less efficient means of promoting productivity. Business performance will increasingly depend on monitoring the revenue/cost ratio and on achieving more for fewer resources. This will inevitably involve reorganization, redesign of facilities, self-service, better scheduling, etc. – many of the tactics used by the manufacturing sector. The hospitality industry of the 1980s is ill-prepared in education and attitude for such a shift in operational emphasis: 'Traditionally the development of hotel managers encourages a "being there" style and discourages reflection and planning. Their "hands on" bias may make them reluctant to spend time on, and even afraid of, paperwork and figure work.'[52]

Productivity measurement in the 1990s will undoubtedly require greater emphasis upon analysis and planning. The industry will also need to maintain and strengthen its work in team building and internal marketing. Thus the challenge for the future will be to achieve an effective integration of revenue-maximization and cost-reduction techniques. It should not be forgotten that productivity is a ratio and that its management requires attention to both the numerator and the denominator.

SUMMARY

Strategies for increasing productivity can be divided into two groups. 'Contractive strategies' involve analysing and cutting costs, while 'expansive strategies' aim to maximize sales revenue. Neither can achieve its goal on its own. Manufacturing industry has developed a number of successful contractive strategies, but these are currently regarded as being of limited application in hospitality, except in 'production' aspects such as kitchen work. In recent years the hospitality industry has developed a potentially productivity-oriented technique based on interpersonal skills, team building and internal marketing. One approach to productivity is to separate the production and service aspects of the hospitality industry and to approach their management in different ways. An alternative is to redefine staff roles so that all have contact and a 'part-time marketing' role with the customer. However, productivity strategies based on a marketing approach are likely to become less effective due to demographic changes during the 1990s. Competitiveness within the hospitality industry will depend upon the successful integration of expansive and contractive strategies.

NOTES

1. Elfing, T., 'The main features and underlying causes of the shift to services', *Service Industries Journal*, vol. 9, no. 3, 1989, pp. 337–56.
2. Medlik, R., 'Profit from productivity in tourism', *Tourism*, vol. 61, Jan./Feb. 1989, p. 14.
3. Johnston, R., 'Service industries: improving competitive performance', *Service Industries Journal*, vol. 8, no. 2, 1988, pp. 202–11.
4. Olsen, M., 'Issues facing multi-unit hospitality organizations in a maturing market', *Proceedings of the Launch Conference of the Journal of Contemporary Hospitality Management*, Dorset Institute, 1989, pp. 64–75.
5. Worland, D. and Wilson, K. 'Employment and labour costs in the hospitality industry: evidence from Victoria, Australia', *International Journal of Hospitality Management*, vol. 7, no. 4, 1989, pp. 363–77.
6. Dittmer, P. and Griffin, G.G., *Principles of Food, Beverage and Labour Cost Controls for Hotels and Restaurants* (3rd edn), chapters 18 and 19, Van Nostrand Reinhold, London, 1984.
7. Adam, E. E. and Ebert, R. J., *Production and Operations Management* (3rd edn), Prentice-Hall, Englewood Cliffs, NJ, 1986.
8. Kotas, R., 'Nature and significance of market orientation in the hotel and catering industry', in Kotas, R. (ed.) *Marketing Orientation in the Hotel and Catering Industry*, Surrey University Press, 1975.
9. Kotler, P., *Marketing for Non-profit Organizations*, Prentice-Hall, Englewood Cliffs, NJ, 1975 pp. 43-4.
10. Ibid.
11. Ibid., pp. 56–60.
12. Ibid.
13. Bell, M. L., *Marketing: Concepts and Strategy* (2nd edn), Houghton Mifflin, Boston, Mass., 1972, p. 52.
14. Buckley, J. W., 'Goal – process system interaction in management', in Thomas, W. E., *Readings in Cost Accounting, Budgeting and Control*, South-Western Publishing Co., Cincinatti, Ohio, 1978, p. 11.
15. Kotler, P., *Marketing Management: Analysis, Planning and Control* (5th edn), Prentice-Hall, Englewood Cliffs, NJ, p. 333.
16. Nightingale, M., 'Determination and control of quality standards in hospitality services', M.Phil. thesis, Surrey University, 1983.
17. Lewis, R. C., 'When guests complain', *Cornell HRA Quarterly*, Aug. 1983, pp. 23–31.
18. Marris, T., *How to Research Your Market*, English Tourist Board, 1980, p. 23.
19. Wilson, R. M. S., *Management Controls and Marketing Planning*, Heinemann, London, 1982.

20. Sevin, C. H., *Marketing Productivity Analysis*, McGraw-Hill, New York, 1965.
21. The discussion is based on Coltman, M., *Hospitality Management Accounting* (2nd edn), Van Nostrand Reinhold, New York, 1982, pp. 193–6.
22. Harrington, J., *Hotel Management Accounting and Control Systems*, Northwood, London, 1981.
23. Peters, T. J. and Waterman, R. H., *In Search of Excellence,* Harper & Row, New York, 1982, p. 32
24. Kaplan, R. S., 'Measuring manufacturing performance: a new challenge for management accounting research', *Accounting Review*, vol. 58, no. 4, 1983, pp. 686–705.
25. Simmonds, K., 'The accounting assessment of competitive position', *European Journal of Marketing*, vol. 20, no. 1, 1986, pp. 16–31.
26. Geller, A, N., 'Tracking the critical success factors for hotel companies', *Cornell HRA Quarterly*, Feb. 1985, pp. 76–9.
27. Merricks, P. and Jones, P., *The Management of Catering Operations*, Holt, Rinehart and Winston, London, 1986, chapter 9.
28. Schafheitle, J. and Light, N., '*Sous vide* cooking and its application to cook-chill: what does the future hold?', *Journal of Contemporary Hospitality Management*, vol. 1, no. 1, 1989, pp. 5–10.
29. Milson, A. and Kirk D., 'The caterer as a process engineer', in Glew, G. (ed.), *Advances in Catering Technology*, Applied Science Publishers, Barking, 1979.
30. Coltman, op. cit.
31. Kotschevar, L., 'Some basic factors in food service planning', *Cornell HRA Quarterly*, May 1968, pp. 104–13.
32. Gamble, P. R. and Kipps, M., 'The conception and development of a microcomputer-based catering information system', *International Journal of Hospitality Management*, vol. 2, no. 3, 1983, pp. 141–7.
33. Jones, P., 'Quality, capacity and productivity in service industries', *International Journal of Hospitality Management*, vol. 7, no. 2, 1988, pp. 104–12.
34. Witt, C. A. and Witt, S., 'Why productivity in the hotel sector is low', *Journal of Contemporary Hospitality Management*, vol. 1, no. 2, 1989, pp. 28–34.
35. Martin, C. A. and Clark, B. R., 'The use of production management techniques in the tourism industry', *Service Industries Journal* (forthcoming).
36. Kotas, op. cit.
37. Pickworth, J. R., 'Minding the P's and Q's: linking quality and productivity', *Cornell HRA Quarterly*, May 1987, p. 42.
38. Hayes, D. K. and Huffman, L., 'Menu analysis: a better way', *Cornell HRA Quarterly*, Feb. 1985, pp. 64–9.
39. Lockwood, A. and Jones, P., 'Approaches to the measurement of accommodation performance', *Proceedings of the Launch Conference of the Journal of Contemporary Hospitality Management*, Dorset Institute, 1989, pp. 44–56.
40. King, C. A., 'Service quality assurance is different', *The Consultant*, Winter 1986, pp. 27–31.
41. Martin, W. B., 'Defining what service quality is for you', *Cornell HRA Quarterly*, Feb. 1986, pp. 32–8.
42. Mill, R. C., 'Managing the service encounter', *Cornell HRA Quarterly*, Feb. 1986, pp. 39–43.
43. Thompson, J. D., *Organizations in Action*, McGraw-Hill, New York, 1967.

44. See, for example, Faulkner, E., 'Will quality circles work in American foodservice operations?', *Restaurant and Institutions*, 15 Sept. 1983, pp. 149, 150, 151, 152, 156.
45. Internal marketing theory is reviewed by Jones, P., 'Internal marketing', *International Journal of Hospitality Management*, vol. 5, no. 4, 1986, pp. 201–4.
46. Price, P., 'Customer care in licensed retailing', *Proceedings of the Launch Conference of the Journal of Contemporary Hospitality Management*, Dorset Institute, 1989, pp. 76–85.
47. Wyckoff, D. D., 'New tools for achieving service quality', *Cornell HRA Quarterly*, Nov. 1984, pp. 78–91.
48. Willborn, W., 'Quality assurance audits and hotel management', *Service Industries Journal*, vol. 6, no. 4, 1986, pp. 293–308.
49. Sasser, W. E. and Arbeit, S., 'Selling jobs in the service sector', *Business Horizons*, Jun. 1976, pp. 61–5.
50. Gummesson, E., 'Marketing organization in service businesses: the role of the part-time marketer', Conference: Current Issues in Service Research, Dorset Institute, 1988 (issued as a separate paper to participants).
51. Olsen, op. cit., pp. 67–8.
52. Guerrier, Y. and Lockwood, A. J., 'Work flexibility in hotels', in Johnston, R. (ed.), Proceedings of the 3rd Annual International Conference of the Operations Management Association, University of Warwick, January 1988, pp. 160–75; quoted by Witt and Witt, op. cit., p. 33.

5

Quality as a strategic issue

Paul Gamble and Peter Jones

THE HOSPITALITY INDUSTRY IN THE 1990s

> In the '90s, the battle for market share will become an all-out war. This will be the most competitive decade in the history of the lodging industry. Every hotel and lodging company must become more market driven, improving their product, improving their service and examining their price in an effort to create a unique, sustainable, competitive advantage in the local marketplace and a perception of greater value for their guests.[1]

This view of the 1990s was given by Robert C. Hazzard, chief executive officer of Quality International, the company that has adopted the word quality as its brand name. The remark was made in the context of the hard-pressed United States hospitality market where problems of oversupply in the late 1980s have produced a very aggressive competitive situation. Yet significantly perhaps, the word 'quality' does not figure in the list of factors mentioned. This may be because it is assumed that quality is an implicit factor in a market-driven situation, especially when associated with a desire for improvement. Improvement always seems to imply higher quality.

However, many service industries, not least the hospitality industry in the USA and to a growing extent in Western Europe, compete in mature markets using techniques based not so much on quality as on price. Based on Levitt's seminal paper on product life-cycles,[2] price is often a major determinant of competitive position, especially during what is known as the 'stable maturity' phase of a market's development.

According to Porter,[3] where this is true there is some kind of price/quality/variety trade-off inherent in such a strategy. This raises the question of whether the hospitality industry is not so much focusing on quality as a competitive tool but rather is trading off quality for price and variety.

At one level, this supposition would seem to be borne out. There was a more or less remorseless growth in capacity in each of the world's major tourism regions during the 1980s. Europe, the USA and Asia/Pacific all experienced rapid expansion in the available hotel stock at all levels. More or less at the same time, evidence of price competition has been growing. Most acutely this has occurred in the USA where, since the late 1980s, pricing techniques such as yield management have come to the fore. The essence of yield management is to vary price very frequently so as to regulate demand for services. In this technique price, not quality, is considered to be a primary determinant and regulator of demand.

There have also been some increases in variety, mainly concentrated on the product surround. While there is nothing to indicate that the fundamental character of hotels and restaurants has changed, some differences can be observed in the style by which products were offered during the 1980s.

Physical facilities. At one level in the USA quality is suggested by large capital investments. Multi-storey atria have become a commonplace feature of expensive operations. This is associated with the emergence of the so-called fantasy hotel, a unit with elaborate physical features such as glass elevators, wrap-around parking garages, revolving roof restaurants and advanced personal communications equipment.

Elsewhere, rocketing land costs have forced a reconsideration of the value of public space. The large lobbies and even ballrooms have begun to shrink so as to release more personal space in guest rooms. The trend is most well established in the budget sector where so-called all-suite hotels with limited public space, restricted service and larger guest rooms have emerged. Here the quality connotations of the word 'suite' are used to disguise lower personal service levels.

Technology. To some extent, an attempt has been made to equate high technology with high quality. Computer technology in particular has become well established as a tool in the operation of hotel services, especially reservation and billing systems. Other guest services such as communications, in-room entertainment and security are also now heavily dependent on microelectronics.

Service. Finally, the customer has been made even more responsible for some aspects of quality with a continuing move towards self-service. Thus guests are responsible for their own service levels. Self-service room bars (mini-bars), breakfast buffets, self-checkout and even self-valeting have become more common.

While the move to self-service is consistent with a broad cultural trend in the West, there are signs that not all of these features are welcomed by guests. Quality trade-offs are sometimes noticed. The new atria have been described as 'guest-holding corrals'. Buffet-style self-service introduces problems of food holding, appearance and customer convenience that have not always been solved and which have sometimes been ignored. Both of these service features represent ways of coping with poorly trained staff. Atria provide for bigger queues; buffets offer a buffer between production and service.

Indeed, the service style offered by inexperienced or undertrained staff may lead to complaints about social skills, competence and speed. One way of dealing with this is to keep the staff away from the customers. Technology or design can achieve such a separation, although sometimes they may result in undesirable side-effects. Hotel technology intended to support service quality can actually be seen as a barrier to good service – especially when hotel staff may use it as an excuse for poor performance or where its apparent complexity defies rapid comprehension by tired travellers.[4]

QUALITY AND THE SERVICE SECTOR

The phenomenon of apparently poor service quality is encapsulated by Koepp in an article published by *Time* magazine.[5] Koepp's complaints, which range widely over a number of service industries, seem to fall into two main areas. The first of these is essentially that service industries have taken too literally Levitt's suggestion that they learn the lesson of manufacturing industries.[6] Levitt argued that service industries should seek to remove the idiosyncratic variety formerly regarded as characteristic of human providers of services, through the application of design and technology.

Uniformity and consistency should be maintained by rigid adherence to tightly defined procedures and methods. The fast-food industry is a prime example of such methods.

The second problem is that service industries do not seem to understand where benefits are being sought or where value might lie in service products. In turn, this might be explained by two phenomena. Firstly, organizations seem to find it easier to concentrate their training on technical rather than social skills. Thus the front-desk clerk is taught how to work the computer terminal but not how to cope with a distraught guest. Secondly, service providers do not understand which services are important because they conduct insufficient or poor research.

Perceptions of the product by the provider are based on what the product is like now. Such research as is carried out tends largely to reinforce these perceptions and is often methodologically unsound. It may be biased deliberately to give false reassurance or simply through lack of proper research training on the part of the managers. Guest comment cards are a prime example of bad research. Nevertheless, they are a popular device and may well support the illusion that a broad and representative sample of customer opinion is being canvassed.

It is also quite possible to encounter research which purports to have conventional academic integrity, but which has been biased to suit current marketing promotions. Lewis[7] gives the example of reports which purport to 'prove' that a clean or comfortable room is the most important characteristic which influences customer preferences when they select a hotel. He goes on to raise the interesting question of the preferences of that small proportion of survey respondents who do not tick this box on the survey form. Is it to be assumed that they prefer dirty or uncomfortable rooms?

TOWARDS A DEFINITION OF QUALITY

On this basis, it might be suggested that quality is whatever standard of service might result from some application of technology to resources. In effect, management chooses a style of operation and supports that style by an investment in physical facilities, personnel and product offerings. The rightness of these managerial choices is then reinforced by conducting research which measures customer reactions only to what is being offered, not to what might be offered.

Exactly how far this process of quality trade-offs can go is illustrated by trends in other service industries. Large retail stores concentrate their so-called service personnel around cash points and focus jobs on payment collection not customer support. Banks introduce an increasing range of automated services such that customer interaction with staff inside the bank is reduced. Airlines redesign their routes on a hub-and-spoke principle, moving passengers in accordance with concentrations of planes, not necessarily in accordance with concentrations of journeys.

Jones and Lockwood[8] stress that quality must be regarded as a key result area of hotel operations rather than as a residual outcome of several other decision processes. In other words, they recommend that a proactive approach be adopted towards quality and that it be seen as a kind of cornerstone which holds the other elements of the production and service system in place.

Definitions of quality are notoriously hard to produce. Most people would consider themselves perfectly capable of judging the difference between a good steak and a virtuoso performance on the grill, but when it comes to specifying the constituents of high quality they might have more difficulty. Jones and Lockwood adopt for their definition of quality that of the British Standards Institute (BSI). According to the BSI, quality is 'the totality of features and characteristics of a product or service that bear on its ability to satisfy a given need'.[9]

This definition highlights the problem. Superficially it seems complete, but it is in fact rather vague. Indeed, the definition might serve as an example of poor quality by appearing to provide for quality trade-offs so long as the basic product or service offering impinges on some aspect of fitness for purpose. It also fails to distinguish between what might be called purposeful quality and residual quality.

The quality of a service or product is largely determined by the extent to which customer needs have been incorporated into the product and the extent to which customers perceive that those needs have been met.[10] Customers themselves are part of the service experience and they bring to the product a set of expectations and perceptions which are quite outside the control of the service provider. Nevertheless, these expectations must somehow be identified.

A more useful definition of quality is that offered by Wyckoff: 'Quality is the degree of excellence intended and the control of variability in achieving that excellence in meeting the customers' requirements.'[11] Wyckoff's definition introduces a more positive dimension, following the approach laid down by writers such as Peters and Waterman[12] in their search for excellence. The definition is useful because it also introduces three important ideas.

The first idea is the notion of designing quality into products. Design quality refers to the standard to which management resources and monitors a product. It is probably the most critical element in a quality strategy. Much has been written about quality control, but the control approach, to which the hospitality industry in particular is attracted, suffers from the overwhelming disadvantage that it comes too late. Quality must be designed into products; it cannot be inspected into them at some later point. Design quality is therefore the starting position for quality management.

The second idea is that of limiting but perhaps not eliminating variability. It might be argued that a personal service business such as a hotel or restaurant which seeks too rigid an adherence to a standard approach loses some of the opportunity to respond to customer needs as they become apparent during a service interaction. It is in this area especially that personal service surpasses technological service. An automated teller machine (ATM) has a preprogrammed range of functions which cannot be varied. Thus the notion of conformance quality is introduced.

The third idea is that of fitness for purpose, or the extent to which the product meets total customer needs. In hospitality services the substantive need for rest or for food as fuel is often secondary to peripheral needs. Since it is quite unusual for people in developed economies to be driven to wants such as food or shelter by environmental pressures, it is often these peripheral needs that are the basis of customer satisfaction. Thus a shopper uses a restaurant as a place to rest, a business traveller uses a hotel as a surrogate office. Referring back to Lewis's contention made earlier, travellers probably have basic expectations about standards of comfort and cleanliness in a hotel. They are neither surprised nor remarkably pleased to see these expectations met. They are simply not dissatisfied. To create satisfactions, the service product must go some way to meeting social or psychological needs. The product must move towards the notion of total quality.

ENSURING QUALITY

Total quality management (TQM) requires managers to take a much broader perspective of service products. It requires primarily the management of processes as well as outcomes. This important lesson was discovered by Japanese manufacturing companies.[13] Even a company engaged in manufacturing typewriters or motor cars needs to pay attention to the cleanliness of its offices, the punctuality of its mail service or the accuracy of its typed letters. This sends a quality message to all employees that is much more credible than endless exhortations from senior managers to work harder and do a better job. Many employees in the hospitality business are often asked to maintain high quality standards while the back-of-house areas in which they have to work are dirty or ill-equipped.

TQM emphasizes an open exchange of information at all levels of the company, and employees are encouraged to become involved in the process by which the product is created. One well-known aspect of this is the idea of quality circles. Quality circles (QCs) draw heavily on Japanese cultural traditions, and it has been suggested that for this reason they will not work so well in non-Japanese companies. It is evident that some aspects of a QC can be made to work in other countries and in other companies. However, they must be prepared to adapt to the concept of empowering work groups to meet, discuss and solve certain production or service delivery problems.

In a sense, perhaps the most difficult aspect of a QC for some managers is a perceived loss of control. This may present extra difficulties for hotel companies. Few studies have examined closely the culture of hospitality organizations, but from both Shamir[14] and White[15] a picture emerges of bureaucratic, hierarchical organizations controlled in an authoritarian manner by department heads who report to an all-powerful general manager. The military model of hotel organizations based on control systems, 'taking names' and directive supervision is widely practised all around the globe.

A more open, participatory management style is also made more difficult by the differentiation observable in hotels. Shamir remarks that even medium-sized units may have as many as 10 different departments and that a single department like a kitchen might have up to 23 job titles and 10 hierarchical levels. Such differentiation is commonly associated with a wages and salary structure that seeks to minimize the rewards available to service staff and so apparently undervalues both personal skills and personal service. Once again, this introduces an inconsistency between what is said ('we are a people organization that believes in our staff') and what is done ('we are paying you low wages because we do not think that you are worth very much'). Total quality management is rendered difficult if not impossible in such a climate.

Problems of quality control

Gaps between the manifest and the extant service system are the focus of quality control techniques. Parasuraman, Zeithaml and Berry[16] identify five key areas where management of service quality must occur:

- *Consumer expectations – management perceptions*. As suggested earlier, the nature of the service which is expected by the customer may not be properly understood by management.
- *Management perceptions – service quality specifications*. Sometimes the policy service level set by management is too low in relation to customer needs. Thus,

for example, management may decide that a five-minute delay at a check-in desk is acceptably short. In practice, tired customers may find this to be excessive.

- *Service quality specifications – service delivery*. Alternatively, management may have understood fully the needs of the customer but failed to design and resource an organization capable of delivering it. So, for example, a fast-food restaurant may be equipped with a conveyorized broiler that can deliver 600 burgers per hour and set a quality standard of serving each customer within 50 seconds of arrival. However, if in surge demand conditions the restaurant customers arrive at the rate of 20 per minute then the service standard cannot be met.

- *Service delivery – external communications*. Advertising messages can sometimes influence customer expectations. One of the UK's largest hotel companies once used an advertising slogan to the effect that its staff had 'the biggest smile in Europe'. Since the company was unable to deliver a friendly smiling service consistently, the campaign backfired and was withdrawn.

- *Expected service – perceived service*. If customer expectations of service are matched by the service experience, it is likely that the service level will be favourably perceived. This is one of the reasons why hotels maintain guest history systems. A customer returning to a hotel after some time, to discover that his or her preference for a room near the lift with a large writing table has been 'remembered', may well be pleasantly surprised to find that the level of service has gone beyond expectations.

Quality control systems are normally designed to focus on potential gaps between actual and planned service. Several well-established techniques are available to managers who wish to monitor the match between planned and actual service levels. These include process flowcharts, Pareto charts (ABC analysis of the 80:20 rule), critical incident tracking, fishbone diagrams and statistical quality control charts.

It is at this juncture that the issue of design quality reasserts itself. The concern here is that of training. A true service culture depends on all staff being properly trained to understand the policy service level which they must support. Furthermore, unless some form of measurement is employed, there is no means by which either the current position or the effect of management decisions can be related to planned results. Measurement implies the systematic collection of reliable data and the application of an appropriate technique.

Unfortunately, hospitality managers are not noted for their rigour in either area. Witt and Witt[17] observed that in a broad sample of hotel managers, 76 per cent seldom or never used any operations management technique. In fact only 11 per cent of managers claimed to do so frequently. It is also unlikely that such managers are able to draw on reliable data for their quality control measurements. Hotels and restaurants are prone to collect quality measurement data by methods which are statistically unreliable and generally invalid. The ubiquitous guest comment cards left in hotel bedrooms and the practice of restaurant managers asking customers if everything is 'all right' are examples of bad practice. However, examples of best practice are not unknown. The Levy Restaurant Company of Chicago employs an external agency to contact a statistically representative sample of guests within 5 to 10 minutes to their arrival at a restaurant. Willing participants are then called between 24 and 48 hours after the meal to determine their considered reactions to product quality.

IMPLEMENTING QUALITY

Developing a quality strategy

The state of strategic thinking and the relationship to 'quality' as a strategic issue often appears confused. As Michael Porter points out: 'There are no substitutes for strategic thinking. Improving quality is meaningless without knowing what kind of quality is relevant in competitive terms.'[18] In her review of some of the published literature on quality in the service sector Barbara Lewis has identified a recent trend in considering service quality as the critical factor in providing a differential advantage over competitors.[19]

The use of terms such as 'competitive weapon', 'critical corporate priority' and 'quality as a major component of mission and competitive advantage' indicates that at least in the literature the quality of service has strategic implications. The reinforcement of this view in industry has been noted by Leonard and Sasser, who claim that 'quality has become a major strategic variable in the battle for market share'.[20]

The management cynic would suggest that this focus on quality as a major issue is the latest in a long line of management fads that has included operations research (OR), management by objectives (MBO), organizational development (OD) and quality assurance (QA). However, any manager will admit that not getting it right first time is a cost to the business, and that this failure has implications not only for that occurrence but for a significant number of subsequent sales. In the case of a hotel product, for example, the impact on repeat and referral business and on the overall reputation of the hotel could be very significant and directly related to long-term financial performance.

It could be argued that consumers are becoming increasingly aware of the price versus quality equation and that wider experiences and expectations are forcing the hospitality businesses to address service quality not as a fad of the management theorist but as a necessary response to customer demands. Quality has a heightened profile as a consumer issue. It is no accident that within the hospitality arena the multiplicity of hotel and restaurant guides are attempts to classify the product offerings in qualitative terms, and that in the food industry the consumer's concept of quality is becoming increasingly synonymous with that of food safety.

Moores in his exposition on the management of service quality does draw some definitions together in attempting to answer the question: what is service quality?[21] In this he cites the earlier work of Nightingale and the use of such terms as 'customer quality standards' and 'customer service standards', highlighting what he considers the key aspects of defining quality by drawing a direct relationship between the 'evolving expectations of the customers' and the organization's ability to satisfy those expectations. However, no matter how good the understanding may be of customer quality standards, as Moore points out the service provider is actually the person who ordains just what service standards are being offered. On that basis, if the provider has a differing perception of the quality of the offering from that of customers then a mismatch between offering and expectations is going to occur. It could be argued that establishing a quality standard is an attempt to minimize that mismatch, but that this in turn is rather more of a marketing and operational issue than one of strategic interest to the organization.

A degree of tension becomes apparent when viewing the operational and strategic perspectives, and it is therefore not surprising that quality as a strategic issue is featured in positioning the product, the company or the offering and that it is the service provider in the operational sense who is interpreting those signals in terms of quality standards.

It appears that what is lacking in this is an underlying vision or philosophy of quality, recognized at all levels in the organization and apparent in the delivery. The quality component of the service provided must be recognized by the customer as being entirely appropriate in terms of the exchange that has taken place in the service encounter.

How can the concept of a vision or philosophy of quality be related to the concept of strategic planning? As Porter relates, strategic planning came to prominence in the 1960s and quickly became a feature not only of the corporate organization but also of the curriculum of any business management course.[22] The focus on planning for the functions of the business and the resultant budgets and five-year plans have led to criticisms of the overall process, the major one being that strategic planning has often obscured strategic thinking.

One of the powerful arguments often put forward against strategic plans is that Japanese companies do not prepare them and yet are still very successful. Dale and Asher,[23] in reporting on a mission by 18 executives to Japan to study total quality control (TQC) activities, noted that the Kansai Electric Power Co. Inc. had developed a long-range management 'vision' of future opportunities. This was not formulated as a strategic plan but was very much a 'vision statement' for the company to look to the future. Proverbs XXIX seems to support this kind of strategic planning: 'where there is no vision the people perish'. This is equally true in the business context, and could be rewritten as 'where companies lack vision and strategic thinking the shareholders could lose their money'.

Mintzburg has proposed an alternative to the conventional strategic planner, recommending 'a pattern recogniser, a learner if you will – who manages a process in which strategies (and visions) can emerge as well as being deliberately conceived'.[24] He uses the verb 'to craft strategy' as a process of synthesis: 'To manage strategy is to craft thought and action, control and learning, stability and change.'

Adopting Mintzberg's crafting and analogy, it is possible to suggest that quality in the strategic sense can be crafted into a vision that could be shared by both the provider and the customer. Where such a sharing exists in terms of expectations and the resultant provision, no mismatch will occur and a commitment to quality will emerge. A number of writers have highlighted a commitment to quality as being essential if quality is to begin to influence the corporate culture (vision).

High quality service at the front line starts in the minds of top management: this service concept must find its way into the structure and operation of the organisation . . . there must be a customer orientated culture in the organisation and it is the leaders of the enterprise who must build and maintain that culture.[25]

The thoroughness of shared commitment, and the consistency of execution that makes the difference between ordinary service and quality service . . . commitment to quality service must be part of the organisational culture . . . we are all responsible for quality service, from the chairman down to the mailroom clerk and we make it work by making it clear that it's everyone's responsibility – everywhere all of the time.[26]

Another interpretation of this commitment can be found in the work of Tom Peters, who suggests that 'most quality systems fail for one or two reasons: They have a system without passion, or passion without system.'[27] Such a view of quality does take on, again in Peters' view, a 'moral dimension' with the suggestion that it should be recognized as a virtue – something for its own sake – not just a profitable strategy.

Quality is a strategic issue

It could be argued that to accept the premiss that quality is a strategic issue is to negate the view that quality is much more of a visionary component embedded into the fabric and philosophy of the enterprise. To achieve that vision, as Berry *et al.* state, 'requires leaders not just managers', and true leaders

- have a vision of the business;
- communicate their vision of the business/lead by example;
- are entrepreneurial;
- are obsessed with excellence.[28]

The implication of this view is that any process designed to improve 'quality' as a separate, almost stand-alone programme within any organization would be most unlikely to succeed. Therefore while quality may be viewed by hospitality organizations as a strategic issue, the realization of that quality objective may not be attainable without a shift in the corporate culture of the organization. Implementing a quality programme as an operational control mechanism to trade off quality against price or as a tool to position the product may bring a limited short-term response but is most unlikely to impact on the quality vision or ethos that the organization exhibits.

QUALITY STRATEGIES

On the basis of the propositions put forward in forming a definition of quality in the hospitality context, it would be realistic to ask the question of whether or not organizational strategies can be developed to recognize and improve the quality component of the service product. The positive dimensions found in Wyckoff's definition of designing quality into products, limiting but not eliminating variability and fitting the product to customer needs could form the basis of a vision of the appropriateness of quality that could be shared by the provider and the customer.

For the strategic planner it must be recognized that a process control type of approach to quality introduced 'strategically' is most unlikely fundamentally to change the quality component of the service product. The introduction of a more quantifiable monitoring and control mechanism would provide an early warning for the element of the service product where additional training may be required, but this must be seen against a philosophy of quality throughout the company and the willingness of the staff to support that philosophy. The nature of the strategic decision as opposed to the cultural decision may well be to decide and define on the appropriateness or fitness for role of the service product. In this context it could be argued that quality has a dimension that could be quantified in terms of high or low quality appropriate to the service product. This dimension of positioning the quality component in strategic terms does not seem to have been widely addressed – the word 'quality' is generally used to imply seeking some improvement on the current situation.

With the acceptance that quality is a major issue for hospitality organizations, the one major factor that will influence the organization's ability to adapt and succeed is, in Peters' words, the 'passion'. Quality as a strategic issue is not about developing quality assurance programmes or implementing quality control techniques; it is about developing, communicating and sharing the ownership of a vision of the total quality of the service product; it is about crafting into the fabric of the organization the recognition that to achieve the appropriate quality is the responsibility of all.

NOTES

1. Rowe, M., 'The chains plan for the nineties', *Lodging Hospitality*, vol 46, no. 1, 1990, p. 87.
2. Levitt, T., 'Exploit the product life cycle', *Harvard Business Review*, Nov./Dec. 1965, pp. 81–94.
3. Porter, M., *Competitive Strategy*, Free Press, New York, 1980.
4. Marshall, A., 'Hotels must tune in to business traveller needs', *Hotel and Motel Management*, vol. 205, no. 2, 1990, pp. 20 –2.
5. Koepp, S., 'Why is service so bad? Pul-eeze! Will somebody help me?', *Time*, 2 Feb. 1987.
6. Levitt, T., 'A production-line approach to service', *Harvard Business Review*, Sep./Oct. 1982, pp. 41–52.
7. Lewis, R., 'Ethics and integrity in research', *Hospitality Education and Research Journal*, vol. 13, no. 1, 1989, pp. 55–8.
8. Jones, P. and Lockwood, A., *The Management of Hotel Operations*, Cassell, London, 1989, pp. 149–67.
9. British Standards Institute, BSI 4778, *BSI Handbook 22*, HMSO, London, 1983.
10. Murdick, R.G., Render, B. and Russell, R.S., *Service Operations Management*, Allyn & Bacon, Boston, Mass., 1990, p. 56.
11. Wyckoff, D.D., 'New tools for achieving service quality', *Cornell HRA Quarterly*, Nov. 1984, pp. 78–93.
12. Peters, T.J. and Waterman, R.H., *In Search of Excellence: Lessons from America's Best Run Companies*, Warner Books, New York, 1982, p. 114.
13. Ingle, S. and Ingle, N., *Quality Circles in Service Industries*, Prentice-Hall, Englewood Cliffs, NJ, 1983, p. 27.
14. Shamir, B., 'Between bureaucracy and hospitality: some organizational characteristics of hotels', *Journal of Management Studies*, Oct. 1978, pp. 285–307.
15. White, M., 'Management style in hotels', *HCIMA Journal*, vol. 11, Oct 1973, pp. 9–11.
16. Parasuraman, A., Zeithaml, V.A. and Berry, L.L., 'A conceptual model of service quality and implications for future research', *Journal of Marketing* (US), Fall 1985, pp. 44–6.
17. Witt, C.A. and Witt, S.F., 'Why productivity in the hotel sector is so low', *Contemporary Journal of Hospitality Management*, vol. 1, no. 2, 1989, pp. 28–34.
18. Porter, M., 'Corporate strategy: the state of strategic thinking', *The Economist*, 23 May 1987, pp. 21-3.
19. Lewis, B.R., 'Quality in the service sector: a review', *IJBM*, vol. 7, no. 5, 1989, p. 4.
20. Leonard, F.S. and Sasser, W.E., 'The incline of quality', *Harvard Business Review*, 1982, pp. 163–71.

21. Moore, B., 'The management of service quality', in Jones, P. (ed.), *Management in Service Industries*, Pitman, London, 1989, pp. 263–71.
22. Porter, op. cit., p. 23.
23. Dale, B. and Asher, M., 'Total quality control: lessons European executives can learn from Japanese companies', *European Management Journal*, vol. 7, no. 4, 1989, pp. 493–502.
24. Mintzburg, H., 'Crafting strategy', *Harvard Business Review*, Jul./Aug. 1987, pp. 66–75.
25. Albrecht, K. and Zemke, R., *Service America! Doing Business in the New Economy*, Homewood, Ill., Dow Jones–Irwin, 1985, pp. 33–40.
26. O'Connell, L., 'Achieving quality service in your store credit operation', *Retail Control*, Nov. 1986, pp. 56–64.
27. Peters, T., *Thriving on Chaos*, Macmillan, London, 1987, p. 82.
28. Berry, L., Bennett, R. and Brown, C.W., *Service Quality: A Profit Strategy for Financial Institutions*, Homewood, Ill., Dow Jones–Irwin, 1989, pp. 2–7.

6

The application of retailing strategies to the management of hospitality

John Lennon

INTRODUCTION

The beginning of 1990 saw a number of leading UK retail companies reporting a reduction in profitability. Half-year results for the Next group showed a 50 per cent reduction in profit, while the Storehouse group (incorporating British Home Stores, Mothercare and Habitat) reported a 63 per cent reduction. Similarly, retail companies which showed miraculous growth in the 1980s, such as Tie Rack and Sock Shop, are now faring badly. At a time when there are examples of poor performance, predictions of modest growth and increased competition, it might seem curious to attempt to draw strategies from retailing and to relate and develop them in a hospitality context. Yet that is precisely what this chapter aims to do. The current performance of certain operators in this sector should not colour consideration of the retail sector as a whole. Indeed a number of examples of hospitality companies utilizing retailing techniques and knowledge are readily identifiable. This chapter will hopefully point the way for further cross-fertilization and provide a foundation upon which to advance debate.

The chapter begins with a brief introduction to the retailing industry, emphasizing its significance to the economy rather than concentrating on detailed statistical analysis. The second section looks at successful retail/hospitality, retail/leisure examples of transfer of operational strategies and techniques. The chapter ends with an examination of examples of strategic retail management techniques which it is felt could have wider application in a hospitality context.

THE RETAIL INDUSTRY: AN OVERVIEW

Retailing represents a very large sector of the UK economy.[1] At a time when UK manufacturing industry was declining, UK retailers were arguably among the most innovative and successful in the world. Estimated employment in retailing is included under the government classification of distributive trades at over 2 million. In addition, the distributive trades account for a further 1.2 million employed in the wholesaling and repair areas.[2] In terms of expenditure, retail outlets accounted for 42 per cent of consumer spending in 1986.

Historically, there has been a reduction in the total number of retail outlets. Thus although the size of the retail industry as an employer has expanded and the level of sales turnover has grown, the actual number of retail outlets has diminished. The major reason for this is the growth of the multiple retailer at the expense of the small, independent retailer. The UK retailing industry is dominated by large companies with multiple outlets accounting for an increasing amount of total sales. However, it would be wrong to suppose that new entrants to the retailing industry are prohibited. The 1980s saw a number of new entrants develop and grow rapidly. Admittedly, fashion trends favouring casual clothing and the development of specialist 'niche' retailers accounted for many such entrants. Among the major barriers to entry facing new operators in the retail field is the absence of economies of scale which arise from the volume of purchasing and distribution available to larger operators. Other barriers include difficulty in obtaining prime site locations and in developing a store design, merchandising and marketing programme targeted at an identified market segment.

Yet despite the considerable challenges facing new retail development, a number of significant operations have emerged. It is simplistic to assume that rising interest rates and a reduction in consumer spending in the late 1980s and 1990 have spelt the end for new operators such as the 'niche' retailer. For example, Knickerbox is claiming sales rises from £1.7 million in 1987/88 to an expected £10 million in 1990/91 with profits having trebled during the same period. Consequently, the company has been able to raise £2 million through Candover Investments to expand its market presence significantly.[3] Knickerbox, unlike other 'niche' retailers such as Sock Shop International and Tie Rack which have arguably captured greater media attention, has developed a product which is considered an essential rather than a luxury. Some 75 per cent of customer purchases are of the planned rather than impulse category. Thus while Sock Shop and Tie Rack reported large losses, Knickerbox in the relatively safer underwear market continues to survive on the 'niche' principles of small items with high mark-up, displayed in prime locations with floor space at a premium. Furthermore, the underwear market (estimated at £1.5 billion) is considerably larger than that of hosiery and ties. Thus Knickerbox need only capitalize on a small share of a large market dominated by Marks & Spencer.

Yet retailing is now considered a mature industry. It is characterized by increasing price competition and falling gross margins and returns.[4] Growth in terms of volume is expected to be modest. High interest rates coupled with the revaluation of rating under the uniform business rate system are contributing to a long and continuing period of underperformance by the stores sector, while the supply of new selling space is in excess of the demand. All of these factors are putting considerable pressure on retail properties to achieve required returns.[5]

Beaumont,[6] and Davies, Gilligan and Sutton[7] draw attention to a growing concentration of ownership in the retail food sector and the retail sector generally. As Sparks notes: 'The retail sector is shrinking in terms of number of outlets and businesses, although not volume, but the sector as a whole is increasingly dominated and controlled by large companies.'[8] Thus although numerically the retail sector is still characterized by single-outlet small traders, in terms of sales turnover the large multiples continue to grow at the expense of these single outlets.

The retail industry incorporates a variety of outlets. Segal-Horn[9] classifies the retailing industry into six distinct groupings:

- department store groups, e.g. House of Fraser;
- general multiples (variety chain stores), e.g. Woolworth;

- specialist multiples (focused chain stores), e.g. Superdrug;
- independents/small operators (ranging from single outlets to small regional chains);
- co-operatives;
- mail order.

However, in recent years such distinctions are becoming difficult to sustain as the increasing overlap between the first three groupings has caused a 'blurring' of classification. Many of the large multiples have been shifting their market shares and attempting to penetrate a number of sectors simultaneously, such as groceries and food, clothing and footwear, and household goods.

In terms of structure the largest sector of the business is food retailing, with the major food retailers (Sainsbury, Asda, Safeway, Tesco) dominating the marketplace. In this sector one also has to consider certain of the so-called mixed business stores such as Marks & Spencer, which has made food retailing a large and successful part of its operation. The next largest sector by sales turnover is the mixed retail business, which once again shows evidence of concentration of ownership. The major players in this sector include both department store groups and the general multiples. Other sectors include: drink, confectionery and tobacco retailers; clothing, footwear and leather goods retailers; household goods retailers; other non-food retailers; and hire and repair businesses.[10]

Development and trends in retailing

Dawson and Sparks[11] divide trends in retailing into changes in business organization and changes in the operation of retailing. In terms of the former, business organizations have been seen to grow considerably. Many of the large retailers are now among the largest companies in the UK. This growth of large companies and the development of new retailers such as Sock Shop and Tie Rack is linked to an ability to raise finance on the Stock Exchange. As a consequence, such companies are not by and large owned by the individuals in charge of their day-to-day operations. However, company performance and ultimately share prices are of vital importance to survival. In addition, concentration of ownership and the mergers taking place in the financial world mean that ownership of retailing companies is being concentrated into a small number of institutions.

Emphasis on style and design, image and lifestyle marketing illustrates the competitive techniques used to receive a high share quotation. These are combined with new management methods reinforced by optimum use of new technology to improve management information and control systems. For example, Augustus Barnett, the off-licence chain operated by Bass plc, constitutes a chain of small outlets nationwide which are not operated by small businessmen and women but are merely branches of a corporate brand which operates standard display, discount and training procedures. Such outlets are controlled centrally by management and are required to achieve weekly sales and profitability targets and to ensure that expenses at unit level are well within budget. Thus by improving management information systems and managing small branch outlets effectively, Bass plc operated an off-licence division which achieved sales growth above industry averages in 1989 despite difficult trading conditions.[12]

Segal-Horn[13] notes that other favoured corporate strategies among retailers include diversification into other service sectors not previously considered part of retailing.

The movement by Marks & Spencer plc into financial services is a good example. Anything within the service sector may be viewed as a potential retail market. Thus banks and insurance companies are facing new and increased levels of competition for customers. A good example of an alternative corporate strategy is the multi-format segmentation practised by Next plc. The various Next chains offer a range of produce from fresh flowers to lingerie, from hairdressing services to brasseries, all under the malleable Next logo. The common theme throughout the chain is the Next corporate emphasis on design and style.

The changes in retail operation identified by Dawson and Sparks[14] include the decline of the small retail outlet and the polarization of retail growth formats. In small-scale operations, target markets are selected so that the retail operation will appeal directly to the identified segment. For example, in the discount food market, 'Lo-Cost offer produce' has little appeal outside the identified target market. At the larger end, there has been considerable growth of generalist stores offering a variety of produce to a wide audience, while at the same time there has been the development of large stores appealing to specifically targeted markets, e.g. Toys 'R' Us.

The relocation of retail outlets has also been recognized as an important change in retailing. Schiller[15] has carried out some analysis of this change and has identified the following developments:

- a movement away from the high streets and town centres as the food store operations grew to superstores and hypermarkets;
- the development of retail warehouses and retail parks usually on the periphery of towns and cities;
- a movement away from towns altogether, to purpose-designed shopping sites with an emphasis on high standards of design, cleanliness, parking and access.

It is notable that these last two developments offer considerable competition to the traditional town centres with their potential problems of parking, access and space for development. However, the continued availability of sites for out-of-town development is becoming questionable.[16] There is past evidence of considerable resistance from local planning authorities to such developments. In contrast the prospect for town centre regeneration combining with the development of retail centres, often in pedestrian areas, is more encouraging. Such retail developments are seen as an integral part of the townscape and are viewed as an intrinsic part of tourist information briefings. A good example would be the Princes Square development in Glasgow, a city receiving considerable attention for its efforts at urban redevelopment and regeneration.

THE RETAIL/HOSPITALITY TRANSFER

In essence there would appear to be a degree of commonality between the hospitality and retail sectors. Both constitute large proportions of the service sector, employ large numbers of people and are essentially consumer led. Both have experienced growth since the Second World War, show indications of concentration of ownership and evidence considerable variation in outlet size and location. Certain branded shops like certain hotel chains are competing for the attention and time of relatively affluent sectors of the market. Such customers are increasingly unwilling to endure conditions for shopping, accommodation, dining, etc. which are of a lower standard than their place of work or their home. Thus commonality is greater than mere structure. In fact the commonality of the consumer increases the potential for comparison and competition.

The retail industry and the hospitality industry have both experienced key changes in the business environment. The long period of inflation in the 1970s provided many retailers with the illusion of growth without its reality.[17] Many hotel and catering companies, like many retail companies, were managing their operations very inefficiently. As inflation declined throughout the 1980s, coupled with a recession and its effect on consumer spending, managements in both of these service sectors found it very difficult to operate inefficient outlets. The environment had become increasingly competitive, and improved management systems reinforced by specifically developed technology were essential for survival. In both the retail and hospitality sectors, budgetary controls, centralized decision making, greater emphasis on design, better control of stock levels and greater appreciation of the importance of marketing were seen to varying degrees as good management practices.

Another common variable faced by the hospitality and retail sectors both now and in the future is that of demography (see Table 6.1). The shift in the UK age profile, and indeed the age profile of all the advanced industrial economies, is of importance to both sectors. The changing nature of the UK population affects both service sectors in terms of changing the consumer profile and the availability of labour. Evidence already exists that retailers are extending their recruitment for potential management to Europe. As competition for UK graduates increases, it is inevitable that organizations will adapt traditional recruitment patterns.

Table 6.1   *Key UK age groups with projections to 2031 (millions)*

Year	0–19	20–29	30–59	Over 60
		Age Group		
1989	15.0	9.2	21.3	11.8
2001	15.8	7.2	24.2	11.9
2031	15.3	7.4	22.2	16.3

Source: Office of Population Censuses and Surveys, *OPCS Monitor: Population Estimates*, HMSO, London, 1988.

In respect of the consumer, shifts in store image and marketing are becoming apparent by a number of retailers. For example, the Lewis Shops Group management has made a conscious decision to replace its 260 branches of Chelsea Girl with the River Island Clothing Company.[18] Chelsea Girl has long been associated with the throwaway, cheap Saturday-night fashions which characterize the youth mass market. The image of the new outlet is a cross between an English country house and a Long Island beach house. It utilizes wooden mannequins, mock Turkish rugs, brass lamps, antique trunks and fresh flowers to create an environment suitable for selling to the post-teen market. A new buying team has been introduced to provide merchandise that utilizes more natural fibres and greater variation in colour, and offers a more relaxed approach to dressing. Yet the Lewis 'value for money' philosophy remains in the competitive approach to pricing which has been adopted. This represents a clean break with past teenage identification, considerable investment in refurbishment and the introduction of a new brand into a highly competitive, somewhat depressed marketplace. A parallel for such a conscious shift in orientation among other retailers and among hospitality operators is difficult to locate. Yet it is clear that in the arena of mass market fashion such a gamble will be observed closely.

The growth of the 30–59-year-old working population (see Table 6.1) is of considerable importance to both retail and hospitality sectors. There will be an increase of 1.25 million in the number of individuals in their fifties by the end of the century. A further factor arising out of this relates to the social revolution which has already taken place in home ownership. Currently over two-thirds of the population own their own homes. The Halifax Building Society has predicted that this will rise to three-quarters of the population during the 1990s.[19] Even if this is not the case, a large number of people who are already home owners will stand to inherit property from their parents. On the basis that many of the individuals who inherit property will possess homes that are quite adequate to the needs of themselves and their families, such inheritance will constitute a substantial increase in personal wealth. Clearly these affluent consumers will be targeted by financial institutions and the leisure industry as well as by more traditional vendors such as retailers and hospitality operators.

The increase in female economic activity has formed the basis for much retailing strategy which has been targeted at the working woman.[20] Clear evidence of such strategy is already apparent in the women's clothing market. However, it is apparent that a number of hospitality outlets are also seeing the female consumer as an important market previously underexploited. Hotel operators are attempting to tailor their product to suit the female traveller. For example, Crest Hotels were voted the best group catering for the lone woman traveller in the 1989 Hotel of the Year awards. Furthermore, other developments such as the emergence of the dual-income household, the spread of earlier retirement and the growing proportion of healthier, more active pensioners are all factors which both retail and hospitality strategists will have to consider carefully in the years ahead.

On examination there would appear to be a number of successful examples of the hospitality sector borrowing and incorporating retail techniques and principles in both management and marketing. Grand Metropolitan plc under the chairmanship of Allen Sheppard made a string of disposals and acquisitions to narrow the company range of interests. In 1988 Grand Metropolitan disposed of the Intercontinental hotel chain but retained a number of hospitality outlets as part of its retailing division.[21] The company now has three clear divisions: food, drink and retailing. Branded retailing operations are now considered to be a major area of long-term opportunity for the group. However, the retailing division also incorporates Pearle (an eye-products retailer) and the Dominic Group (a specialist retailer of alcoholic drinks), as well as recognizable hospitality interests such as Burger King, Berni, Chef & Brewer and Clifton Inns. What is interesting is that this company is not drawing any distinction between hospitality and retailing, but rather is developing branded retail operations which are targeted to achieve pan-European or international recognition.[22] Recent indications are that Grand Metropolitan is to pursue this policy of emphasizing retailing still further. After a thorough review of its hospitality operations, some 70 hotels, restaurants and pubs which are considered to be poor long-term investments are to be disposed of. However, despite such reorganization, no brand names are to be divested.[23]

A good example of the retail/tourism relationship can be seen in the management and operation of retail and tourist visitor attractions. Retail outlets at such locations are now being recognized as important revenue-generating centres. Menzies[24] offers

Port Solent, the Victoria and Albert Museum, and the Tussauds group as successful
examples of this interface. The Tussauds group employed merchandising professionals
from the major multiples to advise on retail development at their visitor attractions.
The siting of the retail units in Tussaud group properties was considered of key
importance: they are located at the entrance so that customers have to pass them on
the way in and out, thus doubling exposure to merchandise. In this way the group
expects retail sales per head to increase by over 200 per cent. In the case of the
Victoria and Albert Museum, V & A Enterprises manages three retail units. V & A
Enterprises pays rent and service charges to the museum and channels profits back to
the museum via covenant. The company has successfully marketed itself through mail
shots, catalogues and joint ventures with high street retail outlets. Through such joint
ventures, merchandise carrying designs held by the museum can achieve greater
market exposure and increase sales turnover. Lastly, the development of marina
complexes provides an example of the retailing/leisure crossover. Port Solent,
Portsmouth, is an 84-acre complex which incorporates berthing for over 900 boats,
residential accommodation, a 144-room Marriott Hotel, 30 restaurant/retail units,
office suites and a marine industry complex. The marina provides the focus for
shopping, housing and leisure, and is a clear example of the integration of previously
distinct sectors.

Further successful examples of hospitality/retail transfer in a leisure context can be
seen in the development of multi-activity entertainment centres. Coral Entertainments,
a subsidiary of Bass Leisure, have achieved significant profit growth with 'The Point'
in Milton Keynes.[25] This was a joint venture between Bass and UCI which opened in
1986 at a cost of £8 million. It constituted the UK's first multiplex cinema operation.
Construction of a second 'Point' multi-entertainment centre at Bracknell, Berkshire,
is currently in progress. This outlet will incorporate a 10-screen cinema, a 28-lane
bowling alley, an amusement arcade, a café bar, a nightclub and 'Papaveros', an
Italian-style restaurant operated by Toby Restaurants, part of the Bass Hotels and
Restaurants division.[26]

More pedestrian examples of retail/hospitality transfer can be seen in the hotel
sector. The Hong Kong Hilton has introduced an illustrated Bedside Shopping Guide
in each of its bedrooms. Prestige merchandise, including clothing, luggage, liquor and
souvenirs, is displayed in the guide. To promote increased sales, goods are displayed
in cabinets near the group check-in areas and shopping guides are placed in the hotel's
restaurant to reach potential consumers who are not necessarily house guests. The
customer simply completes an order form and appropriate goods are mailed to a home
address. The charge is added to the final bill on leaving.[27] Although not the most
innovative retail/hospitality transfer examined, sales in-room have increased considerably. The catalogue was launched in mid-1989 and since then a sales increase of some
400 per cent has been identified during August–October on the same period in 1988.

Thus the separation between retail and hospitality in terms of branding,
development, management and operation is perhaps less apparent than one might
have first believed. However, it is contended here that further application of retailing
management strategy can be developed in a hospitality context. This is examined in
the next section.

RETAILING AND HOSPITALITY: AN APPLICATION OF MANAGEMENT STRATEGY

After the previous discussion it is apparent that many hospitality operators like many retailers are running a portfolio of related and sometimes unrelated businesses. Both have identified numerous target markets and offer a wide range of merchandise and services. However, it would appear that the retail sector is more rapidly able to adapt and refocus its products to achieve sales growth, greater market penetration and improved profitability. The successful retailer utilizes the strategy of 'reconceptualization' for the business.[28] This is the ability continually to refocus aspects of price, product lines and merchandise formats. However, such a policy creates strains on the nature of management within companies. To achieve such regular refocusing a company will need to remain flexible. Yet, conversely, the co-ordination of new concept development requires central strategic direction. Thus there is a push towards centralization which can bring with it inflexibility. Hence the paradox: in order to refocus a company requires considerable flexibility, yet to compete effectively a co-ordinated, centralized strategy must be present. Flexibility must be coupled with strong financial control, purpose-developed technological support and detailed management information systems to ensure the most effective asset utilization. In order to succeed the company will need to sustain high flexibility and high control.

The process of reconceptualization or refocusing brings with it particular difficulties for the retail sector. As a consequence of the relatively low cost of change on dimensions such as type and selection of merchandise, product positioning, location and ambience of display, a great deal of imitation occurs between firms.[29] That is not to say that imitation is a problem unique to retail outlets dealing with low-cost aspects of change. If one considers current UK hotel developments by Marriott, Holiday Inns and Stakis, one can see a degree of commonality. Each of these companies is pursuing a new build policy developing hotels with limited public facilities but superior bedroom accommodation. In each case the new product will provide four-star quality at three-star prices. Indeed, in two of the cases the branding is very close: namely, the Garden Court (hotel development by Holiday Inn) and the Country Court (hotel development by Stakis).

Among retailers a dominant response in circumstances of imitation has been to pursue a strategy of 'enterprise differentiation', which literally means that 'each retail firm attempts to offer a unique set of goods and services to customers and at the same time make certain that these customers view that retail operation as different.'[30] Thus the retailer must continually monitor the environment, identifying the competition and developing and implementing a differentiation strategy. This will be a process of constant re-evaluation as illustrated in Figure 6.1.

Competition in retailing is directly related to actively developing differences in what are essentially similar operations. In utilizing competitive differentiation and market positioning (i.e. the identification and servicing of particular customer requirements) successful retailers orientate their outlets to particular market segments and consumer expectations. A positioning strategy can create a barrier to entry for imitative competitors. As Johnson argues, an established positioning strategy:

> provides the retailer with a unique image in the marketplace, competitors can only expect to imitate it, and must spend heavily, for example, in terms of advertising in order to convince the customer that they can do better: or they must choose to find some other bases of positioning.[31]

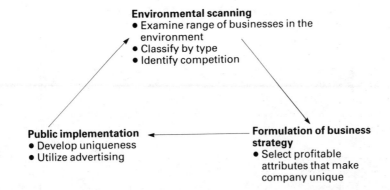

Figure 6.1   *The enterprise differentiation cycle.*
Source: Based on Duncan, D., Hollander, S. and Savitt, R., *Modern Retailing Management: Basic Concepts and Practices* (10th edn), Irwin, Homewood, Ill., 1983

Clearly, the desired result is a reduction in serious competition. An example is the highly successful Body Shop company. This company, which is founded on a strong environmental orientation, has developed a clearly recognizable image and stable position. A number of imitators are in existence, but to date Body Shop remains pre-eminent. However, more successful imitation has occurred by large multiple retailers which have had some success with their promotion of 'natural' beauty produce. The ease with which large multiples can imitate others' strategies will obviously reduce the advantage of positioning.

In the context of the hospitality industry, considerable evidence of imitation exists. For example, the market for the steak meal would appear to have a number of operators involved in supply. Litteljohn[32] argues that such 'me too' imitation in provision will diminish and that 'brand champions' will emerge.

Clearly then, competitive strategy is a core consideration for both the retailer and the hospitality operator. McGee[33] has developed a grid analysis of generic competitive strategies of UK retailers. Companies are positioned on the basis of their strategies, whether cost oriented or differentiation oriented. The position of the company is further moderated by the focus of that company's activities, varying from broad to narrow (see Figure 6.2).

If one were to develop a similar grid analysis of hotel companies, one would find with notable exceptions, such as the budget accommodation sector and the clearly identifiable luxury operators, that there would be a number of claimants for the central position (see Figure 6.3).

Such models can be criticized as simplistic. However, one can identify cost-based, narrow product-focus strategies such as that offered by the budget accommodation sector and the specialist targeted strategies exhibited by luxury operators. Furthermore, such models can illustrate the driving forces and leverage points which reinforce the competitive positioning strategy. Indeed it may be argued that the traditional accommodation sector product in the four-star bracket is being increasingly seen as isolated. It offers neither low cost nor distinctive differentiation. Repositioning may well be advisable as EC and international competition increases.

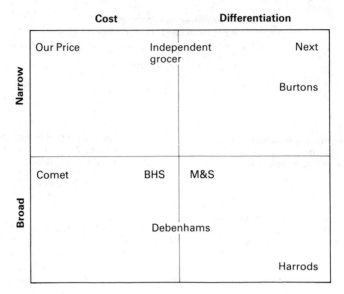

Figure 6.2   *Examples of generic competitive strategies of UK retailers.*
Source: McGee, J., 'Retail strategies in the UK', in Johnson, G. (ed.), *Business Strategies and Retailing*, John Wiley, Chichester, 1987.

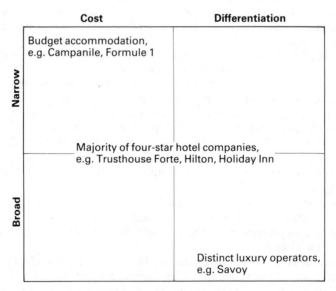

Figure 6.3   *Perceptions of hotel companies' competitive positions.*

Such repositioning will place emphasis on customer service with demands for staff quality at the lower levels. Physical product development and competitive repositioning are limited if they are not combined with consideration of human resources in service sector operations. The retailing industry is labour intensive, yet successful retail operators have been able to develop high levels of customer care while generating considerable cost savings. The use of technology in stock control, stock supply and new customer sales methods is generating considerable productivity gains. However, much of the cost saving has been on staff costs, which can account for over half of total retail overheads.[34] The employment of a greater number of part-time employees has been a recognizable strategy throughout the retail sector. Part-timers are utilized to supplement a small number of core staff at identifiably busy trading periods. Seasonal sales variations are accommodated by forward planning and the early recruitment of temporary seasonal staff. In this way overtime payment can be minimized and National Insurance contributions reduced.

In more successful operations this has not necessarily meant a reduction in customer service. High levels of customer care can be combined with high levels of part-time employment. Customer care considers the relationship between the staff of an organization and the service they provide, and relates it to the customers' perceived requirements. This is essentially a corporate attitude which places customer requirements as paramount. Whereas competitive repositioning and physical product development have capital cost implications, customer care will involve the investment of company resources in staff training. The customer care philosophy requires commitment from all staff to the values of the organization. The philosophy should encourage:

- increased staff commitment to the organization;
- improved customer experience;
- better quality services provided for customers;
- increased customer usage;
- increased repeat purchase.

This, in turn, places requirements on the organization to reinforce the values of the customer care philosophy. In the case of the more successful retailers this has involved:

- the preparation and introduction of new job descriptions and employee specifications which are designed with the customer in mind;
- the redesign of selection, induction, training and appraisal to incorporate the importance of the customer;
- consultation with staff to set objectives and targets for improving customer awareness;
- management and supervision taking an active role in leading by example;
- the introduction and operation of rewards and merit systems for the achievement of targets.

There is without doubt material here for the hospitality operator to consider. However, the hospitality operator must ultimately do more than merely attempt to assimilate and apply models of good practice from the retail sector. Distinctions between business sectors have become increasingly blurred. All aspects of the service sector can constitute a retail market, and retailing constitutes part of the leisure environment as well as providing services and goods for it.[35] Competitive advantage can now be primarily derived from:

- service based on a total organizational commitment to customer care;
- technology based on information and control systems to provide detailed information on consumption, cost allocation and profitability;
- specialization based on clearly defined concepts aimed at target markets;
- property based on location and impact of building.

The retail industry offers excellent examples of business behaviour in continual change as the retailer has constantly to introduce innovations in order to compete.[36] It is thus valuable to return to an overview of macro-retail behaviour to conclude. If one considers retailing in Europe, a number of common trends emerge:

- the multiple retailers have increased their market presence;
- there is an identifiable decline in the total number of retail outlets per head of population;
- there is a clear trend towards the development of self-service, particularly large self-service stores in areas such as furniture and foods;
- there is a growth of large hypermarkets/superstores retailing food and non-food products;
- considerable development of discount outlets is apparent in a variety of areas, e.g. electrical goods, textiles, carpets and furniture.

Furthermore, it is important to note that in the most advanced consumer societies such as the USA, Japan and Canada a number of significant changes have taken place in the retailing system. Such changes may offer certain guidelines for developments in European retailing and for service industries more generally.[37] The most significant changes are as follows:

- The massive increase in computer technology in retailing units of all sizes, to carry out all aspects of financial transactions, stock control, environmental monitoring and overhead control.
- The increase in convenience stores with extended periods of opening and carrying wide varieties of produce.
- The increase in franchised operations which are associated with large retail companies or wholesalers. Franchising is particularly advanced in the USA, with franchise stores accounting for over one-third of the country's retail sales.
- Large multiple corporations have increased their market presence and have introduced some of the most innovative changes in store design.
- There is considerable evidence of the globalization of retailing as large operators extend their geographical market penetration.
- Growth areas would appear to be own-brand retailing, emphasizing value for money and better quality. The lifestyle marketing of products is seen as increasingly more important in competitive environments.

That such changes are associated with retail and not hospitality *per se* does not detract from their importance. Retailing is a very important aspect of the total business world. It is highly competitive and aggressively marketed, and it should not be ignored. The successful examples of retail/hospitality transfer are encouraging. However, the utilization of continual competitive repositioning and the integration of customer care as a key element of human resource management is already established within retailing. If the hospitality operator is to compete then he or she must rapidly assimilate the strategic importance of such operational management and the significance of the changes and trends identified.

NOTES

1. McFadyen, E. (ed.), *The Changing Face of British Retailing*, Newman Books, London, 1987.
2. Sparkes, L., 'The retail sector', in Jones, P. (ed.), *Management in Service Industries*, Pitman, London, 1989.
3. Wilkie, T., 'Knickerbox funded for major expansion', *Independent*, 17 Feb. 1990, p. 15.
4. Johnson, G. (ed.) *Business Strategy and Retailing*, John Wiley, Chichester, 1987.
5. Jackson, A., 'Retailers' future set to stay bleak', *Independent*, 6 Jan. 1990, p. 14.
6. Beaumont, J., 'Trends in food retailing', in McFadyen, E. (ed.), *The Changing Face of British Retailing*, Newman Books, London, 1987.
7. Davies, K., Gilligan, C. and Sutton, C., 'Structural change in grocery retailing: the implications for competition', *International Journal of Physical Distribution and Materials Management*, vol. 15, 1985, pp. 1–48.
8. Sparkes, op. cit., p. 45.
9. Segal-Horn, S., 'The retail environment in the UK', in Johnson, G. (ed.), *Business Strategy and Retailing*, John Wiley, Chichester, pp. 13–22.
10. For a useful summary of the retail sector, see Sparkes, op. cit.
11. Dawson, J.A. and Sparks, L., *Issues on Retailing*, Scottish Development Department, Edinburgh, 1985.
12. Bass plc, *Annual Report* for the year ended 30 September 1989.
13. Segal-Horn, op. cit.
14. Dawson and Sparkes, op. cit.
15. Schiller, R., 'The coming of the third wave', *Estates Gazette*, 1986, pp. 648–51.
16. McGee, J., 'Retail strategies in the UK', in Johnson, G. (ed.), *Business Strategies and Retailing*, John Wiley, Chichester, 1987.
17. Segal-Horn, op. cit.
18. Mower, S., 'Chelsea Girl grows up and goes away', *Independent*, 17 Feb. 1990, p. 37.
19. Kellner, P., 'So how many? Who, what, when, where and why?' *Independent*, 30 Dec. 1989, p. 33.
20. Johnson, op. cit.
21. Vincent, L., 'The new spirit at Grand Met', *Observer*, 2 Oct. 1988, p. 64.
22. Grand Metropolitan plc, *Annual Report* for the year ended 30 September 1989.
23. *Leisure News*, 'Grant Met emphasises leisure', no. 19, 15 Feb. 1990, p. 2.
24. Menzies, A., 'Retailing and tourism', in *Insights 1989/90*, English Tourist Board, London.
25. Bass plc, op. cit.
26. O'Halloran, M. (1990), 'Bass Leisure to open second "Point" in April', *Leisure News*, no. 19, 15 Feb. 1990, p. 2.

27. Hilton Hiliner, 'Shopping made easy: Hong Kong', Jan. 1990, p. 25.
28. Naisbett, J., *Megatrends*, Warner Books, New York, 1982.
29. Porac, J., Thomas, H. and Emme, B. (1987), 'Knowing the competition: the mental models of retailing strategists', in Johnson, G. (ed.), *Business Strategy and Retailing*, John Wiley, Chichester, 1987.
30. Duncan, D., Hollander, S. and Savitt, R., *Modern Retailing Management: Basic Concepts and Practices* (10th edn), Irwin, Homewood, Ill., 1983, p. 8.
31. Johnson, op. cit., pp. 84–5.
32. Litteljohn, D., *Britain's Catering Industry 1989*, Jordan & Son, Bristol, 1989.
33. McGee, op. cit.
34. National Economic Development Office, Distributive Trades Economic Development Committee, *Employment Perspectives and the Distributive Trades*, HMSO, London, March 1985.
35. Martin, W. and Mason, S., *Leisure and Work: The Choices for 1991 and 2001*, Leisure Consultants, Sudbury, 1982.
36. White, R., 'Multinational retailing: a slow advance', *Retail and Distribution Management*, vol. 12, 1984, pp. 8–13.
37. Dawson, J., 'Change and continuity in Japanese retailing', *Retail and Distribution Management*, vol. 15, 1985, pp. 46–50; Rodgers, D., 'Changes in North American supermarkets', *Retail and Distribution Management*, vol. 14, 1984, pp. 19–23; Kaynak, E. (ed.), *Transnational Retailing*, Walter de Gruyter, Berlin, 1988.

PART 3
MANAGING HOSPITALITY SERVICES

7

Human resource management:
a response to change in the 1990s

Philip Worsfold and Stephanie Jameson

INTRODUCTION

The one certain thing about any view of the future is that it will be wrong in many respects.[1]

A popular theme for management development is 'the management of change'; in the not too distant future managers will have ample opportunity to test the theories related to this theme. The events that occurred throughout Eastern Europe in 1990 might almost be regarded as a portent of the extent of change that we are to experience throughout the 1990s. Whatever the result of events occurring in Eastern Europe it is certain that we are entering a period of rapid and dramatic change that will have a profound effect on the operation of all organizations. These changes are so extensive that some authors have likened them to the agrarian and industrial revolutions.

As in previous periods of change, organizations unable or unwilling to accept the necessity for change will risk sharing the fate of the dinosaurs: extinction. Successful organizations have always recognized the need for a continuous process of development and adaptation to the changing environment. The impending changes, however, present new problems because (a) they are considered by some to be of a greater order of magnitude than those previously experienced by many organizations and (b) the increasing rate of technological change may make a gradual process of adaptation untenable.

In the United Kingdom three major agents of impending organizational change can be identified: population change, the single European market and technological change. All these factors have serious implications for the management policies of all organizations, and as one of the largest national and international employers the hospitality industry will inevitably be involved in many of these changes. In their recent report Howarth and Howarth identify the fact that 'hoteliers regard human resources to be the single most important issue facing the industry into the next century'.[2]

Certainly companies will have to direct much more attention to the recruitment, selection, training, career planning and retention of staff at all levels of the their human resource problems and meet the challenge of tomorrow's market. In the following sections some of the problems that will be of concern to human resource managers are addressed.

LABOUR SUPPLY AND DEMAND

Although future labour demand is difficult to assess, estimates from the CBI predict that the number of vacancies in all sectors of employment will rise from 3.5 million to 3.7 million by the next century. It is generally assumed that the majority of these vacancies will be in the service sectors and that many will be concentrated in the hospitality industry. Recent reports indicate that the United Kingdom hotel sector will continue to expand throughout the 1990s, although at a slower rate than during the 1980s. In an analysis reported by Slattery[3] it is suggested that during the 1990s overseas holiday demand for United Kingdom hotel accommodation will increase by about 47 per cent and United Kingdom holiday demand by about 70 per cent. In contrast, business demand will experience more modest growth. It is suggested that by the end of the century business demand by 6.5 per cent. The analysis produces a total growth in demand of 6.4 million room nights by the year 2000. Such an increase will, of course, be accompanied by an increase in demand for labour. Labour forecasts produced by the HCTB for the five-year period to 1993 predict a dramatic increase in employment opportunities within the hospitality industry resulting in the need to fill 22,500 additional jobs.

Against this background of increasing demand we are currently being presented with images of a decreasing labour supply. In the United Kingdom there was a significant decline in birth rate in the 1970s: from a peak of 1,015,000 births in 1964 the birth rate fell to 657,000 in 1977. A consequence of this slump in birth rate is the much publicized fact that by 1995 there will be a drastic reduction (approximately 20 per cent) in the number of people in the 16–24-year age range. The reduction will not be evenly spread throughout the United Kingdom: anticipated regional differences suggest the percentage decrease in this age range will be greatest in Scotland and the North West, and lowest in East Anglia.[4]

Although media attention has highlighted the potential impact of the 'demographic time bomb' on British industry, the situation is not peculiar to the United Kingdom. Most EC countries will experience a similar decline in the young workforce. West Germany had the lowest birth rate in the EC, resulting in an anticipated decrease among 14–19-year-olds of more than 40 per cent; this picture is now complicated, however, by the recent migration of young families from the East. The reduction in Italy is of the order of 30 per cent whereas France, Spain, Portugal and Greece will fare better than the United Kingdom. Ireland will be the only country without shortages. Outside the EC the USA has already experienced the phenomenon of declining population, and in other developed countries such as Japan a similar pattern can be seen.

Given that the relevant demographic statistics have been available for some years, it is perhaps surprising that the 'demographic time bomb' has only recently attracted widespread media attention. However, if we take into account the fact that the United Kingdom labour force is projected to grow from the present 28.3 million to 29.3 million by the end of the 1990s, that there are at the time of writing 1.7 million unemployed in the United Kingdom, and that unemployment among the under-25s is nearly double that of the over-25s throughout the EC, then the media might be considered by some to be guilty of hype.

Certainly this seems to be the attitude of some managers in the hospitality industry. In a recent survey hotel managers were questioned about what action they might take to counter the difficulty of recruiting staff when the industry was expanding and the number of school leavers was falling: 43 per cent responded that they had not given it any thought.[5] The general response of the major hospitality companies has been to direct more attention to recruitment campaigns, developing links with colleges, and attempting to project an improved image of the hospitality industry.

It is generally acknowledged that industry as a whole will have to seek alternative sources of labour and must consider increasing the employment of women (who may be returning after a substantial absence), of people belonging to ethnic minorities, of older persons and of the long-term unemployed. The hospitality industry has traditionally placed great reliance on young employees, female employees and those belonging to ethnic minorities. If in future these groups are to be targeted by other industries then the hospitality industry will be particularly disadvantaged.

MARRIED WOMEN RETURNERS

The government had advocated that one way in which employers may attempt to compensate for the low supply of young workers is to attract more mature applicants who are not already employed, notably married women. The result of such a policy would be that women would become the largest potential growth group in the United Kingdom workforce. However, a major constraint on the employment of married women is the need for child care arrangements. In a report from the European Commission[6] the child care facilities of the EC countries are placed in three categories. Highest levels of child care are seen in Belgium, Denmark, France and Italy; the lowest levels occur in Ireland, Luxembourg, the Netherlands and the United Kingdom. In the lowest group, 20 per cent or less of children under 3 are in publicly funded care. Information presented by the British Institute of Management[7] suggests that even key employees are rarely offered arrangements for child care. Of 800 women managers surveyed, only 11 per cent were offered crèche facilities. Career break schemes allowing employees extended periods of absence (e.g. two years) for child care are being developed by very few United Kingdom companies.

Although the constraint of child care is beginning to attract some attention from government and companies, little attention has been directed towards other pertinent factors. For example, the extent to which married women wish to take up paid employment and the attitude of families to working women will affect the availability of women for employment. In an EC survey[8] 48 per cent of married (or cohabiting) men expressed the view that their wives should have paid work. However, 16 per cent wanted the women's work to be less demanding than their own and for wives to be responsible for the housework. In the United Kingdom 50 per cent of men questioned preferred their wives to have paid work; 40 per cent preferred their wives not to work. Women's attitudes to married women going out to work have changed significantly over the last two decades. The general reaction regarding women without children was that marriage should not prevent them from working. For women with children at school only 7 per cent considered that women should not work whereas 45 per cent considered that women with children under school age should stay at home.[9]

Reports in the popular press have drawn attention to the problems experienced by married women returners: 'Nearly two out of three women who have gone back to work are being victimised by sexist husbands and nagging children who want them to carry on being dogsbodies at home.'[10] In this article the women returners reported that working conditions had improved during their career breaks and that attitudes towards women were less sexist. However, about two-thirds of women returners identified family pressure as harder to cope with than the new job itself; a third considered that going back to work had damaged their personal relationships.

Particular problems arise in the situation where husband and wife have work they consider of equal value. Mobility of the individuals may be restricted, thereby limiting career development and causing frustration. In the dual career family there is less probability that either partner will benefit from returning to a nurturing home environment. The levels of stress experienced by both individuals may as a consequence be higher and this may result in lower performance at work.[11] All these factors may limit the availability of women for employment.

In addition to the problems of child care there is the problem of training. Many potential women employees are hampered by the fact that they lack recent experience and a knowledge of current methods of work. Less than 5 per cent of the companies in the BIM sample offered refresher courses, updating or retraining in new skills for women returners. For companies to recruit, retain and maximize the potential of women returners it is necessary for them to develop appropriate induction and training programmes. Companies also need to develop methods of retaining links with trained personnel who intend to return to work following an extended period of absence for child care. By providing short courses they can maintain contact with former employees and keep them updated until they return to work.

Finally it is perhaps worth mentioning that one of the reasons suggested for the decline in birth rate is the increasing employment of women. If the decline in birth rate results in greater employment opportunities for women but no improvement in child care facilities then a downward spiral in the birth rate may result.

ETHNIC MINORITIES AND IMMIGRATION

A second group that has been identified for targeting in the new era of competition for labour has been that of ethnic minorities. It is worth noting, however, that cultural or religious observances may inhibit some groups from presenting themselves for employment. Companies that do not already recognize their employment potential may regard ethnic minorities as a new source of labour. Although the hospitality industry already employs considerable numbers of ethnic minorities, they are most often employed in unskilled and semi-skilled positions. It is highly probable that many of these employees are under-utilized, and new training programmes will need to be initiated to maximize their potential.

It seems ironic at a time when the world's population is increasing by a quarter of a million a day that in the United Kingdom there should be so much concern about the 'demographic time bomb'. In both the USA and Europe labour shortages are already being met by means of 'guest' workers. In many cases low-paid, unskilled work is carried out by illegal immigrants. In Europe measures are currently being adopted to improve controls and thereby reduce the levels of immigrant labour. If the declining population leads to shortages of labour in the future then a situation may arise in which immigration is actively encouraged. This again will present a challenge for those concerned with organizing training within the industry.

An additional factor to consider is the recent changes occurring in Eastern Europe. The development of a market economy in these countries will initially lead to high levels of unemployment. Whether employment opportunities in the West will be made available to this group is a matter for conjecture.

POPULATION DECLINE AND THE AGEING WORKFORCE

For the population of a developed country to remain constant the average birth rate must be about 2.1 births per woman; in Western Europe the birth rate is about 1.8. At the same time the average life span in developed countries has gradually increased. These two facts mean that Europe has a declining and ageing population with fewer employees available for work.

To some extent the United States has already experienced some of the problems anticipated in Europe. In 1982 the average age of the workforce was 35 years; by 1995 the average age of the workforce is expected to be over 40.[12] Further ageing of the workforce will occur as a result of the removal of the mandatory retirement age.

A survey carried out by the British Institute of Management identified the fact that over 50 per cent of Britain's current managers are over 40 and that by the year 2000 half the population will be over 50. In the United Kingdom it is not yet illegal to discriminate on the grounds of age with the result that a conscientious and experienced workforce is often neglected. The Director-General of the British Institute of Management says:

> The talents of older managers are all too often wasted. It is too easy for organisations to dismiss their older employees as past it, when they have a will to learn and broader depth of experience than their younger colleagues.
>
> A change of attitude by organisations and individuals is badly needed. Some companies are bordering on the negligent in their treatment and use of the skills of older staff. They compete for younger staff without relevant knowledge, competence or experience, while little thought may be given to retraining or developing older and more experienced staff.[13]

It does appear, however, that opinion is beginning to change in this area and some companies (especially the retail sector) are beginning to recognize the value of recruiting older employees. The introduction of legislation to prevent age discrimination does not appear as unlikely as it once was.

THE SINGLE EUROPEAN MARKET

It is anticipated that the advent of the single European market in 1992 will stimulate a huge increase in competition between companies within the Community. Economies of scale resulting from the larger market and the eradication of customs barriers will increase the opportunities for companies producing both goods and services. Increasing competition will promote the need for greater productivity and may result in the need for restructuring similar to that experienced by other industries such as iron, coal and steel. Some industries may find it necessary to relocate themselves outside the Community.

The effect such changes will have on employment and the availability of labour are unclear, but tentative forecasts suggest that there will be an initial loss of half a million jobs. By 1998, however, it is predicted that the changes will result in the creation of an additional 1.86 million jobs.[14] The number of jobs that will be created in the United Kingdom is anticipated to be of the order of 385,000.[15]

A factor that complicates predictions of labour availability is the freedom of movement of the workforce throughout the European Community that will be engendered by the single market. The demographic changes already experienced by the USA have resulted in migration of the population from the North-East to the South. Kravetz[16] suggests that by the year 2000 there will be 500,000 fewer potential employees in the north-eastern United States as a consequence of migration. If the demographic changes in Europe bring about similar shortages of unskilled and semi-skilled labour then migration will tend to be from southern to northern Europe. The alternative scenario for some industries is to relocate to areas of labour availability, i.e. southern Europe. Skilled labour will also seek those employment markets that offer maximum reward. It is estimated, for example, that increased employment opportunities on the Continent will result in a net loss of graduates from the United Kingdom.[17]

These changes in availability of labour will be accompanied by additional longer-term changes affecting the rights of employees. The Community Charter of Fundamental Social Rights adopted by eleven of the member states of the European Community in 1989 is essentially a statement of intent. The plan for implementing the charter has been published and this will, in the fullness of time, lead to the issuing of directives. One of the aims of this action is to counteract the risk of social dumping within the European market: that is, attempting to attract capital investment into an area by keeping the cost of labour low by means of poor conditions of employment. The charter will eventually bring about changes in many areas of working life, including working conditions, remuneration, industrial relations, consultation and participation, and training. The extent of these changes, the time frame for their implementation and their eventual impact on UK conditions of employment is at present unclear; suffice it to say that changes must be anticipated.

It has been predicted that the stimulus to business provided by the single European market will result in a dramatic increase in demand for hotel accommodation on the continent.[18] Those hotel companies that have anticipated the demand and increased their exposure to the Continental market will be presented with the opportunity for continued expansion. Such expansion will in turn increase the need for companies to create a more international management style.

THE IMPACT OF NEW TECHNOLOGY

The process of development and economic growth in industrialized countries has resulted in a movement of the working population from primary industries (e.g. agriculture and fishing) to secondary industries (manufacturing and production) and then to tertiary industries (financial services, professional services, hospitality and leisure). Today the primary sector accounts for only about 3 per cent of the working population, and although there has been a recent upturn, the secondary industries have failed to keep pace with the development of tertiary industries. Forecasters such as Naisbitt[19] and Jones[20] argue that the increased use of computer-based technologies will have considerable impact on patterns of employment, the numbers of staff employed, the skills required by staff, the extent of their motivation, job satisfaction and the level of turnover. They argue that even highly complex operations, at present performed by skilled employees, will be undertaken by robots with advanced sensory capabilities.

A popular interpretation of this trend is that the future will provide employment for only a few fortunate individuals,[21] whereas other authors consider that the prediction of a society 'where most goods and services are produced by information technologies and robot manned factories overstates the transforming power of microelectronics and underestimates the capacity of economies to create new jobs as technological change destroys old ones'.[22]

Certainly the evidence so far suggests that the new technologies more than compensate for the decline in old industries. Despite the creation of jobs in the new industries, however, the changing pattern of job availability brought about by technological change may exacerbate the problem of rising unemployment. In general the introduction of computer technology and automation decreases the demand for unskilled and semi-skilled workers while increasing the demand for technical specialists and white-collar workers. The result is the displacement of unskilled and semi-skilled staff and those staff with inappropriate skills who are unable or unwilling to retrain.

Those workers displaced by new technology may be seen as a source of labour for the hospitality industry. However, workers displaced by computer-related technologies are often unwilling to accept lower-paid jobs in the tertiary sector. Others are unable to move to areas where tertiary employment is available.

Given the anticipated employment changes resulting from the introduction of new technology it has been argued that it is not a shortage of labour that should concern us but a shortage of skills. The automation of routine jobs and the deskilling of traditional areas of work will be accompanied by a greater demand for employees able to deal with the increased mental content of work. It is argued that this demand will rise at a rate that cannot be met by the level of education and training prevailing in the United Kingdom. This could prove particularly damaging to opportunities for economic growth in the United Kingdom; there is an overwhelming need for better education and training.

It is now generally recognized that the development and application of new technology is changing both the demand for skills and patterns of work. For example, many employees may find themselves working from home: one estimate suggests that 10.5 million employees could do their work from home by 1995. It is difficult to see how the concept of home working could apply to employment in the hospitality industry, although the occasional need for temporary office accommodation may create new market opportunities for the industry. On the other hand, the improvement in distance communication brought about by the telecommunications revolution may result in fewer meetings, fewer conferences and less business travel. Such changes should, of course, concern the hospitality industry.

The impact of new technology on the employment practices of industry has so far been rather uneven. A number of industries have experienced considerable gains in productivity with the increasing application of new technology, e.g. telecommunications, financial services, tourism and air transport. The hospitality industry has yet to experience similar changes. Contrary to the views of many people in the hospitality industry, the introduction of new technology has become a major factor in the continuing success of the service sector. We need only look at the use of automatic banking facilities to see how new technology can augment personal service and for some customers provide a complete service. Hospitality managers may, in the future, be required to have an interest in automated systems and IT in addition to the psychology of the service encounter.

The shortage of skilled personnel exacerbated by demographic trends may actually accelerate the introduction of new technology to replace labour in the hospitality industry. For example, the increasing use of more complex automated front-office systems could eventually remove the need for front-office staff altogether. On the food and beverage side, the decoupling of meal production from service could be increased either by the development of centralized meal production units in the hospitality industry or by the supply of ready-prepared products by the food industry. This trend together with the increasing use of automated technology to reconstitute meals produced elsewhere will reduce the need for kitchen porters but may also mean that machine operatives are employed rather than chefs.

The catering sector will also meet increasing competition from the retail food sector supermarkets because they will be able to supply the consumer with an increasing range of quality prepared meals at lower cost; it is possible that budget-priced establishments will respond to this competition by increased use of vending.

With the introduction of automation employing sophisticated methods of quality control the product can become consistently high in quality. Customer selection of the product will then depend to a much greater extent on the quality of the service given by the human factor in the service equation. Consider, for example, a much simplified model of the variables contributing to customer satisfaction in a restaurant. They are (a) product (meal) quality, (b) the service element and (c) the environment. As technology reduces the potential for variation in quality of the product, greater emphasis is placed on the environment and the service element. Of these the environment is relatively easy to improve. It is the service element that will eventually provide a successful company with competitive advantage.

The result of these changes would mean that a number of skilled operations would disappear. People-intensive jobs will be least affected by the introduction of new technology. The jobs most likely to suffer are those that consist of simple routine repetitive tasks. It will be necessary to identify those jobs placed at risk by the introduction of new technology and to develop retraining programmes which prepare people for relocation within the organization. In addition, the changes have implications for recruitment, selection, training, career development and job design.

Those industries that have introduced new technology have found that it is not only capable of removing unpleasant, boring and repetitive jobs but can also deskill other areas of work. Such deskilling results in a reduction of those job characteristics believed to contribute to the job satisfaction and motivation of employees.

Improving the working environment by a conscious process of job redesign may do much to improve job satisfaction and thereby enable companies to retain staff. Cooley, however, argues that such 'systems which enhance rather than subordinate employees'[23] are less likely to be developed by management because they present a challenge to their power base. Hospitality managers must recognize that increasing use of new technology in the hospitality industry coupled with the need to retain skilled staff makes the introduction of job enrichment programmes a necessity.

ORGANIZATION STRUCTURE AND MANAGEMENT STYLE

Studies of manufacturing companies have shown how the nature of the product, the method of production and the type of customer are important determinants of organization structure. Furthermore, it has been demonstrated that when a change in the use of technology occurs it will bring about a change in the organization's structure.[24]

We have seen that the introduction of new technology may influence the relationship between production and service in the hospitality industry. The adoption of new technology will in turn affect the nature of organization structures within the industry.

Small batch production, for example, is typified by the close proximity of the manager to the production work itself. Control of production relies heavily upon the production personnel themselves without extensive administrative controls. As companies move towards automated production and process technologies, the management of skilled specialists is through committees rather than by instruction down the line. More trained university graduates are employed and the proportion of personnel working directly on production is low. The administrative and managerial component is, therefore, a comparatively large proportion of the workforce.

The changes envisaged in the hospitality industry are not so extensive. It may not be possible or desirable to automate the complete restaurant or hotel experience. Nevertheless the trend is in that direction, and these changes will be reflected in the demand for more skilled personnel, more graduates and new approaches to management.

It is certain, however, that as major hospitality companies increase in size and become pan-European they will need to adopt new management structures. It is anticipated that in the future many companies will adopt a flatter and more decentralized organization structure. As they become more decentralized, the process of co-ordination within the organizations will become more complex; there will be increasing pressure to adopt a matrix structure.

The research evidence that is available suggests that in general the management style prevailing in the hospitality industry is essentially autocratic.[25] At a time when other organizations are increasingly adopting more participative management styles, the retention of an autocratic management style may exacerbate the problem of recruitment and staff turnover experienced by the industry. For example, a study of unemployed workers by Hall and Jones[26] found that those who had previously worked in the industry were deterred from seeking re-employment by levels of pay, conditions of employment and the attitudes of management. In a recent study of the hotel industry,[27] employees were asked what they liked least in their place of employment. Twenty-two per cent of the employees sampled identified problems with middle management as opposed to other conditions of employment. Asked what they liked best about their place of employment, 58 per cent emphasized the team spirit. Unfortunately it is not clear whether or not they considered management to be part of the team.

In the future it will be increasingly necessary for managers to place emphasis on the quality of employees rather than on quantity. In order to recruit and retain this new calibre of employee it will be necessary to adopt a new approach to management. In particular, the manager will have to face the fact that his or her new employees are an important resource and are not easily replaced; they must be perceived as an investment rather than a cost. There must be an increasing emphasis on developing the commitment of employees, and on fully utilizing their potential.

In adopting a more participatory style of management, successful managers will have to manage a more diverse range of lateral relationships from a position that is no longer dependent on formal power. Leadership will be no longer just a buzzword but a necessity; it will be required at all levels of the organization. Successful managers will be those who are able to mobilize and direct the energy of the workforce. In addition, decentralization of organizations will increase the need for managers with initiative, the ability to accept greater responsibility and the ability to take moderate risks.

Successful companies will meet the increasing rate of change and the increase in competition with an emphasis on quality and service in which meeting customer needs is paramount. To maintain a competitive advantage they will need to keep in the forefront of technological development. Above all, they will need to recognize that people are their most valuable resource. Successful companies will be those able to recruit, retain and motivate the talented people required to handle problems in the more complex organizations of the future.

MEETING THE DEMAND FOR GRADUATES

The changing nature of the industry with its greater need for 'knowledge workers' will increase the demand for graduate recruits. In the past, the long-term trend in the supply of graduates to the labour market has been one of continuing growth: the supply of graduates between 1979 and 1988 rose by 25 per cent.[28] However, we are now entering a new phase and the demographic trend is fuelling competition for the declining number of 18-year-olds entering the job market. The Institute of Manpower Studies[29] reports the decline in 18-year-olds to be least severe in those sectors of the population that traditionally participate in higher education. The decline in the number of graduates will, therefore, be less severe than the demographic change in 16–24 year-olds may at first suggest. The IMS indicated that graduate supply will continue to increase until 1992 and then will begin to decline. It is anticipated that there will be a fall in the number of UK students in higher education from 124,000 in 1992 to 113,000 in 1998.

Despite the increase in the supply of graduates between 1979 and 1988 referred to above, 55 per cent of companies employing graduates reported a shortfall of graduate recruits in 1988 and 10 per cent of their vacancies remained unfilled.[30] The problem has developed as a result of increasing demand for graduate recruits; demand has now outstripped supply. This situation will be exacerbated by the predicted decline in the number of graduates available for employment. Recent press coverage reports that 'Demand for new graduates is so intense this year that two-thirds of employers in the UK are experiencing difficulties.'[31]

The Association of Graduate Recruiters, which represents more than 500 employers of graduates, and the Association of Careers Advisory Services are predicting graduate recruitment difficulties for even the best-known companies as the number of young people declines.[32] It is evident that the anticipated growth of the hospitality industry and the predicted changes will increase demand for skilled management in a period of decreasing supply. Sherrel[33] argues that the 21,000 students who qualify each year are insufficient to meet the industry's need for skilled labour.

It is obvious that in such an environment the graduate is in a position to be more selective in his or her choice of employer. The HCTC has drawn attention to the prospect of increasing competition from other sectors of industry seeking to attract the same recruits. There have been reports[34] that other sectors of industry, especially retailing, are 'poaching' the top hospitality graduates. This suggests that at a time when the industry is experiencing a shortfall of qualified hospitality students and graduates, it is also losing some of these to other industrial sectors.

Leslie, in an analysis of available research regarding the employment of hotel and catering graduates, concludes that 'many students on catering related courses do not enter the industry'.[35] He found, for example, that 25 per cent of students graduating with a degree in Catering Administration from the University of Ulster in 1983 and 1984 did not enter the industry.

The questions that naturally arise are: why are students on hospitality courses refusing to enter the industry and, in the light of future demand, how can this 'wastage' be prevented?

It is often argued that the service industries demand a particular type of manager. Normann,[36] for example, identifies service industries as 'personality intensive', which places emphasis on the individual's motivation and skills during the service delivery process. This has important implications for the recruitment of suitable staff, their training, their career development and above all their management. It is frequently suggested that the control and management of these social interactions requires special skills and techniques.[37] It has been claimed that hospitality managers operate in a unique environment and need to possess a number of specific attributes if they are to meet the unique demands made upon them by the hospitality industry.[38]

It is conceivable that individuals selected for degree courses in hotel and catering subjects lack these specific attributes and feel unable to operate effectively in the hotel and catering environment. However, in a comparison of the personality profiles of managers and hospitality degree students,[39] only relatively small differences were observed. For example, it was found that degree students may be slightly less uninhibited, less conscientious and more opinionated than hotel managers. It may be argued that the high degree of similarity between the profiles suggests that in general these students possess personality attributes which would enable them to operate effectively within the hospitality industry.

Although graduates may possess the personal attributes necessary to succeed in the hospitality industry, they may still choose not to enter the industry. When considering the process of job choice by hospitality graduates it is worthwhile examining the value of their qualifications in the graduate career market using the classification developed by Brennan and McGeevor:[40]

- *Generalist.* Graduates are equipped with general skills of value to employment but not especially related to any employment field. The process of seeking, obtaining and becoming competent in any job only begins upon graduation.
- *Generalist plus.* In addition to general skills, graduates also have certain specialist skills applicable to work. There is an element of occupational training in this type of degree course and the prospect of a closer tie-up between course content and job recruitment. Like the generalist, the process of seeking, obtaining and becoming competent in a job begins at graduation.
- *Occupational generalist.* Graduates make their first step towards a particular job with their choice of degree course. Their ideas may not be precise, relating to a general employment field rather than a precise occupational role. After graduation, the graduate will still face choices about further specialization. From

the employers' point of view the graduate has demonstrated commitment to a broad field of employment and has knowledge and skills of specialist value to work.

- *Occupational specialist.* These graduates have received a partial training for a job and their degree qualification regulates entry into it. Their choice of career occurs at the point of entry to higher education. After graduation there are likely to be clearly defined steps to acquire full professional status and a job.

From the viewpoint of the hospitality industry those graduates completing a hospitality degree can be located in the occupational generalist category: that is, at the time of degree choice they do not have precise occupational goals in mind, but have demonstrated commitment to a broad field of employment in their choice of degree. In addition, during their course they will acquire industry-specific skills and knowledge. Upon graduation they will still face choices concerning further specialization or type of employer. A study of graduates in the labour market by Chapman[41] highlights the fact that graduates acquiring skills and knowledge applicable to work have greater job opportunities. Thus hotel and catering graduates should have a market advantage within the hospitality labour market.

It must be recognized, however, that from the viewpoint of many other industries those completing hospitality degrees may be considered to fall into the generalist or generalist plus category. They will possess a number of transferable skills such as those identified as desirable by the Standing Committee of Employers of Graduates: communication skills, adaptability, data and problem solving, leadership and team working. That these skills are in demand has been shown by David Hind, who in a study of advertisements for graduate recruits found that 38 per cent made explicit reference to personal transferable skills.[42] Employers who do not require graduates with specific disciplines but are seeking graduate entrants with transferable skills may well see hotel and catering graduates as suitable employees.

The HCTC suggests that the rejection of the industry as a viable employment proposition results from an unattractive employment package. Other employment sectors are offering more competitive employment packages which live up to prospective employee expectations. For companies to be effective in the present recruitment market, Curnow rightly argues that employers 'must remain competitive by offering work with a suitable location, benefits package and career prospects – that live up to the candidates' expectations'.[43] Mabey suggests that graduate recruits and their employers often have conflicting expectations of each other. He states: 'There is a costly and ironical mismatch between graduate resources, potential and aspirations on the one hand and the needs, requirements and opportunities of industrial employers on the other.'[44]

The extent to which a graduate wishes to gain access to a company will depend on the ability of the employer to offer a job package that matches the expectations and aspirations of the graduate. In a mismatch situation, it is unlikely that graduates will apply to an employer. If graduates are appointed and the opportunities provided by employers fail to meet their aspirations, the resulting disillusionment leads to low levels of job satisfaction, low commitment to the organization and increased staff turnover. The mismatch therefore has serious economic, organizational and social consequences since it affects the ability of employers to attract, recruit and retain graduate employees. There is obviously a need for a reduction in the level of mismatch between graduate aspirations and expectations and job reality. To quote Pearson and Pike:

Good graduates are going to be an increasingly scarce and expensive resource in the 1990s. Recruiters and employers need to ensure that they are ready now and will be flexible enough in the future to compete in this challenging environment.[45]

The ability of employers to attract graduates is of particular importance at the moment. The opportunities presented to graduates are, therefore, of fundamental importance. The fact that graduates will be a precious commodity in many member states of the EC should also encourage UK companies to develop European recruitment and training programmes. Although at the moment European graduate recruitment is still the exception, in some countries it may soon become the norm. Companies such as Trusthouse Forte which have already established an international recruitment programme are at an advantage.

HUMAN RESOURCE MANAGEMENT: THE NEED FOR CHANGE

In the past the hospitality industry has been able to obtain employees whenever it chose from a relatively permanent pool of mobile labour. The mobility and/or availability of this labour has, in many sectors, encouraged a lack of interest in human resource issues despite the variable quality of performance obtained from such employees. Personnel policies, when present, have been primarily concerned with the administration of a cost rather than the development of a resource.

If the hospitality industry is successfully to accommodate the changes brought about by the introduction of new technology, demographic changes, a new calibre of employee and the single European market, it must of necessity undergo a culture change. Personnel managers within the industry will have to adopt the role of change agent if such changes are to be successfully implemented. Change may initially be resisted; the traditional methods of work will be seen to have considerable virtue, to be what the customer wants or to be the only way of providing a service. In bringing about a culture change the whole range of personnel practices will need to be employed.

Howarth and Howarth state that 'The image of the industry is not perceived as being attractive in many countries and is therefore low on the list of those wishing to develop careers.'[46] Certainly those attempting to recruit employees into hospitality would welcome a better image for the industry. Unfortunately the industry's idea of promoting a better image does not always appear to be related to improving real conditions of employment.

What is wrong with the conditions of employment, and how will they disadvantage the industry when competing for employees?

Pay

The hospitality industry has a reputation for low levels of pay; unfortunately in many cases this reputation is justified. In a survey of the unemployed, Hall and Jones[47] found that over half of their sample had previously been employed in the hospitality industry. Level of pay was identified as the most significant reason for leaving. Although for the majority of positions pay is set at unattractive levels, the perception of pay levels will differ among different groups. Young employees without dependants may be more willing to accept lower pay rates, especially if they consider the employment to be temporary. In contrast, older workers with dependants will be more concerned with seeking longer-term secure employment with higher rates of pay. It is from this latter group that the hospitality industry will need to recruit in future.

Despite statements to the contrary, it also appears that pay has a low level of organizational priority. Croney[48] reports that, although corporate managers of hotel groups stressed the importance of paying competitive rates to motivate employees, the pay systems employed by the companies were 'largely informal, inconsistent, ad hoc and subjective'. There were in fact no formal job evaluation procedures in any of the hotel groups surveyed.

If the hospitality industry is to improve its image then it must introduce systems of pay determination that reduce subjectivity.

The working day and social life

Long and unsociable hours are often identified as a deterrent to employment in the hospitality industry. Relatively little attention, however, has been directed towards employees' attitudes to different patterns of work. A survey of people already working in the industry (room maids) found that only about 14 per cent were dissatisfied with evening and shift work; thus shift work in itself was not perceived as a problem among this group.[49] In contrast, a survey of attitudes of the unemployed to work in the hospitality industry[50] found that evening work and shift work was seen as undesirable by about 52 per cent of the sample. Split shifts, however, were identified as undesirable by 75 per cent of the sample. One of the major disadvantages of split shifts is disruption of social life, and any action designed to reduce their incidence should prove beneficial when recruiting staff. Attempts to redirect recruitment towards older employees and women returners may be frustrated by the requirement for shift work and work during unsocial hours.

At general manager level the hours worked are often long and unsocial. Evidence suggests, however, that it is not the number of hours worked or their unsocial nature that is seen as the main disadvantage. It is the unpredictability of the hours and the effect of that unpredictability on the manager's social life.[51] This was particularly the case for married managers with children. While younger managers may accept these conditions in their desire to further their careers, in older managers this is clearly a reason for considering employment out of the industry. In addition, high mobility is expected of all hotel managers wishing to advance their careers; they may be required to move, on average, every two years. This is not feasible in many dual-career families and has often restricted the career development of married women managers. A way of resolving these problems needs to be found. Changes in the management structure, career pathways and nature of commitment expected from senior management may be required in the future if the hospitality industry is to recruit and retain talented management.

Following the trend in other industries, the hospitality industry is beginning to experiment with new patterns of work. The industry has always employed part-time and casual seasonal staff to match variations in demand. Increasingly it is employing permanent part-time staff who are part of the establishment and are provided with similar benefits to full-time staff.[52] Some companies have begun to experiment with job share schemes[53] and the provision of workplace crèches. With the prevailing demographic scenario these trends will need to continue.

JOB DESIGN AND JOB SATISFACTION

In a study of motivation and job satisfaction in hotel workers it was found that most managers perceived money as the main motivator of their employees. This 'economic' view of the employee lacked congruence with the views of their subordinates, who also identified responsibility and job satisfaction as important.[54] The response of the subordinates reflects the 'human relations' theories which lead to ideas concerning job enrichment. Increased job satisfaction resulting from job enrichment could be a major factor in staff retention.

At the present time there is little evidence of functional flexibility such as job rotation, job enlargement or multiskilling within the hospitality industry.[55] Job rotation and job enlargement can both result in job enrichment provided the employee is not just required to do a greater range of boring jobs. In future, however, the increased use of technology will require jobs to be broadly based and employees will need to become multiskilled: they will need to be trained in a number of operational areas. The need for multiskilling will present human resource managers with an opportunity to design jobs enriched with higher levels of task variety, task significance, autonomy and customer contact.

Because of multiskilling and the increasingly personality-intensive nature of the industry, a high proportion of staff will come into contact with the customer. All will need additional social skills training.

RECRUITMENT AND SELECTION

Although corporate managers of hospitality companies may be aware of the need for an effective recruitment and selection process, this awareness is not always reflected in policy at unit level. In their survey of 50 hotel companies, Lockwood and Guerrier[56] found that in all but one company the general manager of the hotel was given almost total freedom to staff his or her own hotel subject only to certain financial constraints. In another study,[57] research at unit level reveals that all the units followed informal selection methods. The appointment of staff was invariably delegated to the line manager. Sometimes the personnel department carried out preliminary interviews, but it was often only concerned with administration of the line manager's decision. The high turnover rates prevailing in many areas of hospitality have in the past encouraged employers to concentrate simply on filling a vacancy with any available applicant.

Preparation for the process of recruitment appears in many cases to be minimal; the analytical determination of job requirements is frequently absent. In a study of hotels Croney found that 'job analysis was rarely carried out and . . . job specifications were not written down but were left to the discretion of the interviewer'.[58] Another study of industrial catering units[59] found that the majority of unit managers did not employ the job descriptions produced by head office. In only one case was this because the manager felt they were inadequate and had produced more comprehensive job descriptions for his unit.

Managers in the 1990s will have to be concerned with the retention and training of staff rather than continuous recruitment. Selecting employees of the right calibre will mean adopting new approaches to selection that focus not only on the current performance of candidates but also on their potential. Companies will need to consider carefully the employment criteria for all jobs and develop appropriate, reliable and valid methods of selecting staff. Implementation of new approaches to selection will require additional training of those concerned with the recruitment process.

DEVELOPING THE POTENTIAL OF THE WORKFORCE

Evidence suggests that many applicants seeking employment want jobs with career opportunities.[60] For example, in their survey of room maids Saunders and Pullen[61] found that career prospects were considered fairly to very important by 66 per cent of their sample. At the managerial level a survey of the graduate recruitment process[62] found that the most important influence on graduates' initial decision to apply to a company was their perception of career opportunities offered by the company (93 per cent rated very important) and good training facilities (86 per cent very important).

It is not unusual to think of graduates in terms of career development: the term 'graduate' is commonly associated with skilled and managerial positions within organizations. Less attention is directed to the possible career development of other groups. In a survey of management opinion on staff retention only 9 per cent of management considered that career development was an important factor.[63] Hall and Jones found that 'apart from chefs, and to a limited extent male waiting staff, none of the hard to fill occupations had a formally defined career structure'.[64] With an increasing need to retain and develop the full potential of staff, all employees must be given the opportunity of career development. Companies must establish career paths for all staff with potential.

The anticipated emphasis on staff retention will mean that staff must be considered in terms of investment. The successful company will be concerned with maximum utilization of the entire workforce. This will be achieved only if measures are taken to identify the potential of individual employees. At present appraisal is all too often restricted to senior positions in the company. Formal methods of appraisal can be employed to measure performance, identify ability and maximize the effectiveness of training. There is an urgent need to establish systems of appraisal and succession planning for all employees and to make full use of the information obtained. Effective appraisal will only be possible with appropriate training for all those involved in its implementation.

Training and induction

Comparisons of the level of training in the UK and in other EC countries continue to appear in the popular and the trade press. Invariably these comparisons identify a severe training gap in the United Kingdom. Speaking of the hotel sector, S. Mascilo comments: 'training is not seen as a problem – with a few exceptions there isn't any'.[65] A number of surveys suggest that what training there is in hotels is restricted to simple on-the-job techniques.[66] For example, a survey of south coast hotels found that 75 per cent of operative staff had not undertaken any off the job training since their induction'.[67]

A far higher priority must be given to training and developing staff. Special training programmes will need to be developed if greater numbers of ethnic minorities or women returners are to be employed. Changes in management structures may mean that line mangers will need training if they are to take responsibility for staff development. In addition, retraining of older managers to implement the new human resources approach will be particularly important. In the words of Howarth and Howarth: 'education and training are seen as the cornerstones of future success in hotel keeping. The re-training of an older labour force displaced from other industries and the continuing development of existing employees are matters which should not be ignored.'[68]

EUROPE AND HUMAN RESOURCE MANAGEMENT

The common European market presents a number of problems for human resource management whether or not a company expands into the Continent. It is certain that future legislation will eventually have some influence on individual rights and working practices within the UK. Companies that expand into continental Europe will find an increasing need to develop consistent employment policies throughout the company. The degree to which acquired companies will be able to develop compatible systems will vary greatly.

Expansion of UK companies into continental Europe also carries with it the implication that staff will move from country to country with the same employer. In future senior appointments of pan-European companies will only be for those who have worked in more than one country.

Language presents a particular problem for British managers, who unfortunately are less proficient in languages than other Europeans. Languages are clearly essential for the hospitality industry, and in the larger Continental hotels it is not uncommon for the manager to speak several languages. In future greater emphasis will need to be placed on languages in the education and training of potential managers in the UK. Another way in which companies may overcome language and cultural barriers in the future is by extending graduate recruitment programmes across Europe. At the moment few firms operating from the UK have recruited European graduates; it is anticipated that more companies will embark on a co-ordinated programme of European recruitment.

STRATEGIC HUMAN RESOURCE MANAGEMENT?

A trend that can be identified in UK industry over the last ten years is that of personnel management being excluded from major managerial decisions.[69] It is debatable to what extent personnel management in the hospitality industry has contributed to major managerial decisions. It appears that in many cases the majority of personnel decisions are seen as the concern of unit managers who in turn may delegate responsibility to junior management. The image of the personnel manager in a hotel is of a young (stereotypically female) manager with little experience or few qualifications in personnel management who spends 90 per cent of his or her time attempting to recruit new staff to replace those contributing to the typical high turnover figures for the industry. It can be argued that a significant proportion of human resource management within the hospitality industry leaves much to be desired, and that the focus of attention needs to be redirected from the overwhelming concern with recruitment of staff to the training and development of existing staff, from quantity to quality of staff, and from autocratic management of staff to participation and leadership.

Armstrong directs attention to a phenomenon of UK industry which appears particularly prevalent in the hospitality industry: that is, the ascendancy of the accounting profession. He points out that 'over the last two decades there has been an increase in the sophistication and prominence of accounting controls in British Companies' and that 'whilst this has been good news for qualified accountants interested in managerial careers, it poses problems for those who believe that the personnel function has a part to play in the formulation of overall company strategy'.[70]

There is in many sectors of the hospitality industry an overriding concern with financial indicators of performance. The resulting preoccupation of unit managers with the 'bottom line' can prevent appropriate action in the area of human resources. This tendency is exacerbated by the career structure of unit managers in some companies. In a survey of the hotel managers of a large UK hotel group it was found that the unit managers expected to move about every two years to gain experience and promotion.[71] With this degree of mobility the unit manager's concern is more likely to focus on short-term profitability rather than long-term staff development and stability.

Increasing emphasis on the service component at a time when skilled staff are in short supply means that the quality of staff has never been so important. Competitive advantage will accrue to those companies that employ a strategic approach to human resource management. Those sectors of the hospitality industry that have not already done so must focus on human resource management at a strategic level; only then will they be able to bring about the necessary changes in company culture and implement appropriate responses to the problems previously outlined.

NOTES

1. Handy, C., *The Future of Work*, Blackwell, Oxford, 1985, p. xiii.
2. *Hotels of the Future: Strategies and Action Plan*, International Hotels Association/ Howarth & Howarth, London, 1988.
3. Slattery, P., 'Structural theory of business travel', *Conference Proceedings, International Journal of Contemporary Hospitality Management*, Dorset Institute, Poole, 1990, vol. I, pp. 70–80.
4. Central Statistical Office, *Social Trends*, vol. 19, HMSO, London, 1989.
5. Richards, R. and Cunningham, N., *Bournemouth Catering Industry*, BCI/The Training Agency, Bournemouth, 1990.
6. Phillips, A. and Moss, P., *Who Cares for Europe's Children?*, Commission of the European Communities, Brussels, 1988.
7. British Institute of Management, *Survey of Women Managers*, BIM, London, 1989.
8. Commission of the European Communities, *Men and Women of Europe in 1987. Supplement No. 26: Women of Europe*, Brussels, 1987.
9. CSO, op. cit.
10. Freeman, V., 'Mum's job sabotaged by families', *Today*, Apr. 1990.
11. Davidson, M. and Cooper, C., *Stress and the Woman Manager*, Martin Robertson, Oxford, 1983.
12. Kravetz, D., *The Human Resources Revolution*, Jossey-Bass, San Francisco, 1988.

13. 'You're never too old at 40!', *Management News*, no. 61, Oct. 1989, p. 3.
14. Commission of the European Communities, *Studies on the Economics of Integration. Research on the Cost of Non Europe: Basic Findings*, vol. 2, Brussels, 1988.
15. Commission of the European Communities, *Nouveaux domaines et nouvelles formes de croissance de l'emploi luxembourg: étude 27/86*, Brussels, 1988.
16. Kravetz, op. cit.
17. Pearson, R. and Pike, G., 'The graduate labour market in the 1990s', IMS report no. 167, University of Sussex.
18. Slattery, op. cit.
19. Naisbitt, J., *Megatrends*, Warner Books, New York, 1983.
20. Jones, B., *Sleepers Wake!: Technology and the Future of Work*, Wheatsheaf, Brighton, 1982.
21. Pearson, op. cit.
22. Pang, E.F., 'Employment, skills and technology', in Gustavsson, B., Karlsson, J. and Räftegård, C. (eds), *Work in the 1980s*, Gower, London.
23. Cooley, M.J.E., 'Problems of automation', in Lupton, T., *Human Factors*, IFS Publications, Bedford, 1986.
24. Woodward, J., *Industrial Organisation: Behaviour and Control*, Oxford University Press, Oxford, 1980.
25. Worsfold, P., 'Leadership and managerial effectiveness in the hospitality industry', *International Journal of Hospitality Management*, vol. 8, no. 2, 1987, pp. 145–55.
26. Hall, M. and Jones, P., 'Meeting aspirations: unemployed people and the hospitality industry', *Conference Proceedings International Journal of Contemporary Hospitality Management*, Dorset Institute, Poole, 1990, vol. I, pp. 42–58.
27. Richards and Cunningham, op. cit.
28. Anon., 'Increasing graduate supply', *Industrial Relations Review and Report*, no. 441, Jun. 1989, p. 3.
29. Pearson and Pike, op. cit.
30. Anon., 'Recruiters compete more aggressively for graduates', *Personnel Management*, Mar. 1989, p. 81.
31. Thomas, D., 'Graduate shortage pushes up starting pay', *Financial Times*, Jul. 1989.
32. Association of Graduate Recruiters, reported in Thomas, op. cit.
33. Sherrel, S., 'Staff crisis?', *Caterer and Hotelkeeper*, no. 12, Feb. 1989, p. 17.
34. Churchill, D., 'Hotel and catering: you have to love the lifestyle', *Financial Times Career Choice Supplement*, 1989, p. 49.
35. Leslie, D., 'Industrial placement, recruitment and training', International Association of Hotel Management Schools, Autumn Symposium, 1988, p. 5.
36. Normann, R., *Service Management: Strategy and Leadership in Service Businesses*, John Wiley, New York, 1984.
37. Powers, T., *Introduction to Management in Hospitality Industries*, John Wiley, New York, 1984.
38. Shamir, B., 'Between bureaucracy and hospitality: some organisational characteristics of hotels', *Journal of Management Studies,* Oct. 1978, pp. 285–307.
39. Worsfold, P. and Jameson, S., 'Back to the future: a response to demographic projections?', *Conference Proceedings, International Journal of Contemporary*

Hospitality Management, Dorset Institute, Poole, 1990, vol. II, pp. 51–69.
40. Brennan, J. and McGeevor, P.A., *CNAA Graduates: Their Employment and Their Experience after Leaving College, Summary Report*, CNAA Development Services, publication no. 13, 1987.
41. Chapman, A., *Just the Ticket? Graduate Men and Women in the Labour Market Three Years after College*, HELM working paper no. 5, 1989.
42. Hinds, D., *Bulletin of Teaching and Learning*, Sep. 1987, pp. 12–13; reported in Green, S., 'Biological science graduates: employment prospects and flexibility', *Biologist*, vol, 36, no. 4, 1989, pp. 209–13.
43. Curnow, B., 'Recruit, retrain, retain . . .', *Personnel Management*, Nov. 1989, pp. 40–7.
44. Mabey, C., *Graduates in Industry*, Gower, Aldershot, 1986, p. 3.
45. Pearson and Pike, op. cit., pp. 55–6.
46. *Hotels of the Future*, op. cit., p. 21.
47. Hall and Jones, op. cit.
48. Croney, P., 'An analysis of human resource management in the UK hotel industry', International Association of Hotel Management Schools, Autumn Symposium, Leeds, 1988.
49. Saunders, K. and Pullen, R., *An Occupational Study of Room-Maids in Hotels*, Middlesex Polytechnic, 1987.
50. Hall and Jones, op. cit.
51. Worsfold (forthcoming).
52. Lockwood, A. and Guerrier, Y., 'Underlying personnel strategies in flexible working', International Association of Hotel Management Schools, Autumn Symposium, Leeds, 1988.
53. Anon., 'How we plan to diffuse the demographic time bomb', *Communicater*, no. 62, Oct. 1989, pp. 8–9.
54. McDowell, D., Fawcett, S. and Morelli, D., 'A report on the congruency found between motivational factors identified through research in the catering workplace and those identified by management theorists', International Association of Hotel Management Schools, Autumn Symposium, Leeds, 1988.
55. Lockwood and Guerrier, op. cit.
56. Ibid.
57. Croney, op. cit.
58. Ibid., p. 9.
59. Worsfold, unpublished report on personnel management in an industrial catering company, 1987.
60. Hall and Jones, op. cit.
61. Saunders and Pullen, op. cit.
62. Keenan, A. and Scott, R.S., 'Graduate recruitment. How graduates "select" companies: a note', *Personnel Review*, vol. 14, no. 1, pp. 12–14.
63. Richards and Cunningham, op. cit.
64. Hall and Jones, op. cit., p. 53.
65. Mascilo, S., 'Management, the hospitality industry and the 1990s', in *Managing Skill Shortages in the Hospitality Industry of the 1990s*, Conference Papers, Blackpool and The Fylde College, 1989.
66. Kelliher, C. and Johnson, K., 'Personnel management in hotels: some empirical observations', *International Journal of Hospitality Management*, vol. 6, no. 2, pp. 103–8.
67. Richards and Cunningham, op. cit., p. 19.

68. *Hotels of the Future*, p. 24.
69. Hunt, J., 'Hidden extras: how people get overlooked in takeovers', *Personnel Management*, Jul. 1987, pp. 24–8; Daniel, W., 'Four years of change for personnel', *Personnel Management*, Dec. 1986, pp. 35–7.
70. Armstrong, P., 'Limits and possibilities for HRM in an age of management accountancy', in Storey, J. (ed.), *New Perspectives on Human Resource Management*, Routledge, London, 1989.
71. Worsfold, op. cit.

8

Consumer strategies for assessing and evaluating hotels

Richard Teare

INTRODUCTION

The characteristics of service firms, and in particular hospitality operations, where employees both produce and deliver consumer services, suggest that the role of marketing is potentially much broader than in manufacturing. This is because consumers are continually influenced by interactions with staff and the environment in which service delivery takes place. Although service staff may see themselves as full-time specialists in accommodation or food and beverage, they also act as part-time marketers[1] as their behaviour affects consumer choice.

The aim of this chapter is to explain and illustrate some of the strategies used by consumers to assess and evaluate hotels. The illustrations are drawn from an empirical study of the consumer decision process for hospitality services.[2] Four of the sections deal with assessment issues which occur during service delivery, referred to below as the consumption stage of the decision process. These are:

- assessment criteria;
- the consumption environment and design effects;
- hotel services;
- personal rating systems.

The remaining two sections are concerned with the evaluation of hotels during the post-consumption stage of the decision process. These consider:

- sources of satisfaction;
- sources of dissatisfaction.

ASSESSMENT AND EVALUATION: A REVIEW OF THE RESEARCH EVIDENCE

The relationship between product expectations and experience

Investigating changes in consumer satisfaction associated with consecutive purchase behaviour, LaBarbera and Mazursky[3] found that prior satisfaction plays a significant role in mediating intentions and actual behaviour. Although consumers may not always recall evaluations, they conclude that they will always think of past satisfaction prior to making a repurchase decision, thereby linking expectations with experience. Historically, however, a certain degree of ambiguity has existed in the literature regarding the expectancy construct. Olson and Dover define expectation as 'the perceived likelihood that a product possesses a certain characteristic or attribute, or will lead to a particular event or outcome'.[4]

The difference in expectations and perceptions of quality and service held by customers, managers and staff in the hospitality industry has been investigated by Nightingale.[5] His findings suggest that efforts to improve consumer satisfaction may be seriously impeded by perceptual differences. Managers and staff tend to focus on tangible elements of the product in their role as service providers, whereas consumers often have a wider set of expectations which are not always easy to anticipate. To some extent, as Burnkrant and Cousineau have argued,[6] this may be explained by the influence of word-of-mouth communications on the formation of expectations. They found that recommendations from people who are known to be familiar with a particular product category have a significant influence on the way in which products are perceived by others.

A reference standard may be used by consumers for making attribute-based product comparisons. This is usually described in terms of experiences which fall above or below a reference point experience. For example, LaTour and Peat[7] found that prior experience and product satisfaction are linked by product attribute comparisons. Swan and Jones Combs[8] and Howes and Arndt[9] found that product attributes are likely to be assessed according to their perceived product importance, suggesting that consumer satisfaction consists of many differently weighted individual satisfactions. Howes and Arndt argue that consumers often seek 'bundles or clusters of satisfactions', especially from service products where the consumer actively participates in the service provision. Further evidence is provided by Westbrook,[10] who concludes that consumers add together their experiences so that high levels of satisfaction from some sources compensate for lower levels from others.

The relationship between satisfaction and evaluation

Reviewing the literature on consumer satisfaction, McNeal[11] found that it has been defined in numerous ways. He concludes that the term 'consumer satisfaction' is most frequently used to refer to the fulfilment of a motivating state or the meeting of an expectation, through the purchase of a product or service.

In a study concerned with the measurement of tourist satisfaction with a destination area, Pizam, Neumann and Reichel defined satisfaction as 'the result of the interaction between a tourist's experience at the destination area and the expectations he had about that destination'.[12] They found that satisfaction was derived from the evaluation of tourist product components such as accommodation, eating and drinking experiences, destination accessibility, attractions, cost and services. The outcome: satisfaction (or dissatisfaction) was derived from the weighted sum total of comparative assessment ratings, guided by expectations and reference standards.

Lounsbury and Hoopes[13] found that an important dimension of tourist satisfaction is relaxation and leisure. This is related to the way personal plans work out in practice, emotional and physical well-being, the 'pace of life' experienced, opportunities for familiar and new leisure activity participation, and the feeling of enjoyment associated with each experience.

The majority of studies concerned with consumer satisfaction subscribe to one of two viewpoints: firstly, that satisfaction results from the confirmation of expectations and dissatisfaction from disconfirmation; and secondly, that satisfaction/dissatisfaction is derived from measurements made against experience-based norms.

The confirmation/disconfirmation of expectations

Confirmation/disconfirmation begins prior to brand purchase and use, when the consumer formulates expectations about brand performance in a given situation. After using the brand, the consumer compares perceived actual performance with expected performance. Confirmation of expectations, leading to a feeling of satisfaction, occurs when the two perspectives coincide or when perceived brand performance exceeds expectations. Disconfirmation occurs if perceived brand performance falls below expectations, leading to a feeling of dissatisfaction.

Oliver[14] concludes that expectations provide a standard against which product performance can be measured, thereby influencing subsequent product preferences and behavioural intention. Westbrook and Cote[15] support this view, suggesting that the consumer compares actual experience with prior expectations, noting any performance disparity. This information provides the basis for assessing relative satisfaction or dissatisfaction with the overall experience.

Experience-based norms

Woodruff, Cadotte and Jenkins[16] propose a model for conceptualizing consumer satisfaction which replaces expectations with experience-based norms as the standard for comparing brand performance. They suggest that after using a brand the consumer will note how it performed. When there are many attributes to consider, overall brand performance may be determined by a combination of beliefs about the brand's various performance dimensions.[17] In this way, beliefs are either strengthened or weakened according to how closely actual brand performance matches expected brand performance.[18]

Experience-based norms provide a frame of reference for evaluating performance. There is also some evidence to suggest that they are better predictors of satisfaction than evaluations based solely on brand expectations.[19] As experience will vary from different product categories, two types of experience-based norm are hypothesized:

- a brand-based norm in situations when one brand dominates the consumer's set of brand experiences;
- a product-based norm in situations when the consumer has had experience with several brands within a product class, but does not have a specific reference brand.

Experience-based norms are utilized in different ways during the decision process, ranging from single norms for familiar, low-involvement products, to multiple norms associated with important events such as the purchase of a car or holiday. When actual brand performance is close to the norm, it is described as being within an acceptable latitude of performance. If, however, brand performance is considered to be outside the latitude of acceptance, dissatisfaction occurs.

Comparing the two explanations, Woodruff, Cadotte and Jenkins regard the experience-based norms viewpoint as more realistic because norms provide an integrated frame of reference derived from evaluations of prior experience.

ASSESSING HOTELS DURING SERVICE DELIVERY

A key theme of this chapter is the interrelationship between consumption and post-consumption evaluation. As noted earlier, these terms are used to describe stages in the consumer decision process following pre-purchase. A degree of consistency of approach and integration between the three stages is provided by the consumer's prior product category experience. As the consumer acquires product knowledge, evaluations are encoded in memory for future use. The store of information acts as a personal rating mechanism or system for comparing, assessing and evaluating future product category purchase decisions. For instance, experienced hotel users might be expected to make confident purchase decisions using well-established information search and selection strategies. Conversely, inexperienced hotel users may feel more uncertain during decision making, and seek guidance from a variety of expert sources of opinion. The four definitions listed in Figure 8.1 are used to define experienced and inexperienced hotel users.

Experienced hotel users
- Very extensive prior hotel experience over a number of years and in a variety of different usage contexts and places, including overseas travel.
- Substantial prior hotel experience, mainly in connection with regular hotel short breaks and/or business travel.

Inexperienced hotel users
- Limited hotel experience, mainly in connection with occasional short breaks taken over the last few years and/or infrequent business travel.
- No prior experience of three or four star equivalent hotel accommodation.

Figure 8.1   *Definition of terms.*

The illustrations which follow consist of extracts from computer-based models of consumer decision making for hotels. These are referred to as maps, and they show the relationships between numbered ideas. Arrows are used to depict causal relationships and lines to show bi-directional links. Finally, a minus sign (−) is used to signify a relationship with the second pole of a dichotomous idea.

Assessment criteria

The experienced hotel users in the study reported that initial impressions of an hotel provide a reliable indication of whether expectations are likely to be fulfilled. This is because many of the events which occur on arrival and during the reception and registration period are similar on each occasion. Map 1 illustrates this by showing the connection between fulfilment of expectations (48) leading to a satisfactory experience (52), and recurrent events such as the need for car parking space (50) and helpful front-hall staff (49, 51). The motive for establishing assessment criteria (45) is

provided by the desire to assess from the very beginning of the consumption period
how well the hotel compares with the standard of facilities at home (47).

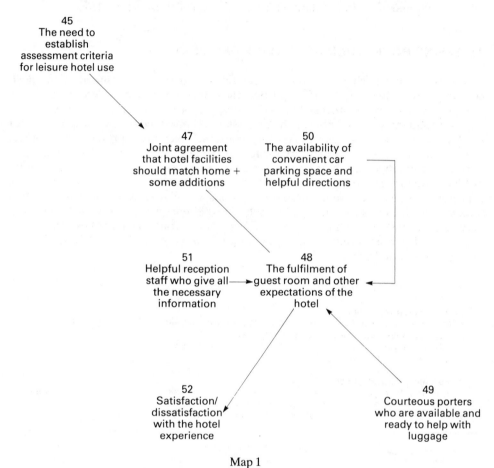

Map 1

The initial interactions between hotel staff and the consumer are particularly
important because they may affect how the consumer feels about the hotel throughout
the stay. If the consumer is experiencing travel-related stress or fatigue, he or she will
be especially vulnerable, and may find it difficult to compensate for negative
impressions arising from operational or interpersonal problems. Map 2 provides an
example of the range of expectations associated with the formation of a favourable
impression of an hotel (66). Important to all customers is the need to feel welcome on
arrival (67, 70). Experienced consumers also reported using other measures to make
an early assessment of the hotel. These included how staff react (71), how well
prepared the hotel is (68), and how attentive the staff are (69).

Although the perspectives of male and female partners may differ, all the
respondents in the study acknowledged the need to establish criteria and undertake
some form of assessment during consumption. Though the underlying reasoning
varies, Map 3 illustrates how important elements of the consumption experience are

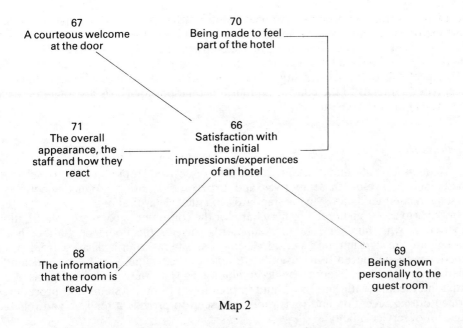

Map 2

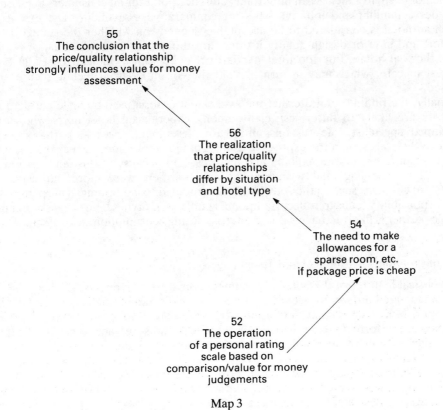

Map 3

recognized. In the example a respondent identifies the influence of comparisons with prior experience, and value for money judgements on personal assessment or rating (52). This leads to recognition that price should equate with standards and facilities, and the 'need to make allowances' if a cheaper guest room is more sparsely furnished (54). Accepting that price–quality relationships are likely to differ by situation and hotel type (56) leads to the conclusion that this relationship exerts a strong influence on value for money assessments (55).

Implications

The findings indicate that assessment criteria are derived from a number of sources. These include pre-purchase motives and expectations, prior product experience, personal recommendations, living standards and lifestyle aspirations.

In order to assess an hotel, it is necessary for the consumer to compare consumption experiences with familiar reference standards such as the home or another hotel throughout the consumption period. Using assessment criteria derived from prior experience, experienced hotel users were able to determine quickly and efficiently whether an hotel was likely to be acceptable. This is because assessments based on initial interactions with hotel staff and impressions of hotel systems and procedures formed during reception and registration are seen to provide a realistic and reliable indicator of service quality.

The home environment is an important reference point for all consumers because it provides a familiar and intuitive basis for comparative assessment. The extent to which an hotel is considered to be acceptable depends on whether the standards of comfort and interior design quality it offers are thought to be as good as, or better than, those at home. Inferior hotel standards may be seen as indicative of a lack of interest or care, which may in turn prevent the consumer from feeling secure and relaxed.

Finally, the findings indicate that the assessment criteria used by male and female partners are likely to differ, especially among experienced hotel users who have developed specialist role responsibilities for assessment. Female partners were particularly interested in the expressive aspects of interior design, such as the use and quality of different fabrics, colours and textures, and because of this tended to take the lead in assessing quality standards. Male partners were more interested in functional concerns such as the control of guest room air conditioning. This pattern of role responsibility tends to reflect traditional gender stereotypes, and suggests that the female partner is likely to have a dominant role during consumption stage assessment.

The consumption environment and design effects

The physical features of the hotel environment convey design effects which are likely to be interpreted differently according to the prior expectations and experience of the consumer. Map 4 shows that the business traveller may have 'no real expectation of extraneous comforts' (13) because the hotel is viewed as 'a place to sleep in rather than relax' (15). However, this example also shows that the functional consumer expects to find an 'inherently cold' atmosphere in the hotel (12), which may lead to a negative impression of the guest room (16). The respondent suggests that a more positive impression is created if a feeling of warmth can be conveyed by the décor, furnishings and design of the guest room (17).

In contrast, the leisure traveller aims to spend more time in the guest room and around the hotel for the purpose of relaxation. Tolerance of obstacles to relaxation such as poor décor and design is consequently lower, especially among female partners who, as already noted, are inherently more interested in design features.

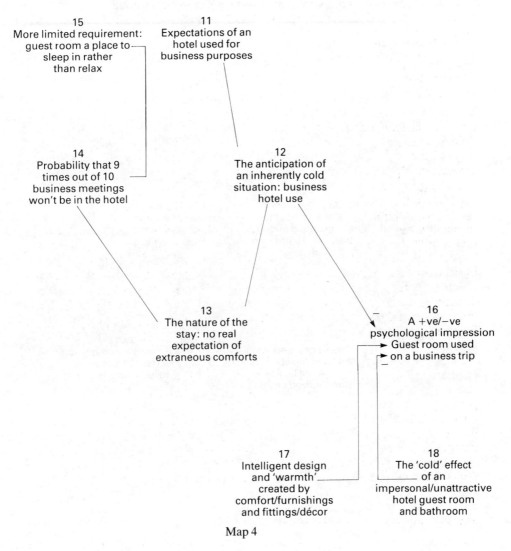

Map 4

Overall, inexperienced hotel users were favourably impressed by the guest room design standards and facilities that they encountered. This is illustrated in Map 5, where assumptions about the nature of standardized design (17) are challenged by unexpected features such as the level of guest room control (31, 32), radio and telephone extensions (30), and the standard of guest room preparation (33). A positive experience of this kind may become a reference point for future assessments, with the incorporation of new product information leading to the revision of expectations.

The example also illustrates how a new experience can act as a learning stimulus, prompting the consumer to gather further information to facilitate more accurate differentiation between hotel types and styles. As the new information becomes integrated with existing product knowledge, the consumer's confidence in the reliability of selection and assessment criteria will thereby improve.

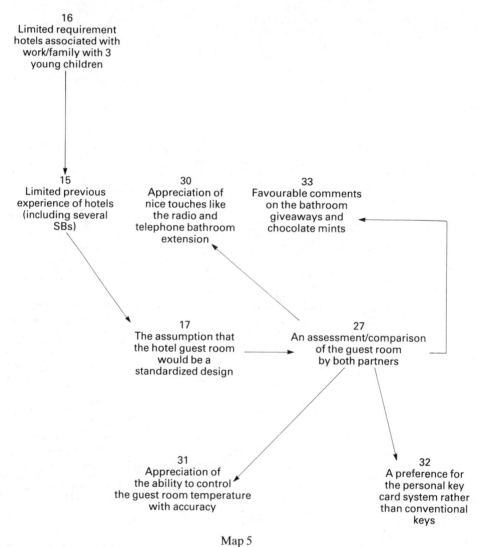

Map 5

Implications

The findings show that design effects can have a powerful impact on the consumer, especially if the consumption environment is perceived to be cold and impersonal. This is often the experience of business travellers, who equate 'coldness' with standardized design and impersonal service. In these circumstances, the customer is likely to react by spending as little time in the hotel as possible.

However, the leisure traveller is likely to want to spend more time in the hotel in order to relax. In these circumstances, the consumer determines the 'warmth' of the consumption environment by undertaking a detailed assessment of interior design features. As noted earlier, if the standard of design implementation is considered to be inferior to the home, the consumer is unlikely to be able to relax. Conversely, the effective use of space, colour schemes and well-maintained furnishings and equipment are conducive to relaxation. This is especially important to the female partner, who is more sensitive to, and appreciative of, attention to detail and 'individuality' in the design, implementation, servicing and maintenance of the guest room and public areas of the hotel.

Hotel services

Attaining consistency in service delivery is complicated by the frequency and variety of service interactions which occur during the consumption period. Although difficult to quantify, many hotel operators attempt to measure the effectiveness of service components using self-completion guest questionnaires. The experienced hotel users interviewed in the study did not consider this to be a meaningful way of collecting data. This viewpoint reflects the belief that objective, factual data and subjective, personal response data should be collected and analysed using appropriate methods. For instance, experienced hotel users were often critical of hotel restaurants. As the nature of the criticisms varies, it is difficult fully to appreciate the range of views on this subject by relying solely on self-completion guest questionnaires.

Service interactions have a critical role to play in making the consumer feel welcome, and in preventing him or her from feeling isolated or alienated in an unfamiliar environment. This is illustrated in Map 6, which shows how 'an acute awareness of open space' (49) can lead to a 'feeling of detachment' (50), resulting in a more critical assessment of the hotel (51). In these circumstances, hotel staff have an essential role in compensating for the emotional reaction evoked by the atmosphere of the building (52).

In assessing service delivery, hotel users with international travel experience were able to identify perceived strengths and weaknesses by referring to cultural differences. This is illustrated in Map 7, where uniformly high standards of accommodation in the USA (46, 48) accounted for a less tolerant attitude towards inconsistent standards in the UK (47, 52). The key cultural difference in service delivery relates to staff attitudes, which are seen to be positive and courteous in the USA (49, 50) and rather negative and unhelpful in the UK (52, 53).

Implications

The duration and complexity of the hotel consumption experience means that service interactions are difficult to standardize and control. Experienced hotel users even perceive differences in the friendliness of hotel staff which they attribute to the design and atmosphere of the building. If, for example, the building conveys an impersonal feeling then hotel staff may also appear to be formal and distant. The combined effect is sufficient to make the consumer feel isolated or even alienated as soon as an impression of 'coldness' has formed.

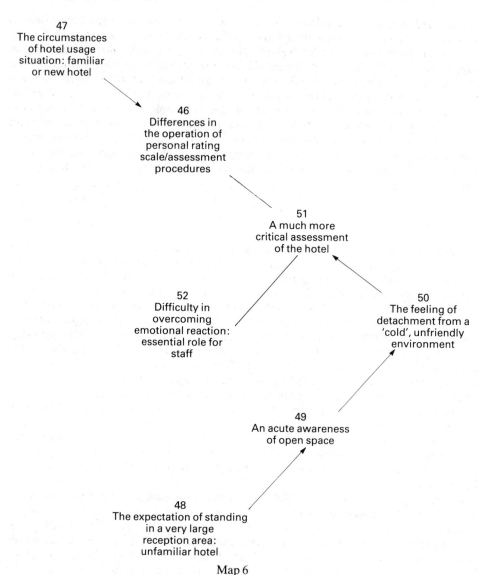

Map 6

To prevent this from happening, appropriate ways of monitoring and assessing the effectiveness of service delivery are necessary, so that the views of consumers can be incorporated into the design of systems and procedures. As business and leisure hotel users have different requirements, hotel staff therefore need to know how to respond accordingly.

It is also important to note the distinction between the service expectations of experienced and inexperienced hotel users. Whenever experienced users have international travel experience, their definition of 'good service' may include reference to service characteristics experienced in different countries. For example, hotel accommodation and service in the USA is frequently perceived to be of a higher

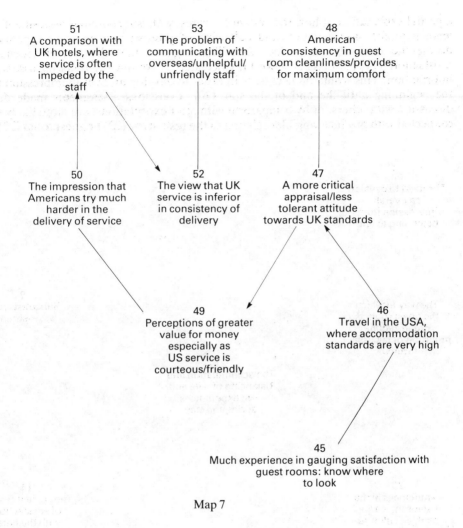

51
A comparison with
UK hotels, where
service is often
impeded by the
staff

53
The problem of
communicating with
overseas/unhelpful/
unfriendly staff

48
American
consistency in guest
room cleanliness/provides
for maximum comfort

50
The impression that
Americans try much
harder in the
delivery of service

52
The view that UK
service is inferior
in consistency of
delivery

47
A more critical
appraisal/less
tolerant attitude
towards UK standards

49
Perceptions of greater
value for money
especially as
US service is
courteous/friendly

46
Travel in the USA,
where accommodation
standards are very high

45
Much experience in gauging satisfaction with
guest rooms: know where
to look

Map 7

standard than in the UK. This is because the 'service culture' is different, and because American attitudes towards service are perceived to be more positive than in the UK.

Personal rating systems

During consumption, the consumer receives and stores information from many sources. This facilitates the formation of impressions which can be assessed in relation to established criteria and expectations. To facilitate an overall evaluation of the consumption experience, the consumer must integrate these impressions and assessments. This procedure constitutes a personal rating system which has two interrelated functions. It provides a mechanism for organizing, storing and assessing experiences as they accumulate, and it facilitates post-consumption evaluation.

The efficiency of the personal rating system may depend on how sensitive the consumer is to impressions formed at conscious and subconscious levels. Map 8 offers a partial explanation of how the system operates, with 'subconscious assessment' (19) leading to the 'accumulation and balancing of positive and negative experiences' during the consumption period (21). This suggests that the 'current feeling of satisfaction' (14) (or dissatisfaction) is calculated by continually updating assessment information. This would be necessary in order to develop an overall impression from the beginning until the end of the stay (20). Conscious assessments made during discussion with others, or by comparison with prior expectations, are more likely to be connected with product tangibles relating to the restaurant (23) or guest room (22).

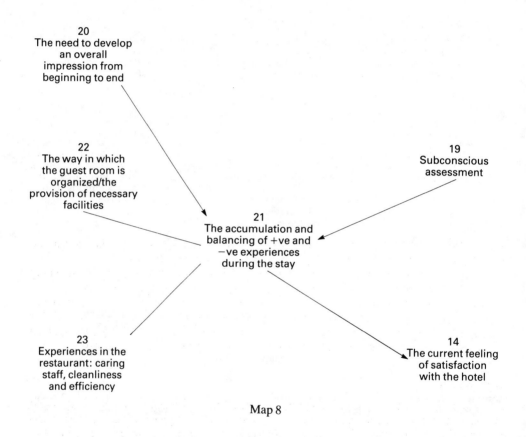

20
The need to develop
an overall
impression from
beginning to end

22
The way in which
the guest room is
organized/the
provision of necessary
facilities

19
Subconscious
assessment

21
The accumulation and
balancing of +ve and
−ve experiences
during the stay

23
Experiences in the
restaurant: caring
staff, cleanliness
and efficiency

14
The current feeling
of satisfaction
with the hotel

Map 8

Experience-based learning has an important role in the refinement of the personal rating system, enabling the consumer to assess and categorize hotels more accurately. This is illustrated in Map 9, where the female partner in particular has developed a routine for assessing the guest room. The map shows a division of responsibilities which is gender related. The female partner is concerned with the assessment of quality and cleanliness in the guest room, and the male partner with checking that all the electrical appliances are functioning correctly (80). The shared responsibility for assessment is related to the perceived need to check the room immediately, in case it has not been prepared properly or equipment is faulty (81).

Inexperienced hotel users also undertake role specialization during assessment,

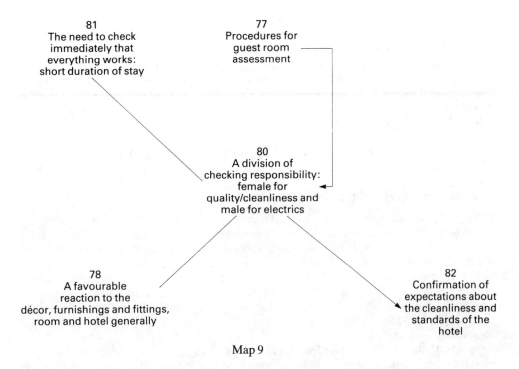

81
The need to check
immediately that
everything works:
short duration of stay

77
Procedures for
guest room
assessment

80
A division of
checking responsibility:
female for
quality/cleanliness and
male for electrics

78
A favourable
reaction to the
décor, furnishings and fittings,
room and hotel generally

82
Confirmation of
expectations about
the cleanliness and
standards of the
hotel

Map 9

although role tasks are often unclear or imprecisely defined. This suggests that limited prior experience may account for the absence of role specialization.

When a reference standard has become established, inconsistent performance may cause disappointment and lead to a reappraisal of beliefs about the brand. This is because consumption assessments must exceed the minimum acceptable level in order to form a new reference standard and generate brand-based confidence. If, for example, a newly established reference standard is disconfirmed by a substandard experience, the consumer's perception of the brand may be affected as a result.

Implications

The personal rating system provides the integrating mechanism for individual assessments made during the consumption period. It also provides a link with post-consumption evaluation, which draws on stored assessment ratings to determine the overall level of product satisfaction. As this information improves product familiarity and knowledge, it is also likely to affect subsequent pre-purchase expectations and selection criteria.

The personal rating system also unifies subconscious reactions to the consumption environment and conscious assessments of product tangibles, such as the equipment provided in the guest room. The overall measure of satisfaction is thereby updated as new assessments are made. Experienced hotel users, who have an established frame of reference, are more likely to assume specialist role responsibilities during assessment. Whenever role specialization was used, the objective was to undertake a rapid and systematic appraisal of the hotel.

Evidence suggests that inexperienced hotel users undertake assessment more tentatively. Consequently, the overall measure of satisfaction with the hotel at different points in time may be less certain. Role specialization was also reported, although assessment tasks and responsibilities were not clearly defined. These findings indicate that the extent of product familiarity and knowledge affects the operation of the personal rating system and limits role specialization during assessment. This view is supported by the numerous learning experiences referred to by inexperienced hotel users during service delivery.

POST-CONSUMPTION EVALUATION OF THE HOTEL EXPERIENCE

Sources of consumer satisfaction

During post-consumption evaluation, the consumer faces the task of reconciling the individual assessments which have accumulated during consumption. Even if the overall evaluation is favourable, it may involve assimilating, accepting or compensating for minor sources of dissatisfaction.

The relationships in Map 10 illustrate how satisfaction (or dissatisfaction) with an hotel experience (71) is determined by reconciling assessment ratings. Clustered around the dichotomous variable 'satisfaction . . . dissatisfaction with an hotel' are the contributory factors leading to a feeling of satisfaction (82) or dissatisfaction (72, 73, 74, 75).

In this example, the respondent found it easier to list factors which would cause dissatisfaction, believing that positive experiences add to, and negative experiences subtract from, the final evaluation (49). A series of favourable service interactions (51, 52) lead to 'the accumulation of positive experiences' (48) and as no potential sources of dissatisfaction are encountered, a favourable evaluation occurs (46, 47, 50).

Implications

The findings indicate that consumer satisfaction is derived from two main sources: firstly, from the accumulation of positive assessments within the personal rating system; and secondly, from the psychological impact of consumption. If, for example, a consumer feels relaxed and refreshed at the end of the consumption period, this 'end state' will have a positive effect.

The purpose of post-consumption evaluation is to determine an overall, enduring measure of satisfaction (or dissatisfaction) with the consumption experience. In this respect, the personal rating system has an important role, as the individual assessments integrated within the system provide a moving average measure of satisfaction.

The post-consumption evaluation period begins at the end of the consumption stage, and may take several days to complete. During this period, the consumer reflects on, and evaluates, the temporary measures of satisfaction made during the consumption period. This may also involve reconsidering sources of dissatisfaction. This is to determine whether they were compensated for by subsequent experiences, or whether they remain influential, and thereby reduce the overall level of satisfaction.

As might be expected, when brand loyalty was reported, it was closely associated with positive prior experience. However, the effect of a positive evaluation on

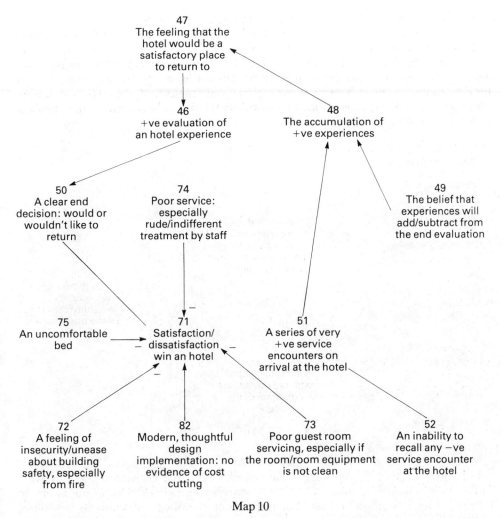

Map 10

inexperienced hotel users was more pronounced than for experienced hotel users. This was because consumers with limited prior existence often felt surprised by their own favourable reactions to an hotel. When this happened, pre-purchase preferences were reinforced and a reference standard for making future comparisons was established.

Sources of consumer dissatisfaction

There are some circumstances in which dissatisfaction with one or more aspects of the hotel experience can lead to a feeling of disappointment which the consumer is unable or unwilling to express. If, for example, the source of dissatisfaction is of a confrontational nature, such as an argument with an hotel staff member, the emotional energy generated is likely to be discharged in the form of a verbal complaint. In contrast, dissatisfaction arising from less emotional sources may lead to a feeling of disappointment which is not expressed.

This is illustrated in Map 11, where dissatisfaction is caused by a poor standard of guest room furnishing and décor (23). This disconfirms expectations (25) and leads to a decision to complain (72). However, the desire to complain immediately is not strong enough, and the situation is resolved by a decision not to return to the hotel again (73). The consequences of passive dissatisfaction are potentially more serious for the producer. This is because the complaint is not registered, the consumer decides not to return, and the reasons may be communicated to others without the producer ever knowing what had happened.

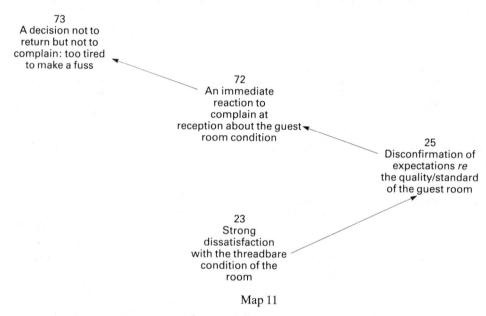

73
A decision not to return but not to complain: too tired to make a fuss

72
An immediate reaction to complain at reception about the guest room condition

25
Disconfirmation of expectations *re* the quality/standard of the guest room

23
Strong dissatisfaction with the threadbare condition of the room

Map 11

When expectations of the hotel experience have not been fulfilled, post-consumption evaluation may reveal ways of modifying the decision process to avoid future disappointment. Map 12 depicts learning outcomes which are likely to influence future decision making. The respondent identifies a brochure as the source of the mismatch between expectations and experience (65, 66, 67). He realizes this only after he accepts that he had not considered the risk of disappointment from this source before.

Implications

The findings indicate that dissatisfaction is commonly associated with indifferent service and poor design and quality standards. As noted earlier, these factors are considered to be symptomatic of an uncaring approach to the management of service delivery and the consumption environment. Dissatisfaction may be manifest in a feeling of disappointment that standards and facilities are not as good as expected, or as good as those available at home. The consumer may also feel insecure if the fabric of the building appears neglected, or alienated if hotel staff are perceived to be uncaring.

When dissatisfaction arises from poor service, interactions with hotel staff can

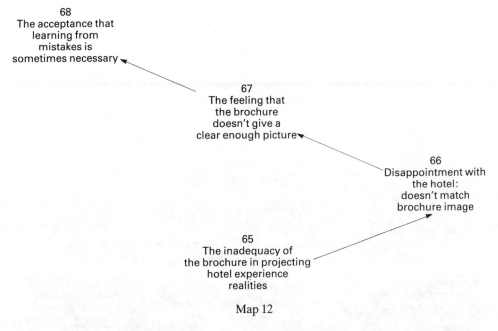

68
The acceptance that
learning from
mistakes is
sometimes necessary

67
The feeling that
the brochure
doesn't give a
clear enough picture

66
Disappointment with
the hotel:
doesn't match
brochure image

65
The inadequacy of
the brochure in projecting
hotel experience
realities

Map 12

invoke strong emotional reactions. In these circumstances, the consumer is more likely to make a verbal complaint at the time when dissatisfaction occurred. In contrast, disappointment relating to less confrontational issues such as poor guest room servicing may be internalized if the consumer does not feel sufficiently motivated to complain. This is potentially more damaging for the producer, as the source of dissatisfaction is not reported, and yet the consumer may communicate this to others.

Experienced hotel users were generally more confident about their ability to resolve sources of dissatisfaction. This is because they have a notional idea of what constitutes 'ideal service', enabling them to recognize unacceptable practices. Inexperienced hotel users do not have this advantage, and are inclined to be more hesitant about complaining. This is because they feel less certain about the distinction between good and bad service, or because they are less confident about their ability to resolve the issues responsible for the dissatisfaction they are experiencing.

A CONSUMER FRAMEWORK FOR ASSESSING AND EVALUATING HOTELS

To summarize from the empirical data, Figure 8.2 depicts the procedures used by consumers for selecting, assessing the evaluating hotels. The framework also shows the interrelationships between the three stages of the decision process.

During the pre-purchase stage, two factors are especially influential in determining strategies for information search and selection. These are prior product experience and the consumer's preference structure.

Preference structure has been defined as a combination of internalized environmental factors (such as cultural norms and values, family and reference groups, financial status and social class) and affective judgements, influenced by factors such as

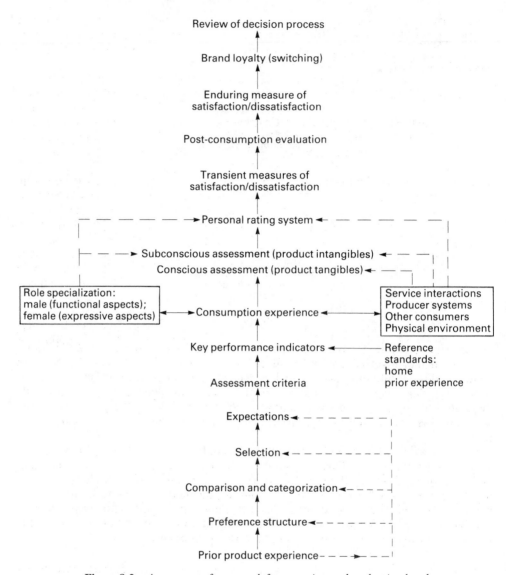

Figure 8.2   *A consumer framework for assessing and evaluating hotels.*

personality, lifestyle and purchase motives.[20] As the interrelationships between these contributory factors are complex and difficult to isolate, prior product experience offers a more practical way of identifying the various types of decision-making strategy. Those adopted by experienced and inexperienced hotel users are explained in the final section.

The experienced hotel user is able to draw on recollections of prior experience when comparing choice options during pre-purchase. In this way, the consumer can select an hotel using an established procedure, and formulate realistic product performance expectations. The relationship also extends to the use of assessment criteria during consumption, which are based on key performance indicators and reference standards derived from prior experience. The inexperienced hotel user does not have this advantage, and may have to rely on comparative assessments made against other familiar reference points such as the home.

Consumption experiences consist of interactions between the consumer and the producer, producer systems, other consumers and the physical environment.[21] Assessments are either made consciously and deliberately while checking product tangibles such as furnishings and fittings, or subconsciously in reaction to product intangibles such as atmosphere and design effects. Subconscious impressions are mainly responsible for the psychological impact of the consumption experience on the consumer.

As many individual assessments take place during the consumption period, consumers may respond by developing role responsibilities. For instance, experienced hotel users tend to adopt specialist roles whereby female partners concentrate on assessing expressive aspects and male partners functional aspects of the consumption experience.

As individual assessments occur, they are integrated within the consumer's personal rating system and used to determine transient measures of satisfaction (or dissatisfaction) with the consumption experience. The combined set of measures is evaluated during the post-consumption period. The purpose of this is to determine the final, enduring measure of satisfaction. In the event of a positive evaluation, brand loyalty is reinforced. If the final evaluation is negative, the consequence is likely to be a desire to change brands. In both cases, a review of the decision process is likely to ensue so that existing product knowledge can be updated.

CONSUMER STRATEGIES: AN EXPERIENTIAL PERSPECTIVE

The matrix in Figure 8.3 summarizes reported differences between hotel users with extensive and limited prior experience associated with:

(1) pre-purchase influences on the operation of the personal rating system;
(2) consumption stage assessment procedures;
(3) post-consumption stage evaluation.

Extensive experience and pre-purchase influences (1A)

Product familiarity enables the consumer with extensive prior experience to use established selection criteria during pre-purchase. The product information encoded within a personal category system also facilitates experience-based comparison. This means that experienced hotel users may be able to categorize hotels by size, age, ownership and other relevant variables. Category-based information guides consumer choice and influences the formation of realistic expectations and relevant assessment criteria.

Extensive experience and consumption stage assessments (2A)

Extensive prior experience enables the consumer to assess the consumption experience against predetermined key performance indicators. For instance, experienced

Personal rating system	Prior product experience	
	Extensive (A)	Limited (B)
Pre-purchase influences (1)	Established procedures for product classification and categorization facilitate close links between selection and assessment	Expectations derived from product information and personal recommendations shape assessment criteria
Consumption assessments (2)	Clearly defined role responsibilities and experience-based assessment criteria facilitate rapid and confident assessment	Imprecise role responsibilities and uncertainty about appropriate assessment criteria lead to greater dependence on the home as a basis for assessment
	Comparisons against key performance indicators provide the basis for measuring transient satisfaction	Transient measures of satisfaction/dissatisfaction lead to the discovery of key performance indicators
Post-consumption evaluation (3)	Predetermined task definition: enduring satisfaction/dissatisfaction evaluated against experience-based performance norms and in relation to the overall psychological impact of consumption	Reactive task definition: enduring satisfaction/dissatisfaction evaluated against learned performance indicators and psychological reactions to the consumption experience

Figure 8.3   *Experiential consumer strategies for assessing and evaluating hotels.*

hotel users reported that interactions with hotel staff, systems and procedures during reception and reservation provide an early indicator of service quality.

The use of key performance indicators and role specialization enables the consumer to focus on important transient measures of satisfaction (or dissatisfaction) quickly and confidently.

As the assessment criteria for key performance indicators are derived from prior experience, it is easier and more efficient for consumers to develop role responsibilities for assessment. The findings indicated that role specialization among experienced hotel users is commonplace and tends to reflect traditional male/female decision-making roles. Gender-related domains of expertise equate with the female partner's interest in expressive aspects of the consumption experience and the male partner's interest in functional aspects.

Extensive experience and post-consumption evaluation (3A)

For consumers with extensive prior experience, the final, enduring measure of satisfaction (or dissatisfaction) with the consumption experience is determined with reference to established performance norms. Experienced hotel users reported making evaluations against a measurement scale representing a spectrum of prior experience ranging from the least to the most satisfactory experience. In this way, prior product experience provides a frame of reference within which product evaluations can be made.

The psychological impact of the consumption experience is also indirectly related to prior experience. If, for instance, an experienced hotel user feels alienated by the 'cold' consumption environment, he or she may feel tense at the end of the consumption period. If the ideal psychological 'end state' is a desire to feel relaxed and refreshed, the conflict between actual and ideal states may cause the consumer to feel dissatisfied.

Limited experience and pre-purchase influences (1B)

The consumer with limited prior product experience cannot anticipate the consumption stage in the same way as the consumer with extensive experience. This is because expectations relating to product performance are largely derived from non-personal information sources. Consequently, assessment criteria are less formalized, and the consumer is not as well prepared to interpret product performance or determine transient measures of satisfaction as key performance indicators are less familiar.

Limited experience and consumption stage assessments (2B)

When the consumer has limited prior experience, it becomes necessary to make comparative assessments using familiar reference standards such as the home. As assessment criteria are likely to have been derived from product literature or personal recommendations, they may need to be adapted. This occurs as the consumer begins to discover for him or herself key performance indicators during the measurement of transient satisfaction (or dissatisfaction) with the consumption experience.

Limited experience and post-consumption evaluation (3B)

Post-consumption evaluation occurs in the context of learned performance indicators and salient positive and negative recollections from the consumption stage. As the consumer may find it difficult to evaluate transient measures of satisfaction (or dissatisfaction), it is a more reactive process than for consumers with extensive product experience.

Summary

In general, experienced hotel users are more critical and more aware of operational deficiencies than inexperienced hotel users. However, they are less sensitive to service delivery inconsistencies because they are more confident of their ability to deal with problems which may arise.

Inexperienced hotel users feel that they are less in control, and because of this they are more reluctant to complain, even if they feel dissatisfied. If, for example, minor sources of dissatisfaction create a feeling of tension, this may overshadow more positive aspects of the consumption experience. Dissatisfaction caused by ineffective service is especially potent. This is because inexperienced hotel users may lose self-esteem if service delivery is perceived to be unfriendly or threatening. These issues are illustrated in Chapter 9.

NOTES

1. Gummesson, E., *Marketing: A Long-Term Interactive Relationship: Contributions to a New Marketing Theory*, Marketing Technology Center, Sweden, 1987; Gummesson, E., 'Marketing organization in service businesses: the role of the part-time marketer', in Teare, R., Moutinho, L. and Morgan, N. (eds), *Managing and Marketing Services in the 1990s*, Cassell, London, 1990.
2. Teare, R., 'An exploration of the consumer decision process for hospitality services', in Teare, R., Moutinho, L. and Morgan, N. (eds), *Managing and Marketing Services in the 1990s*, Cassell, London, 1990.
3. LaBarbera, P.A. and Mazursky, A., 'A longitudinal assessment of consumer satisfaction/dissatisfaction: the dynamic aspect of the cognitive process', *Journal of Marketing Research*, vol. 20, Nov. 1983, pp. 393–404.
4. Olson, J.C. and Dover, P., 'Effects of expectation creation and disconfirmation on belief elements of cognitive structure', in Anderson, R.E. (ed.), *Advances in Consumer Research*, vol. 3, Association for Consumer Research, Ann Arbor, Mich., 1976, pp. 168–75.
5. Nightingale, M., 'Determination and control of quality standards in hospitality services', M. Phil thesis, University of Surrey, 1983; Nightingale, M., 'The hospitality industry: defining quality for a quality assurance programme – a study of perceptions', *Service Industries Journal*, vol. 5, no. 1, 1985, pp. 9–22.
6. Burnkrant, R.E. and Cousineau, A., 'Informational and normative social influence in buyer behavior', *Journal of Consumer Research*, vol. 2, Dec. 1975, pp. 206–15.
7. LaTour, S.A. and Peat, N.C., 'Conceptual and methodological issues in consumer satisfaction research', in Wilkie, W. (ed.), *Advances in Consumer Research*, vol. 6, Association for Consumer Research, Ann Arbor, Mich., 1978;

Latour, S.A. and Peat, N.C., 'The role of situationally produced expectations, others' experiences and prior experience in determining consumer satisfaction', in Olson, J.C. (ed.), *Advances in Consumer Research*, vol. 7, Association for Consumer Research, Ann Arbor, Mich., 1979.

8. Swan, J.E. and Jones Combs, L., 'Product performance and consumer satisfaction: a new concept', *Journal of Marketing*, vol. 40, Apr. 1976, pp. 25–33.

9. Howes, D. and Arndt, J., 'Determining consumer satisfaction through better profiling', *European Journal of Marketing*, vol. 13, no. 8, 1979, pp. 284–98.

10. Westbrook, R.A., 'Sources of consumer satisfaction with retail outlets', *Journal of Retailing*, vol. 57, no. 3, 1981, pp. 68–85.

11. McNeal, J.U., 'The concept of consumer satisfaction', *Management Bibliographies and Reviews*, vol. 3, 1977, pp. 231–40.

12. Pizam, A., Neumann, Y. and Reichel, A., 'Dimensions of tourist satisfaction with a destination area', *Annals of Tourism Research*, Jul./Sep. 1978, pp. 314–22.

13. Lounsbury, J.W. and Hoopes, L.L., 'An investigation of factors associated with vacation satisfaction', *Journal of Leisure Research*, vol. 17, no. 1, 1985, pp. 1–13.

14. Oliver, R.L., 'Effect of satisfaction and its antecedents on consumer preference and intention', in Monroe, K. (ed.), *Advances in Consumer Research*, vol. 8, Association for Consumer Research, Ann Arbor, Mich., 1980.

15. Westbrook, R.A. and Cote, J.A., 'An exploratory study of non-product related influences upon consumer satisfaction', in Olson, J.C. (ed.) *Advances in Consumer Research*, vol. 7, Association for Consumer Research, Ann Arbor, Mich., 1979.

16. Woodruff, R.B., Cadotte, E.R. and Jenkins, R.L., 'Modeling consumer satisfaction processes using experience-based norms', *Journal of Marketing Research*, vol. 20, no. 3, 1983, pp. 296–304.

17. Westbrook, op. cit.

18. La Tour and Peat, 'The role of situationally produced expectations', op. cit.

19. Swan, J.E. and Martin, W.S., (1980) 'Testing comparison level and predictive expectations models of satisfaction', in Monroe, K. (ed.), *Advances in Consumer Research*, vol. 8, Association for Consumer Research, Ann Arbor, Mich., 1980.

20. Moutinho, L., 'An investigation of vacation tourist behaviour', Ph.D. thesis, University of Sheffield, 1982; Moutinho, L., 'Vacation tourist decision process', *Quarterly Review of Marketing*, vol. 9, no. 3, 1984, pp. 8–17; Moutinho, L., 'Consumer behaviour in tourism', *Management Bibliographies and Reviews*, vol. 12, no. 3, 1986, pp. 3–42.

21. See below, Chapter 9.

9

Integrated marketing organization for hospitality firms

Richard Teare and Evert Gummesson

OVERVIEW

The conventional focus of commercial marketing activity is the external environment. Yet for service firms, there are potentially many internal points-of-marketing when employees interact with customers and influence buyer behaviour. Employees in this category thereby act as 'part-time marketers'[1] as they carry out marketing activities, but in contrast to the full-time marketers, they do not work in the marketing or sales department.

This chapter examines the contribution which operations personnel can make to the total marketing effort and some of the implications for the design and delivery of hospitality services. The observations are based on research evidence, examples of effective practice drawn from other service industries and personal experience.

INTRODUCTION: THE CASE OF THE DISILLUSIONED CUSTOMERS

Mr and Mrs Brown and their three children arrived late on Friday evening at the large London hotel which they had booked for a short spring break. They had had a long and tiring drive from Darlington, and had been forced to make several unplanned stops on the way. Anxious about the disconcerting noise coming from under the bonnet of their old Cortina, Mr Brown had reluctantly agreed to expensive repair work which had taken two hours at a motorway service station. Mrs Brown had had a hard time controlling the children during this time, especially as the youngest was suffering from car sickness. When the Browns finally arrived in London, they were beginning to wish that they had stayed at home, especially as they managed to lose their direction half a dozen times before finding the hotel.

The Browns had been looking forward to their weekend in London for months. They had moved house in the previous summer, a troublesome experience which had prevented the family from taking a holiday. Instead, they had promised themselves a spring break in London, which would be an adventure as none of the family had been there before. They had planned to combine sightseeing with some shopping, and had spent several weeks looking at brochures before selecting their first-choice hotel. When the travel agent phoned the operator it was to discover that only the Grand Hotel could accommodate them. It had 950 bedrooms and was more expensive than they had planned, but they decided to go ahead so as not to disappoint the children.

Mrs Brown's first reaction to the hotel was that from the outside it was not what she had expected. She had rarely stayed in an hotel before and she felt intimidated by its imposing façade. They parked the car with some difficulty, and made their way to the large revolving doors which signified the main entrance. Once inside, they felt overawed by the size of the reception area and the bustle of activity. They looked around to decide what they should do next. Mr Brown approached the hall porter's desk and joined a throng of people asking questions about messages, keys, taxis and theatre tickets. The elderly man behind the counter was clearly feeling harassed, and he responded by pointing across the lobby and saying 'You'll have to go over there, sir,' before moving down the counter to deal with the next query.

The reception desk was even busier, and the receptionist who eventually registered the Browns made no attempt to hold a conversation. By this time Mrs Brown was feeling very intimidated, and the children were busily trying to climb a modern sculpture in one of the far corners of the lobby. Mr Brown had intended to ask lots of questions about the opening hours and prices of the restaurants, how to find the nearest Underground station, etc., but he did not feel as though he was in control of the situation, and the receptionist plainly was not in the mood to listen anyway.

After waiting in a long queue to use the hotel lifts, they eventually reached the ninth floor, to be confronted by long corridors running in four directions. On the second attempt Mr Brown discovered how the room numbering system worked and they trekked down to the end of the corridor to find their family room, which was situated opposite a service lift. The room was very disappointing. The carpets were badly stained, and one of the portable children's beds was in need of repair. By now the time was 10 p.m. and Mr Brown tried to order sandwiches and hot drinks from room service, but was told that they would have to wait for up to an hour.

The next morning the Browns received their next disappointment. Despite the elevation, all they could see from the bedroom window were high-rise office blocks and a partial view of a fire station. They were also unsure about where they were supposed to take breakfast, as the 'Welcome Pack' they had been given at registration gave details of the hotel's three restaurants, but did not say which one they were supposed to use. When the lift arrived at the ground floor, they followed a group of Japanese businessmen into the main hotel restaurant, where the supervisor insisted that they must obtain breakfast tickets before they could be served . . .

By now the Browns were feeling like unwelcome guests in the hotel. All the staff they had encountered seemed to be too busy to appreciate their needs, and instead of enjoying the change of environment they felt tense and irritable. They had already decided that the hotel had been an expensive mistake.

The story illustrates what can happen if circumstances conspire against the novice customer. A busy hotel, harassed staff and above all failure to recognize the impact of a succession of hostile messages conveyed by the service environment. What can managers do to improve the effectiveness of their customer support?

INTERFUNCTIONAL DEPENDENCY IN SERVICE FIRMS

Marketing theory and practice has traditionally recognized the marketing mix[2] as a convenient framework for integrating changing business variables. In managing the mix, firms attempt to optimize the relationships betweem the components of product, place, price and promotion. In this sense, the marketing function may be viewed as an independent task, aiming to manipulate controllable factors in response to marketplace conditions and events. However, effective decision-making critically depends on good channels of referral and communication between unit and corporate functions. McKenna[3] observes that when firms do not adequately consider the linkages between all the function they end up with 'broken chains', a situation which can be potentially very damaging. Lee Iacocca encountered this problem when he began as chief executive at Chrysler:

> The manufacturing guys would build cars without even checking with the sales guys. They just built them, stuck them in a yard, and then hoped that somebody would take them out of there. We ended up with a huge inventory and a financial nightmare.[4]

Services marketing theory recognizes that production, marketing, and even service development are often handled by the same people. As a result the marketing function is spread throughout the firm, with operations personnel also acting as part-time marketers. This has important implications for the marketing approach, as customer relations are continually influenced by the behaviour of staff, who in turn differ in their understanding and interpretation of customer needs.[5]

A significant issue for service firms is how to apply marketing expertise to the internal network of interactive relationships in order to achieve integrated marketing organization. It implies the need to recognize what has been described as interfunctional dependency,[6] meaning that all of the activities of a firm are interrelated. Part of this task involves ensuring that operations personnel are well attuned to the mission, goals, strategies and systems of the firm, so that unity of purpose permeates outwards to customers, suppliers, the media and other interest groups. This also helps to strengthen corporate image and generate public confidence among investors and financial institutions which closely monitor financial performance. The importance of this perspective is emphasized by the network/interaction theory of industrial marketing which suggests that:

> A company can be viewed as a node in an ever-widening pattern of interactions, in some of which it is a direct participant, some of which affect it indirectly and some of which occur independently of it. This web of interactions is so complex and multifarious as to deny full description or analysis.[7]

The increasing emphasis on quality in the management and marketing of services[8] is indicative of the desire to adopt a more systematic approach to monitoring the service offering. It is also partly a competitive response to growing Japanese dominance in world markets. Quality has become a key integrating concept, linking corporate strategy, marketing and operations management to customer needs and satisfaction. Hence, the term 'total quality management'[9] embodies a philosophy which aims to focus on customer perceived quality in all aspects of a firm's operations.

Common to the development of services marketing theory, network/interaction theory and the principles of total quality management is the concern with interactive relationships or 'relationship marketing'.[10] Although interpretations differ, service firms aiming to integrate full-and part-time marketing activity need to find ways of combining relationship and marketing mix expertise in order to maintain a customer perceived quality focus.[11]

REQUIREMENTS FOR INTEGRATED MARKETING ORGANIZATION

The importance attributed to effective marketing organization can be illustrated with reference to a study of 128 major European firms which were asked to list, in order of importance, strategic marketing issues for the 1990s.[12] Four out of the top eighteen issues related to marketing organization. In rank order, these were:

3. Creating a marketing culture throughout the organization.
4. Adapting company structure to changing market strategies.
5. Recruiting and retaining experienced marketing professionals.
8. Improving the interface between marketing and technological resources.

Although principally responsible for the external domain, sales and marketing professionals also need to take full advantage of the naturally occurring opportunities within the firm to inform customers, persuade them to buy and satisfy their expectations. The work to create and maintain market relationships thereby becomes a joint undertaking between marketing and operations personnel, with the network of contacts inside the firm playing an integral role in the marketing process.

Integrated marketing organization has to occur in professional service firms like management consultancy and accountancy, as new client contacts are made in a variety of ways. Present and former clients are an important source of referral business because they play a central role in enhancing or degrading corporate image. Information provided by former employees may also form part of the network. For example, the management consulting firm McKinsey & Co. receives a sizeable proportion of business from former McKinsey consultants.

The nature of service business activity means that, in addition to the full-time marketers, firms are heavily populated with part-time marketers. Additionally, in some situations, firms organize their marketing by using their own personnel, supplemented by outside specialist support. The need for integration, and less rigid demarcation of marketing responsibility is therefore evident, the network of contacts inside and outside the firm, the formal and the informal, the professional as well as the social, are all part of the marketing process.

THE ROLE OF SERVICE DELIVERY IN MARKETING ORGANIZATION

In contrast to manufacturing, where the production process is under more direct control, service firms have to face the problems of dispersed and variable production, often involving the customer as co-producer. For example, the hotel general manager cannot hope to monitor the many events which occur simultaneously around the building at any given point in time. This presents something of a challenge, because the same people who develop, produce and deliver services often carry out marketing activities too. However, the fact that many people have direct or indirect influence on customers, thereby creating multiple marketing opportunities, can be advantageous. It requires that operations staff view every customer contact as an opportunity to influence customer behaviour and choice.

The naturally occurring contacts between employees and customers have been referred to as service encounters, service interactions or 'moments of truth'.[13] Although more commonly associated with person-to-person contact, these terms have also been used to describe telephone interactions. For example, when IBM Canada began to scrutinize the telephone calls they received from customers, they found that little was known about the range of enquiries they received, or how the calls were handled by employees. The study revealed that in one year, 10 million telephone calls were made by customers, and that 6 million of these calls were handled by operations personnel.[14]

Extending the moment of truth concept, the term *point-of-marketing*, meaning 'an opportunity to influence favourably the customer's present and future purchases', has been introduced.[15] Considered in relation to the process of service delivery and perceived customer benefits, which are key elements of the customer's total experience,[16] it is possible to identify four different types of interaction. These are depicted in Figure 9.1 and described below in relation to hotel points-of-marketing.

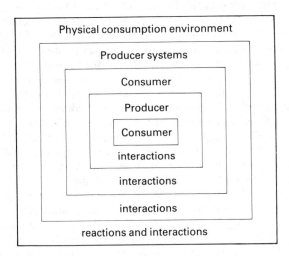

Figure 9.1   *Key elements of the consumption experience for hospitality services.*

Formative interactions between the customer and producer

The interactions which occur between the customer and the producer represent an important indicator of service quality. If, for example, a consumer feels tired and stressed after a long journey, the initial interactions with hotel reception staff will either reinforce or reduce uncertainty about hotel choice.[17] Managers should therefore ensure that the customer receives efficient and attentive service, especially at the initial point of contact.

Interpersonal interactions between customers

In some situations, customers are able to create the service themselves if the producer provides the appropriate systems, environment and staff. This happens to some extent in hotel bars and restaurants, where customers interact and, by so doing, create atmosphere.

Although customer interactions occur naturally, they can be stimulated by using devices such as background music and lighting. However, if they are set at inappropriate levels, or if bar and restaurant staff are too formal, customer interaction may be impeded. Managers should therefore give careful consideration to these contacts as customers who fit together reinforce their own positive experience, and the image of the service provider.

Interactions between the customer and producer systems

The interactions between the customer and producer systems are important because they affect the perceived efficiency of the producer. For example, the value of a computerized reservation system from the viewpoint of the customer may depend on how easy and convenient it is to access and the accuracy of the information it provides. If check-in and check-out times are reduced by the system and it is perceived to be more efficient and accurate than the equivalent manual procedures, the customer may be prepared to accept less personal service in return for the technological benefits.

The impact of the physical environment on the customer

The physical environment in which service delivery takes place is important because it can affect the customer in several ways. Design features in public areas convey impressions of warmth or coldness which may have a psychological impact on the customer. The physical environment also provides the customer with a wide range of information about the product. For example, the implementation of restaurant design conveys impressions about the style of service and the professionalism of the service producer. In restaurant design, retailing techniques can also be used to attract the customer by designing and positioning signs, displays and architectural features so that they convey a consonant theme.

All four types of interaction have contrasting characteristics and may combine in different ways, according to the type and duration of the service production/delivery process. This complex set of interactions has also been called the 'servuction' process,[18] which emphasizes that services are different from products, especially in relation to purchase and consumption behaviour. The hotel environment can be used to illustrate this point.

In the following extract, a customer reflects on his feelings and describes his participative role in the consumption experience at an international airport hotel:

'I recall vividly the feeling of the revolving doors sucking me into a big "factory". It was a factory where I became a "worker". My behaviour, knowledge, and needs would influence the functioning of the factory and the quality of its output. So would my temper, emotions, and degree of sympathy towards the staff. Moreover, I would have to do certain things myself – fill out a registration form, carry my luggage, find my room – while the hotel staff would do other things for me. I would have to interact with other guests, with the system of checking-in and checking-out . . . I would have to do this in different areas: in my room, the restaurant and the lounge.'[19]

As the example illustrates, the servuction process is facilitated or hindered by the customer's willingness to participate and interact with the service provider. Service quality is therefore partly determined by the nature of this collaborative effort, which constitutes a division of labour between customer and producer.

The four types of interaction or points-of-marketing ensure that service environments are unique and distinctive during the servuction process. Interactions during service production and delivery also create the right conditions for 'designed-in' marketing. The increasing emphasis on quality management and the design of services[20] indicates the need to ensure that marketing is actually in-built, so that harnessing the internal market potential becomes second nature to operations personnel. This is achieved by concentrating attention on the naturally occurring points-of-marketing in order to increase the proportion of positive interactions between the customer and the producer. In this way, a more fully integrated marketing organization can be attained. In approaching this task, staff who produce and deliver services should be consulted, as their experience of dealing with customers and operating systems is likely to generate new ideas and suggestions.

INTERNAL MARKETING: THE ROLE OF SERVICE DELIVERY PERSONNEL

As noted earlier, marketing is traditionally associated with the task of persuading the external customer to buy a product or service. However, there are a number of relationships existing within the organization which can be defined as internal marketing activity. For example:

- The customer–supplier relationship between employees inside a firm. In this sense, groups of employees 'service' the needs of other groups as part of an integrated network, processing a product from manufacture to after-sales service.
- The dissemination and application of marketing knowledge, developed initially for external marketing, to the internal market. In this way, operations personnel become more customer oriented, and more aware of the wider implications of their action in servicing customer needs.
- Strategic initiatives to improve the market orientation of service firms. These usually affect both external and internal marketing organization. Typically, more attention is given to the interface between the two, with 'front-line' staff receiving sales and customer awareness training.
- Internal marketing which takes place when profit centres inside a decentralized company trade with each other: for example, when a manufacturing division sells to an overseas subsidiary or a data-processing unit sells computer services to an operating division.

To consider the potential contribution that operations personnel can make to marketing organization, it is helpful to examine in more detail the concept of the internal customer and the value of disseminating external marketing expertise inside the firm.

Customer–supplier relationships inside the service firm are especially important because the boundaries between production and delivery are more fluid than in manufacturing. All employees should see themselves as customers of other employees from whom they receive product components and information through different kinds of interaction. Figure 9.2 illustrates the point that co-operation and effective co-ordination are needed to manage the process of servicing each other's needs. In this sense, employees should see themselves as suppliers to other internal customers who must be satisfied if the job is to be completed properly. This means that every employee contributes to the internal marketing function.

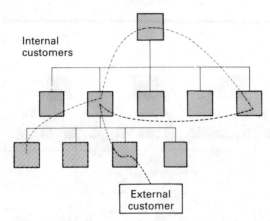

Figure 9.2 *An example of the principle of process management where the internal customers from different departments and tiers form a chain ending with an external customer.*

As stated earlier, to organize the internal customer concept effectively, it is necessary to ensure that all operations personnel, especially those in the 'front line' who are in daily contact with customers, are attuned to the mission, goals, strategies and systems of the firm. By importing and disseminating external marketing philosophy in this way, internal marketing activity can embrace a broader range of ideas about training, education, information and communication. If this is not happening then operations staff are ill-equipped to cope with the main points-of-marketing which occur during interaction with customers. It is also more difficult for them formally to recognize heterogeneous internal market segments, such as the various categories of business and leisure traveller who use hotels. By harnessing the potential that exists within a service firm, integrated marketing activity becomes possible. Figure 9.3 illustrates the numerical advantage resulting from shared marketing responsibility for the interactions with customers inside and outside the firm.

To illustrate the application of this approach to hospitality services, the final section draws on the introductory case to identify how an internal marketing strategy might be developed.

INTERNAL MARKETING ORGANIZATION IN HOSPITALITY FIRMS

Having established the value of spreading the marketing function throughout the service firm, it is essential that the organizational structure is responsive to the internal as well as the external opportunities that arise. This requires empathy with the needs and expectations of customers, careful monitoring of operational procedures, well-designed systems support and effective co-ordination. In this respect, many hospitality firms may benefit from implementing a review process to ensure that service interactions are uniformly positive and effective.

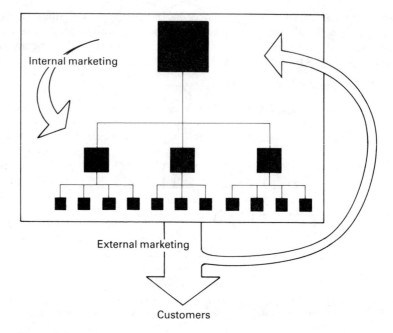

Figure 9.3   *Internal and external marketing and their interdependency.*

In outlining a strategic approach, four stages are suggested: a customer audit, an appraisal of operations personnel in regular contact with customers, a review of support system effectiveness and finally a monitoring process designed to minimize sources of customer dissatisfaction.

Stage 1: Undertake a customer audit

The nature of hospitality services, which must satisfy both physiological and psychological needs, means that customer expectations of, and reactions to, the service delivery environment are complicated and often unpredictable:

Mrs Brown's first reaction to the hotel was that from the outside it was not what she had expected. She had rarely stayed in an hotel before and she felt intimidated by its imposing façade . . . Once inside, they felt overawed by the size of the reception area and the bustle of activity. They looked around to decide what they should do next.

The emotional impact of a hostile environment may also affect initial service interactions. If the staff are not aware of this, and cannot respond appropriately, they are likely to be perceived as impersonal, officious or even uncaring. To prevent unhelpful and unforeseen friction from developing, managers should:

- Monitor the impact of public area design, congestion and related atmospheric effects on customers.

This is likely to require a continuous programme of qualitative research either by personal interview or focus group discussion. In this way, customers can be encouraged to talk freely about their reactions to the consumption environment.

- Ensure that operations are customer-centred, and not adversely affected by fluctuations in business demand.

Meeting this objective requires two kinds of action. Firstly, it needs the setting up of a customer awareness programme to assess interpersonal skill development needs and to provide a means by which information about changing customer expectations can be disseminated. Implementation should include regular small-group discussion meetings so that staff can given an opportunity to develop their own solutions to customer comments and complaints. Secondly, it is necessary to address the problem of fluctuations in business demand by developing a flexible approach to supporting front-line personnel. This could be achieved by redefining operational roles and improving the handling capacity of operator systems. For instance, multi-purpose work stations can be used for both checking-in and checking-out hotel guests. This provides enhanced flexibility during peak time periods.

Stage 2: Appraise the effectiveness of front-line personnel

In the discussion relating to the interaction between operations personnel and the customer, it was established that direct contacts represent natural internal points-of-marketing. If, however, the interactions are not handled sensitively, they can have the opposite effect:

Mr Brown had intended to ask lots of questions about the opening hours and prices of the restaurants, how to find the nearest Underground station, etc. But he did not feel as though he was in control of the situation, and the receptionist plainly was not in the mood to listen anyway.

In order to minimize the risk of alienating customers, managers should:

- Employ staff who have the ability to cope effectively with the work-related pressures of their operational role, and who are sensitive to the differing needs of customers.
- Ensure by monitoring personal development needs that these staff, above all, appreciate their influential role in dealing with customers and can respond positively to every foreseeable kind of service interaction.

These issues imply the need critically to examine recruitment, selection and induction procedures so that new members of staff are fully integrated into cohesive work groups. Development needs may arise from job expansion, preparation for career advancement or advances in system design and implementation. If staff are not developed according to changing circumstances, they may feel unsettled and consequently less sensitive to customer needs.

To maintain the interest, motivation and effectiveness of operations personnel, managers should:

- Ensure that staff have the freedom to initiate effective solutions to customer requests, and wherever possible delegate responsibility to enable them to make rapid decisions.

- Encourage new ideas and approaches, listen to suggestions made by staff and reward them when their suggestions are successfully implemented.

If operations personnel are constrained by too many rules and regulations, they are unlikely to respond to strategic objectives such as improving sales and customer satisfaction levels. In promoting customer awareness it is therefore necessary to give staff the opportunity to deal with customer requests creatively. In this way individual talents and personalities are mobilized in order to solve problems in the best interests of the customer and the employer. The challenge for managers is to provide guidance which emphasizes the need to build customer loyalty and at the same time observes basic rules governing standard company routines and policies.

Stage 3: Review the adequacy of systems support

In most hospitality operations 'back of house' staff support service delivery by using equipment and following procedures to achieve standardized production. This applies equally to administrative functions as well as to kitchens and supply areas. A product-oriented approach is necessary to complete specific tasks, but if front-line personnel also think and act in the same way, they may be unaware that customers sometimes feel confused or even intimidated by the service environment. This can lead to embarrassment and frustration:

After waiting in a long queue to use the hotel lifts, they eventually reached the 9th floor, to be confronted by long corridors running in four directions. On the second attempt Mr Brown discovered how the room numbering system worked . . . They were also unsure about where they were supposed to take breakfast, as the 'Welcome Pack' they had been given at registration gave details of the hotel's three restaurants, but did not say which one they were supposed to use. When the lift arrived at the ground floor, they followed a group of Japanese businessmen into the main hotel restaurant, where the supervisor insisted that they must obtain breakfast tickets before they could be served . . .

To avoid causing unnecessary customer anxiety managers should:

- Design the service production/delivery system so that systems and procedures can be clearly understood by customers.
- Use all available information sources such as brochures, leaflets, in-house magazines, merchandising and signage to support the naturally occurring point-of-marketing.

The interrelationship between service design and the provision of customer information should recognize the different kinds of interaction that take place between customers and staff. If, for example, restaurant service is highly personalized, guidance and information about service procedures and menu items can be provided by the restaurant staff. This means that the customer needs less point-of-sale literature and more information which accurately describes the degree of personalized service, prior to using the restaurant. Conversely, in self-help or self-service situations the customer may need to know how to find and use a particular service. This may seem a trivial concern to service staff, but unfamiliarity may lead to uncertainty and cause the customer to feel that service is impersonal or uncaring.

Stage 4: Minimize sources of customer dissatisfaction

Hospitality firms often rely on customer recommendations and repeat bookings to generate a significant proportion of their future business, yet customer dissatisfaction is often poorly handled:

By now the Browns were feeling like unwelcome guests in the hotel. All the staff they had encountered seemed to be too busy to appreciate their needs, and instead of enjoying the change of environment they felt tense and irritable. They had already decided that the hotel had been an expensive mistake.

A study by the management consulting firm Arthur D. Little revealed that many firms receive complaints from as few as 4 per cent of their dissatisfied customers. The consequences of this are potentially serious, as dissatisfied customers tell on average nine or ten other people; 13 per cent tell twenty or more, and those whose complaint has been resolved, tell on average five people.[21] These findings support earlier studies, and illustrate the need continuously to monitor and improve the procedures used to detect sources of customer dissatisfaction. In approaching this task, managers should:

- Ensure that lines of communication within the organizational structure are always open so that problems can be rapidly identified.
- Monitor and periodically review the mechanisms established for dealing with customer comments and complaints.

Maintaining and improving customer satisfaction is formally recognized as one of the key objectives of the marketing process. By recognizing the internal as well as the external contribution that employees can make, integrated marketing organization provides a clearer perspective on customer priorities and needs. To achieve this, it is necessary to establish the roles to be undertaken by the part-time marketers who work at reception, in the restaurant and in other jobs where service interactions directly influence the customer. Secondly, the process of establishing integrated marketing activity should seek to create a network of relationships within the firm so that a customer–supplier ethos develops between departments and not just at the point of service delivery.

NOTES

1. Gummesson, E., 'Marketing organization in service businesses: the role of the part-time marketer', in Teare, R., Moutinho, L. and Morgan, N. (eds), *Managing and Marketing Services in the 1990s*, Cassell, London, 1990.
2. McCarthy, J.E., *Basic Marketing*, Irwin, Homewood, Ill., 1964.
3. McKenna, R., *The Regis Touch*, Addison-Wesley, New York, 1985.
4. Iacocca, L. (with Novak, W.) *Iacocca: An Autobiography*, Bantam Books, New York, 1984, p. 162.

5. Nightingale, M., 'Determination and control of quality standards in hospitality services', M.Phil. thesis, University of Surrey, 1983.
6. Hutt, M.D. and Speh, T.W., 'The marketing strategy center: diagnosing the industrial marketer's interdisciplinary role', *Journal of Marketing*, vol. 48, Fall 1984, pp. 53–61; Ruekert, R.W. and Walker, O.C., 'Marketing's interaction with other functional units; a conceptual framework and empirical evidence', *Journal of Marketing*, vol. 51, Jan. 1987, pp. 1–19.
7. Ford, D., Hakansson, H. and Johansson, J., 'How do companies interact?' *Industrial Marketing and Purchasing*, vol. 1, no. 1, pp. 26–41.
8. Armistead, C., 'Productivity and effects on quality in service operations'; Piercy, N. and Morgan, N., 'Retailer marketing organizations: strategic developments for the 1990s'; Voss, C., Johnston, R., Fitzgerald, L. and Sylvestro, R., 'Measurement of service performance: empirical results'; in Teare, R., Moutinho, L. and Morgan, N. (eds), *Managing and Marketing Services in the 1990s*, Cassell, London, 1990.
9. Deming, W. E., *Out of the Crisis*, Massachusetts Institute of Technology, Cambridge, Mass., 1986; Buzzell, R. D. and Gale, B. T., *The PIMS Principles*, Free Press, New York, 1987; Garvin, D. A., *Managing Quality*, Free Press, New York, 1988.
10. Levitt, T., *The Marketing Imagination*, Free Press, New York, 1983; Jackson, B. B., 'Build customer relationships that last', *Harvard Business Review*, Nov./Dec. 1985, pp. 120–8.
11. Gummesson, E., 'The new marketing: developing long-term interactive relationships', *Long Range Planning*, vol. 20, no. 4, 1987, pp. 10–20.
12. Larreche, J-C., Powell, W. W. and Ebling, H.D., *Key Strategic Marketing Issues for the 1990s*, INSEAD, Fontainebleau, 1987.
13. Carlzon, J., *Moments of Truth*, Ballinger, Cambridge, Mass., 1987; Petersen, K., *The Strategic Approach to Quality Service in Health Care*, Aspen Publishers, Rockville, Md, 1988.
14. Myles, D., 'Think customer: the IBM-Canada way', American Marketing Association 7th Annual Services Marketing Conference, Arlington, Va, Oct. 1988.
15. Gummesson, E., 'Marketing-orientation revisited: the crucial role of the part-time marketer', *European Journal of Marketing*, Spring 1991 (forthcoming).
16. Grönroos, C., *Strategic Marketing and Management in the Service Sector*, Marketing Science Institute, Cambridge, Mass., 1983; Lehtinen, J. R., 'Improving service quality by analyzing the service production process', in Grönroos, C. and Gummesson, E. (eds), *Service Marketing: Nordic School Perspectives*, Research Report, University of Stockholm, 1985.
17. Teare, R., 'An exploration of the consumer decision process for hospitality services', in Teare, R., Moutinho, L. and Morgan, N. (eds), *Managing and Marketing Services in the 1990s*, Cassell, London, 1990.
18. Eiglier, P. and Langeard, E., *Servuction*, McGraw-Hill, Paris, 1987; Bateson, J. E. G., *Managing Services Marketing*, Dryden Press, Chicago, Ill., 1989.
19. Gummesson, E., 'Service design', *Total Quality Management*, vol. 2, no. 2, Apr. 1990, pp. 97–101.
20. Shostack, L. G., 'How to design a service', in Donnelly, J. H. and George, W. R. (eds), *Marketing of Services*, American Marketing Association, Chicago, Ill., 1981; Dale, A. and Wooler, S., 'Strategy and organization for service: a process

and content model', and George, W. R. and Gibson, B. E., 'Blueprinting: a tool for managing quality in services', in Brown, S. W., Gummesson, E., Edvardsson, B. and Gustavsson, B. O. (eds), *Quality in Services: Multidisciplinary and Multinational Perspectives*, Lexington Books, Lexington, Mass., 1990.
21. Krauss, C. G., 'Customer satisfaction: a bottom line performance indicator', in Surprenant, C. (ed.), *American Marketing Association*, 6th Annual Services Marketing Conference, San Diego, Calif., Sep. 1987.

PART 4
STRATEGY FOR INTERNATIONAL MARKETS

Strategic developments for the 1990s: implications for hotel companies

Paul Slattery with Andrew Boer

INTRODUCTION

In January 1990 Kleinwort Benson Securities published its annual review of the hotel market and, in particular, a prospective view of the future of hotel chains operated by public companies within the United Kingdom.[1] Within this category, the importance of the business traveller both from within the United Kingdom and from overseas was noted (see Table 10.1). It should also be noted that, although this market has exhibited the largest growth of all hotel markets in the last decade, it is projected to grow at around half of the 1980s rate in the next decade. However, it still accounts for two-thirds of hotel room demand and, as such, is of primary concern to planners and strategists.

Table 10.1 *UK Hotels plc: room nights used (millions)*

Demand category	UK residents		Overseas visitors		Total	
	1979	1989	1979	1989	1979	1989
Business travellers	5.7	14.0	2.8	4.7	8.5	18.7
Holidaymakers	2.2	2.6	4.5	6.8	6.7	9.4
Total	7.9	16.6	7.3	11.5	15.2	28.1

Source: Kleinwort Benson Securities, *1990 UK Hotels plc: The Decade Review*, 1990.

THE STRUCTURAL THEORY OF BUSINESS TRAVEL

Central to the assessment of the business demand for hotels is the 'structural theory of business travel', which argues that business traveller demand is determined by the structure of an economy rather than simply by GDP growth. The structural theory identifies three phases.

In Phase I an economy is dominated by single-site companies mostly in extractive and manufacturing industries, and serving local and regional markets. There is a low overall level of business demand for hotels because sales and marketing executives are normally the only ones who travel regularly on business. In economies at this stage a high proportion of demand comes from international business travellers to major cities in the economy, while in all but the largest countries indigenous business demand is at a relatively low level.

A current example of this would be Eastern bloc countries such as Poland or Hungary, which experience minimal indigenous demand with very few local business travellers and, indeed, also very few local leisure travellers. These economies are usually serviced by *ad hoc* hotels and large franchised hotel brands such as Hilton International, Intercontinental (in capital cities) and Hyatt, all of which are oriented towards overseas visitors.

The theory proposes that two states are necessary for an economy to enter Phase II, when business traveller hotel demand will grow. These two states evolved in the UK economy during the 1980s (having previously emerged in the USA) and were the cause of the substantial growth in business demand.

First, there is growth in the number of multisite companies in the economy as its core moves from primary and secondary to tertiary industries. Such growth is important because it brings with it growth in peripatetic corporate jobs.

The growth of multisite companies and peripatetic corporate jobs has been a feature of the structural changes in the UK during the 1980s, most obviously evidenced by the expansion of nationwide retail multiples. This has required hotels throughout the country to meet the growing demand from UK executives to stay away from home as part of their jobs. Additionally, hotels have been needed as substitute regional offices in which to hold area meetings as part of the committe structure of these companies, as well as providing a centre for a whole range of in-company training courses.

An important feature of the development of multisite companies is that their operation requires peripatetic employees who thus become hotel users. This demand stems from the structure of these companies. It is also no accident that the emergence and growth of multisite firms in the UK economy is matched by the emergence and growth of hotel chains such as Queens Moat Houses and hotel brands such as Post Houses, explicitly committed to meet this demand.

The second state necessary for an economy to enter Phase II is a growth in companies serving national and international markets rather than local and regional markets. An economy dominated by local markets does not produce any significant business demand for hotels. Companies with national and international markets employ people who are involved in the research, penetration and servicing of these markets. This creates a layer of jobs in a firm which involve business travel and staying away from home as a prerequisite.

The 1980s in the UK produced a material growth in the number of companies servicing national and international markets as well as a growth in foreign companies selling into the UK economy. These have provided the impetus to increase business demand for hotel services.

Hotel companies such as Queens Moat House, which emerged around the beginning of Phase II in the UK and is specifically focused on the business market, has increased its room stock by more than 1,100 per cent during the past decade.

Similarly, both Mount Charlotte Thistle and Ladbroke showed a marked growth during the 1980s with an increase in room stock of over 800 per cent.

That there has been a marked growth in demand during the 1980s and an increase in supply in secondary locations and in smaller, more modest hotels may be seen as an indication that Phase II is coming towards its closing stages. It is an important feature of the structural theory that Phase II is a transitional stage with a limited time period – in the case of the UK, less than twenty years. This implies that the 1990s will mark the entry into Phase III, a phase characterized by only marginal growth in business demand.

It is, however, not yet certain at which point an economy moves from Phase II to the plateau of Phase III. It should be noted that there is a limit to the extent to which an economy can be dominated by multisite firms and by firms committed to national and international markets rather than local markets. Additional improvements in transportation – faster trains, more air routes and improved roads – means that more business travel can be undertaken on day trips.

An example of a Phase III economy would be the USA, which has evolved firmly as a service economy with a strong indigenous business demand for hotels in place but growing marginally both in achieved daily rate and in occupancy. Tangible indications of this mature market are the vigorous introduction of sales promotion strategies such as frequent user programmes and high-specification hotel facilities like suites, executive floors and hotel clubs at prices marginally above standard rooms.

A central proposition of the theory is that when the corporate structure of multisite companies and those servicing national and international markets is in place, further growth in demand for business travel is marginal. Changes in GDP or in imports require no more than fine tuning of the corporate structures of companies in an economy, thereby having only a marginal impact on hotel demand.

Hence the logic of the theory determines that Phase III is a plateau and that the three phases of the theory form an S-shaped curve (see Figure 10.1).

To avoid the impact of Phase III, UK hotel companies now have the task of identifying strategies which will protect them from the effects of marginal growth. The following sections will deal with some of the issues facing these companies.

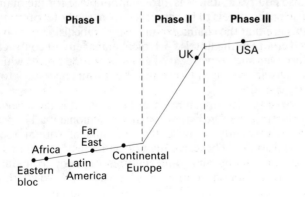

Figure 10.1   *The structural theory of business travel.*
Source: Kleinwort Benson Securities, *1990 UK Hotels plc: The Decade Review, 1990.*

INTERNATIONAL DEVELOPMENT STRATEGY

Given the evidence of saturation in the business accommodation market of both the UK and US hotel industries, many UK hotel chains are actively seeking to expand into and take advantage of the opportunity offered by Phase II growth in other economies. The continental European countries are exhibiting many of the character-istics of economies moving from Phase I to Phase II, a process which will be accelerated by the single market initiative planned for 1992.

One such growth market is that of west Germany, which has experienced a large increase in the number of service sector companies and consequently a move towards the conditions which boost indigenous business demand for hotels. In terms of hotel supply it conforms to the characteristics of the US or UK market at a similar stage – a low level of concentration and insufficient hotels dedicated to the business market in terms of location, size and facilities.

Given the evolutionary nature of the west German hotel market it can be seen that UK hotel companies have several advantages over their foreign counterparts in penetrating this market. Primarily, the cost of purchasing hotels in early Phase II economies is up to 40 per cent cheaper than in the UK. Interest rates are as little as half of those in the UK, and there are also significant tax and financial advantages.

It is the predominant practice within UK chains both to own and to manage hotels. This allows them not only to consolidate all of the hotel profits, but also to benefit from the capital appreciation on the hotels. This is important since UK hotel companies are enabled to revalue their hotels, thus increasing the shareholders' funds annually. This, in turn, allows gearing to be controlled or debt capacity to be increased. Thus Trusthouse Forte revalues one-third of its assets every year, Stakis revalues all of its assets every three years and Queens Moat Houses revalues all of its assets annually.

Another advantage of UK Hotels plc over its foreign competitors is the ability to raise equity through rights issues and the issuing of shares in payment for assets. Companies which have used this method of funding to assist their international expansion include Ladbrokes and Queens Moat Houses. In comparison, in continental Europe and the USA there are very few public companies involved in the hotel market, and the prevailing conditions in these capital markets constrain the extent to which companies can raise equity capital. It is also commonplace for the management of US and continental European hotels to be separated from the hotel property.

The implications of this are that the chains expand using franchising or management contracts with little or no equity in the hotels. A typical management contract is based on 3 per cent of hotel turnover and 10 per cent of gross operating profit, which means that a multitude of contracts are required to produce the profits necessary to produce the cash flow needed for expansion.

Given the potential size of the European market, however, it is inconceivable that UK companies pursuing a strategy of growth through international market penetration will have the capability consistently to raise the amounts of capital required to purchase all of their acquisitions. These companies will thus be inclined towards management contracting, franchising and joint ventures in order to maintain their growth rates. Thus Hilton International continues its international growth through the medium of management contracting, and Holiday Inns continue to be franchised in the ratio of ten franchised units to one company hotel.

BRANDING STRATEGY

The increase in demand in the UK market during the 1980s and the consequent concentration on growth strategies have tended to detract many companies from the need to develop balanced and structured portfolios which will equip them for some of the challenges of the 1990s.

Many of the major companies have, however, developed structured portfolios and strategies based around hotel brands. Examples are Accor, Marriott, Holiday Inns and Hilton International. Hotel brands appear to be central to their strategies in the 1990s and particularly in facilitating growth on the international market. The strategy of branding is not, however, homogeneous and a distinction may be made between 'international' hotel brands and 'national' hotel brands.

The international brand strategy tends to be used by companies which develop hotels only in major cities in various countries and which are directed largely towards international travellers as opposed to drawing on the domestic demand generated by the host country. This leads to a very low level of penetration in a country, and usually a very wide geographical coverage. Examples are Hilton International, Hyatt, Intercontinental Hotels and Sheraton.

The national brand strategy tends to be concentrated in the mid to lower markets and is used by companies wishing to capture primarily domestic demand. This requires far greater penetration of the host country's domestic market and a far greater knowledge of the local economy and its likely future. Examples of the latter strategy are Queens Moat Houses, which trade in the UK with the Queens Moat House hotel brand, in the Netherlands with Bilderburg, and in Germany with Queens Hotels. Similarly, the Trusthouse Forte mid-market brand, Post Houses, is UK specific.

Companies following the national brand strategy will thus have a far greater commitment to the economic and social development of the host country and will need to develop more intricate and involved networks to service their units. In contrast, a company with an international brand strategy will have few sites in many countries. Hilton International is located in 47 countries and Sheraton in 65 countries. Neither attracts many customers from the local population. The adoption of one or other of these types of strategies not only implies a difference in perception of the type of market the company supplies, but also has important implications for the structure and operation of the company.

In summary, then, the UK business accommodation market is likely to experience a sharp reduction in growth during the next decade. Companies which will survive this increase in competition are those which not only will have recognized the limitation of the UK domestic market but also will have been proactive. They will have structured their portfolios to take advantage of growth potential in foreign economies and implemented operating strategies to suit the changing, and more demanding competitive environment.

NOTE

1. Kleinwort Benson Securities, *1990* UK Hotels plc: The Decade Review, 1990.

11

International marketing in the hospitality industry

Simon Crawford-Welch

INTRODUCTION   *statistic expansion*

There can be little doubt that the business of hospitality corporations is international business. The hospitality industry is global in its focus. A study of selected lodging corporations determined the ratio of internationalization (the number of rooms operated abroad by a lodging corporation divided by the total number of rooms operated by that corporation) for the period 1987–90.[1] Findings revealed significant increases in international operations by almost all lodging organizations sampled. For example, the Holiday Corporation is projected to have a 9.6 per cent increase in its internationalization ratio by the end of 1990, Quality International a 6.9 per cent increase, Sheraton a 5.4 per cent increase, Ramada a 13.8 per cent increase and the Marriott Corporation a 20.7 per cent increase.

Lodging organizations are increasing their international focus in every corner of the globe. In the USA, for example, for the period 1989–91, Miyako Hotels (Japan) plan to build a 430-room hotel in Los Angeles; Swissotel Ltd (Switzerland) plans to build a total of 775 rooms in Atlanta and Ontario; and Trusthouse Forte (THF) plans to build a total of over 500 rooms throughout the USA.

In Europe for the same three-year period (1989–91), Accor (France) plans to build over 250 rooms in the UK; Iberotel (Spain) plans to build over 600 rooms in Turkey; Ramada (USA) plans to build over 550 rooms throughout Europe; Scandic Hotels (Sweden) plan to build over 1,100 rooms throughout Europe; and Sol Hotels (Spain) plan to build over 750 rooms in Turkey.[2]

The major source of international expansion from European hospitality firms is the United Kingdom. British hospitality companies with strong international operations and expansion plans are financially sound and a good investment. Particularly favoured are THF, which continues to penetrate continental Europe, Ladbroke, which is expanding with Hilton International, and Queens Moat, which gets 50 per cent of its profits from its hotels in continental Europe.[3]

In the Asia/Pacific arena, despite recent setbacks, China is predicted to experience vast growth in international hotel chains in 1990–1 with examples including Ana Hotels (Japan) building over 1,100 rooms, Hyatt International Hotels (USA) building over 1,400 rooms and Sheraton Hotels Corporation (USA) building over 800 rooms. There will, however, be expansion in additional Asia/Pacific countries with Pullman

International Hotels (France) scheduled to build over 2,500 rooms in the Asia/Pacific region and Accor (France) scheduled to build over 1,250 rooms throughout the Asia/ Pacific region.

Japan will continue to increase its role in the international arena with such major players as Tokyo's Sekitei Kaihatsu Co. Ltd, which acquired the Hotel Bel-Air in Los Angeles for US $110 million in 1989; Tokyo Masuiwaya Co. Ltd, which has already made significant entries in the California market, the Saison Group, which bought Inter-Continental in 1988, and of course the Aoki Corporation which bought Westin Hotels and Resorts in 1988. However, international growth by Japanese chains is not restricted to existing international players. Domestic Japanese lodging chains are also poised to make an impact on the world scene with companies like the New Otani Co. Ltd (15 hotels in Japan) and Hotel Okura (9 hotels in Japan) expanding overseas at phenomenal rates.[4]

Almost identical growth scenarios can be found in the Caribbean/Latin America and Africa/Middle East regions. Sol Hotels (Spain) will open over 2,900 rooms in the Caribbean and Latin America between 1989 and 1991, Ramada (USA) over 1,500 in the same region and Club Méditerranée (France) an additional 580 rooms in Africa in the same period.

The picture is similar in the restaurant industry with organizations such as McDonald's with an internationalization ratio of 22.7 per cent, Kentucky Fried Chicken with a ratio of 28.2 per cent, Pizza Hut with a ratio of 11.2 per cent, Burger King with a ratio of 8.9 per cent and Baskin-Robbins with a ratio of 23.2 per cent, all for the year 1987.[5]

Despite this phenomenal growth in the international operations of hospitality organizations, there has been little attention directed toward the implications of this trend for the functional-level strategy of marketing in the hospitality industry. It is the purpose of this chapter to outline and discuss the implications of internationalization for the functional-level strategy of marketing in hospitality organizations. Definitions of the main constructs being discussed will first be offered in order that a solid conceptual frame of reference be established at the outset. Attention will then be directed toward six related, but distinct, issues which play a significant role in the international marketing decision. These issues are (a) market segmentation, (b) product segmentation, (c) product differentiation, (d) standardization, (e) pricing and (f) distribution.

TERMS DEFINED

Hospitality industry

The definition of the hospitality industry used throughout this chapter encompasses two main industries: the lodging industry and the food service industry. There are arguably other components of the hospitality industry such as bars, gaming and attractions, but the issue of international marketing strategy is most relevant if discussed within the specific context of the above two industries.

Worldwide hospitality demand was estimated to be worth $1,900 billion in 1989 rising to $2,500 billion in 1990. The main components are currently estimated to be holiday tourism worth $750 billion, business tourism worth $550 billion and local hospitality worth $1,200 billion. Sixty per cent of hospitality turnover comes from the G7 countries, which are Canada, France, UK, USA, Japan, Germany and Italy.[6]

Marketing

The term 'marketing' is one of the most consistently misused and abused terms in the hospitality field. As long ago as 1969, a distinction was made between marketing as 'pushing' products and marketing as 'customer satisfaction engineering'.[7] The difference between these two approaches is as different as night and day. The former approach pushes a product on to the market and organizations assume their products are sold, not bought. The latter approach is a philosophy that holds that the task of management is to determine the needs and wants of a market a priori to developing a product. In other words, selling focuses on the needs of the organization, whereas marketing focuses on the needs of the customer.[8]

Many hospitality organizations claim to adopt a marketing orientation when in reality they adopt either an operations orientation (i.e. 'everything would be just fine if the customer did not get in the way'); a product orientation (i.e. 'we have this wonderful product but have not yet determined whether or not there is a demand for it'); a selling orientation (i.e. 'we have seventy rooms to fill, let's go and get the customers'); or some combination of the three.

There are three stages of marketing consciousness.[9] Consciousness 1 views marketing as essentially a business concept; consciousness 2 views marketing as being appropriate to all organizations that have customers; and consciousness 3 views marketing as being relevant for all organizations in their relationships with their publics, not solely their customers. It will be suggested throughout this chapter that, if hospitality marketing is to come of age in today's increasingly fierce and cut-throat operating environment, it must adopt stage 3 of marketing consciousness.

A general definition of marketing is the procedure of planning and putting into action the conception, pricing, promotion and distribution of ideas, goods and services in order that exchanges may be created that are able to satisfy both individual and organizational objectives.[10] For the purposes of this chapter, marketing is defined as communicating to and giving the target market customers what they want, when they want it, where they want it, at a price they are willing to pay.[11]

International marketing

International marketing is replete with terminology that is often contradictory, redundant and/or imprecise.[12] For example, the term 'international marketing' is often used interchangeably, although incorrectly, with such terms as 'transnational marketing', 'foreign marketing' and 'multinational marketing'. While all these terms refer to the process of marketing in more than one country, there are important differences between them. For the purposes of this chapter, international marketing is defined as the performance, in more than one nation, of business activities that direct the flow of a company's goods and services to consumers or users for a profit.

Hospitality marketing

There continues to be a debate in the marketing literature as to whether or not service marketing (of which hospitality marketing is a part) is significantly different from the marketing of consumer goods/durables. There are three broad schools of thought concerning this relationship. First, there is the school of thought that argues that there is no difference between goods and services, and therefore that they are subject to the same marketing techniques.[13] Second, there is a school of thought that argues that the difference between goods and services is a matter of degree rather than absolutes, and therefore that marketing techniques simply need to be adapted.[14] Third, there is the school of thought that argues that goods and services are indeed different and thus require different marketing techniques.[15] The literature is rife with pleas to stop applying manufacturing-oriented marketing strategies to the marketing of services, since they do not produce acceptable performance levels.[16]

This chapter proceeds on the premises that services are indeed different from goods. A service is a deed, a performance or an effort; whereas a good is a device, a thing or an object.[17] The unique attributes of services fall into one of two categories: service product characteristics and service product dynamics. The former include the intangibility of services, their temporal nature and their heterogeneity. Service-product dynamics include the simultaneous nature of production and consumption, short channels of distribution, difficulties in ensuring reliabilities and consistencies, demand fluctuations and imprecise standards. Because of these characteristics which are inherent in the hospitality product, the marketing of hospitality products is, indeed, a special case of marketing at both an operational and a strategic level.

Non-traditional marketing, for example, has a major role to play in the marketing of hospitality products. Non-traditional marketing has two major components: internal marketing and relationship marketing. Internal marketing attempts to apply the philosophies and concepts of marketing that have traditionally been used in the organization–customer relationship to the organization–employee relationship. An internal marketing philosophy recognizes the fact that the employee is the most important individual in the organization, since the employee is the organization in the eyes of the customer. In hospitality organizations there needs to be a high emphasis on internal marketing owing to the high-contract nature of hospitality itself.[18] Relationship marketing should attract, maintain and enhance customer relationships.[19]

Attention will now be directed toward the six issues outlined in the introduction, which have implications for both the formulation and the implementation of international marketing strategy in hospitality corporations.

THE MARKET SEGMENTATION ISSUE

Market segmentation certainly became the buzzword of the 1980s in the hospitality industry. Both researchers[20] and practitioners[21] alike directed increasing amounts of attention and resources to the segmentation issue in the 1980s. There is no reason to suspect that the 1990s will be any different in terms of this preoccupation with segmentation as a viable marketing strategy. Indeed, both the existing and planned proliferation of brand bear witness to this fact.

In the lodging industry, the single brand hotel chain of the 1960s and 1970s is now virtually non-existent. Rather we see an influx of multiple brands and brand strategies. For example, contemporary brand strategies include corporate brand strategies (e.g. Motel 6 (USA), Econo Lodges (USA), Days Inns (USA), Copthorne Hotels (UK), Metropole Hotels (UK), Movenpick Hotels (Switzerland), Iberotel (Spain)); product-line brand strategies (e.g. Comfort Suites, Quality Inns, Quality Suites, Clarion Inns, Clarion Suites, which are all part of Quality International USA); family name brand strategies (e.g. THF Viscount, THF Little Chef, THF Travelodges, THF Exclusive, THF Forte Hotels and THF Post Houses, which are all part of Trusthouse Forte (UK)); and individual brand name strategies (e.g. Hampton

Inns (USA), Cresthill (Hilton International), Dunfey Hotels, Embassy Suites). Segmentation has grown to the extent that there is inter-tier brand segmentation: that is, segmentation of the product within a brand tier, such as in the case of the all-suite segment which is subdivided into limited service all-suite, full service all-suite and extended stay all-suite.

The most common definition of market segmentation is the process by which an organization attempts to match a total marketing programme to the unique manner in which one or more customer groups (market segments) behave in the marketplace.[22] Segmentation is simply a means of achieving efficient resource allocation in an increasingly competitive marketplace. The general aim is to segment markets into distinct subsets of customers, where any subset may conceivably be selected as a target market to be reached with a distinct marketing mix. The basic assumption behind segmentation is that the market is heterogeneous as opposed to homogeneous.

There is general consensus in the literature around four basic approaches to market segmentation: (a) the traditional a priori approach; (b) the clustering/post hoc approach; (c) the flexible approach; and (d) the newer componential approach.[23] The a priori approach uses either product-specific variables or general consumer characteristics as dependent variables (i.e. the basis for segmentation). The clustering approach different from this in that the basis for segmentation is determined not a priori but rather post hoc through the clustering of respondents. It is not uncommon, however, to find some combination of the above two approaches in a hybrid approach, as is the case with sequential clustering. Flexible models of segmentation use conjoint analysis and very often also make use of computer choice simulations, the results of which are then combined to determine segments. Finally, componential segmentation is a unique approach in that the emphasis of the segmentation model is not on the partitioning of the market but rather on the attributes and characteristics of individuals and how these are linked with particular product features.[24] Table 11.1 shows each of the above four approaches in terms of their primary focus, orientation and the dependent variable used as well as major proponents of each approach.

Within the framework provided by the above four approaches to segmentation, there are generally accepted to be five basic models of segmentation: (a) descriptive models, which use geographic and demographic variables as dependent variables; (b) psychological models, which use personality, attitudes, opinions, interests and values

Table 11.1   *Four major approaches to segmentation*

	Method			
	A priori	Post hoc	Flexible	Componential
Dependent variable used	Product specific; general customer characteristics; demographics	Needs; attitudes; benefits sought; psychographics	Consumer behaviour; product attributes	Personality: product attributes
Primary focus	Quantitative	Qualitative	Quantitative/ qualitative	Qualitative/ quantitative
Orientation	Static	More dynamic	Dynamic	More dynamic

as dependent variables; (c) psychographic models, which use lifestyle and product-specific psychographic profiles as dependent variables; (d) behavioural models, which use benefits sought, brand loyalty, user rate, user status and usage situation as dependent variables; and (e) 'other' segmentation models, which essentially include 'hybrid' models of segmentation.[25] Table 11.2 shows the various components of each of these five basic models as well as major studies conducted to date on each model.

Table 11.2 *Components of segmentation models*

Model	Variables used	Major studies[1]
Descriptive segmentation models	Demographic: age	26
	sex	27
	marital status	
	family size	
	Socio-economic: occupation	
	income	28
	education	
	Geographic	29
	Social class	30
	Family life-cycle	31,32
Behaviourally based segmentation models	Volume of usage	33
	Brand loyalty	34
	Use occasions	35
	Benefits sought	22
Psychographically based segmentation models	Lifestyles	36
	Attitudes	37
	Interests	
	Opinions	
	Values	38
Psychologically based segmentation models	Personality	39
	Attitudes	
	Motivation	

[1] Numbers listed refer to notes on pp. 187–93.

Segmentation in the international hospitality industry will continue to be a force to be reckoned with for several reasons. First, conventional wisdom in the field of financial management suggests that firms should develop a portfolio of businesses to balance their earnings stream. In theory, the portfolio is designed so that the return to the shareholder will be stable over the life of the firm. Thus, individual businesses are expected to compliment each other such that when one business is experiencing a downturn the other businesses will be up. It is in response to this type of thinking that hospitality firms began to develop multiple brands. Second, segmentation offers hospitality firms the opportunity to grow in a saturated marketplace. Third, it is often cheaper and financially wiser to build new concepts than to renovate existing hotel room inventory. In the USA for example, it is estimated that over 50 per cent of today's inventory in the lodging industry is old and tired. It is financially more rewarding to develop new properties and concepts than to renovate the existing old inventory.[40]

The most popular segmentation models used in the international hospitality industry are descriptive in nature. The most important of these descriptive models is geographic segmentation. There are three broad approaches to geographic segmentation.

The first approach is national geographic segmentation. In countries like the USA and the UK, hotel companies have traditionally concentrated only on this type of segmentation. Examples are chains like Mount Charlotte (UK), Stakis Hotels (UK), Norfolk Capital Hotels (UK), Econo Lodges (USA) and Motel 6 (USA). The emphasis is clearly on geographic segmentation, usually by place of origin, of the national market with little or no specific provision for the international market.

The second approach to geographic segmentation lies at the other extreme of the continuum and is international geographic segmentation. This approach is far more complex than the first approach for two reasons: (a) it demands a far wider geographic segmentation and (b) it often requires the mixing of diverse market segments. Hotels in Hong Kong and Singapore have long faced the problem of a wide geographic approach to segmentation. It is not unusual to find hotels in these locations simultaneously catering to the needs of nationals from each of the ASEAN countries (Indonesia, Malaysia, Thailand, the Philippines, Brunei and Singapore) as well as nationals from one or several of the member states of the EC (Britain, France, Germany, Spain, Turkey, Greece, Denmark, the Netherlands, Belgium, Italy, Luxembourg, Portugal and Ireland) as well as several additional countries. Such a wide approach to geographic segmentation poses some practical problems. The hotel has to ensure that each market segment is compatible with the other. This would not be the case, for example, with Arabs and Jews. In an attempt to overcome some of these practical problems, many hotels, often by default, have become one-origin hotels: that is, they cater only to Arabs or Americans or Japanese, etc. Examples of the latter are the Nikko Hotel in New York City and the New Otani in Los Angeles, which initially catered primarily to the Japanese market. A hotel has to ensure, however, if it is to become a one-origin hotel, that the segment is large enough to support profitable occupancy levels. In reality this is seldom the case.

The third and final approach to geographic segmentation is a combination of the above two approaches. Lewis and Chambers[41] offer the case of France's Accor chain as an example of such an approach. Accor's Formule 1, Ibis and Novotel concepts segment on the lower and middle portions of the French market, while the Sofitel concept segments primarily on the international market. Another example of such an approach would be Trusthouse Forte: its Viscount chain in the USA caters primarily to the international traveller, while its Travelodge chain caters primarily to American nationals.

There are problems, however, with basing one's approach to segmentation purely on descriptive variables. Descriptive data, by their very nature, are of little analytical worth in that they are not capable of implying causality and are, in turn, poor predictors of behaviour. They are not actionable.[42] For example, knowing that an individual earns over $50,000 per annum is meaningless and useless as a segmentation variable. Knowing how much an individual earns does not tell us what he or she spends that income on. The fact that a group of individuals fall within the same income category does not mean, by virtue of that fact, that they all possess identical or even similar patterns of consumption and expenditure. Descriptive statistical categories are not capable of inferring individual or group values and patterns of expenditure, and are certainly not capable of inferring the reasons behind those purchase decisions. All descriptive statistics can do is summarize qualities about a data set; they are incapable of anything more. Yet they are often misinterpreted and are often the only type of research conducted by hospitality firms as a basis for segmentation.

The same logic can be applied to the practice of geographic segmentation. All Europeans, or even all Britons or all Germans, are not the same: that is, they are heterogeneous in nature. Since market segmentation is founded upon the concept of within-group homogeneity and between-group heterogeneity, it is not feasible to segment markets solely by place of origin. Rather, it may be more beneficial to segment international markets by benefits sought or purpose of visit. Thus a hotel, as is the case of the Hilton Park Avenue in New York City, may cater primarily to the business traveller, regardless of nationality or geographic origin. If hotel companies are to cope with the complexities and subtleties of segmenting international markets, they need to move away from their current reliance upon descriptive statistics and to move toward the use of inferential statistical techniques as a basis for segmentation.

The future of segmentation in the international hospitality industry lies in the use of multivariate statistical techniques such as multiple regression analysis, multiple discriminant analysis, multivariate analysis of variance, canonical correlation analysis, factor analysis, cluster analysis, multidimensional scaling, and conjoint analysis.[43] Multivariate techniques are capable of analysing the association among three or more variables. The multivariate approach allows the researcher to gain a whole host of potentially more fruitful knowledge than is available from descriptive statistical techniques. The benefits of using multivariate statistics to segment markets is apparent in Marriott's development of the 'Courtyard by Marriott' concept, which is currently running at around 20 per cent above the US national average occupancy rate of 63 per cent.[44]

Despite the proven success of adopting a true market approach to segmentation, many hospitality organizations are guilty of claiming to engage in a strategy of market segmentation when in fact they are practising a strategy of either product segmentation or product differentiation. While related, each of the three above strategies is distinct and should serve a different purpose.

THE PRODUCT SEGMENTATION AND PRODUCT DIFFERENTIATION ISSUES

One of the main reasons for the confusion between the above three marketing strategies is that the marketing literature itself is not clear on the difference between each of the three strategies. For example, a review of sixteen contemporary marketing textbooks reveals considerable confusion about the basic purpose, definition of terms and theory underlying the practice of segmentation and differentiation.[45] Five of the texts[46] describe product differentiation as an alternative to market segmentation, and eleven of the texts[47] describe it as a complement or means of implementing market segmentation.

Market segmentation, as defined earlier, is a state of demand heterogeneity such that the total market demand can be disaggregated into segments with distinct demand functions. Product segmentation is a process whereby the product differentiates for the same market, as in the case of the plethora of brands in the lodging industry. In other words, the market is sought to fit the requirements of the product, not viceversa. Product differentiation is defined as a product offering which is perceived by the consumer to differ from its competition in any physical or non-physical product characteristics including price. The differentiation does not have to be real; it can be perceived. Differentiation may be moot when it occurs within the same product class.[48] This scenario is one which is all too familiar in the lodging industry with the evolution of inter-tier brand segmentation, such as the all-suite segment. Differentiation is being pursued to the extent that it does not clarify customer confusion and create brand awareness and loyalty, but rather only serves to enhance customer confusion. A strategy of differentiation cannot be pursued without a strong market positioning programme.

Positioning occurs after the market has been segmented on appropriate variables: that is, not solely on descriptive variables. It is the process whereby a hospitality organization will inform its target markets about its attributes, both objective and subjective, and attempt to differentiate those attributes from those of competitors in the mind of the target market. There are essentially three components of positioning: (a) the creation of an image; (b) the determination of benefits offered; and (c) the differentiation of those benefits. Many chains have been unsuccessful in their attempt to position multiple brands. The success of a multiple brand strategy depends upon creating, and more importantly maintaining, a clear differentiation in the minds of the consumer.[49] However, many lodging firms have failed to create a strong positioning statement for their multiple brands, in that each brand often does not stand for a unique combination or package of goods and services.[50]

The attempt at branding in the lodging industry is indicative of both the product-orientation of many hospitality organizations and their use of descriptive criteria for segmentation purposes. Rather than segment markets according to behaviourally based variables such as benefits sought, many chains have simply attempted, usually unsuccessfully, to provide a single brand for a single market. One exception to this lack of success is the French chain Accor, which has successfully managed to develop and maintain a strong positioning statement which clearly and effectively differentiates each of its Formule 1, Ibis, Novotel and Sofitel brands. Each of these four brands caters to a distinct market and there is little customer confusion. Conversely, Quality International with its Quality Suites, Quality Inns, Clarion Suites, Clarion Inns, Comfort Suites, Comfort Inns and McSleep Inns is an example of an organization that has not developed a strong positioning statement for each of its brands, and there would appear to be customer confusion concerning the difference (actual or perceived) between each of these seven product-oriented brands. Many of the attempts in the lodging industry to create brand loyalty and maximize brand switching costs have failed owing to customer confusion brought about by a combination of a lack of clear positioning statements and poor segmentation strategies.

One of the driving forces behind the whole concept of branding is the creation of a standard product. The reasoning adopted is that the degree of risk experienced by the consumer in the purchase decision will be reduced if he or she is familiar with the package of services and goods being bought. The potential benefits of standardization are, without doubt, attractive to the hospitality operator, and include reduced costs through economies of scale as well as tighter operating procedures leading to increased control over the provision of the product itself. While standardization has historically been confined to the actual physical provision of the hospitality package, it is now being used, with varying degrees of success, in several functional-level strategies, such as administration, finance and marketing. Only the issue of standardization and international marketing will be discussed here.

THE STANDARDIZATION ISSUE[51]

Should international marketing in the hospitality industry be standardized? Though much has been said and written lately on globalization of marketing (34 studies in the last 25 years), we are nowhere close to any conclusive theory or practice.[52] Unfortunately, the proliferation of research in the area of standardization of international marketing does not extend to the hospitality industry, which, to the best of the author's knowledge, has had no research on the subject of standardization of international marketing.

The term 'standardization of international marketing' refers to a common product, price, distribution and promotion programme on a worldwide basis.[53] A protagonist of standardization in the international arena is Ted Levitt. In a seminal and imaginative piece on the globalization of markets, Levitt argues that:

> The globalization of markets is at hand. With that, the multi-national commercial world nears its end, and so does the multinational corporation . . . Everywhere everything gets more like everything else as the world's preference structure is relentlessly homogenized . . . Different cultural preferences, national tastes and standards, and business institutions are vestiges of the past.[54]

There is little empirical evidence either to support or to refute Levitt's claims, although there is one piece of research[55] which does lean in favour of Levitt's arguments. In three related studies of US companies in the European Community spanning 25 years, it was found that the standardization of international marketing practices is relatively high and growing in some cases. Examining the three areas of product, advertising and branding standardization it was found that: (a) there were significant increases in the standardization of products across all EC countries (see Table 11.3); and (b) there was little increase in the standardization of advertising over the 25-year period, but a significant increase in the standardization of branding (see Table 11.4). In other words, standardization of product, brand and advertising did not necessarily move at the same pace, and it proved more difficult to introduce uniformity in the case of advertising than it was for product and brand.

Table 11.3   *Percentage of goods with very substantial product standardization 1973–1988*

	1973	1978	1983	1988
Consumer non-durables	25%	33%	42%	42%
Consumer durables	33%	83%	38%	38%
Industrial goods	50%	69%	33%	33%

Source: Boddewyn, J.J., Soehl, R. and Picard, J., 'Standardization in international marketing: is Ted Levitt in fact right?', *Business Horizons*, vol. 29, Nov./Dec. 1986, pp. 69–75.

In a comprehensive review of the literature on the standardization of international marketing, Jain[56] concluded that: (a) there are two aspects of standardization, process and programme;[57] (b) across-the-board standardization is inconceivable;[58] (c) the

Table 11.4   *Standardization and adaptation in advertising and branding 1973 and 1983*

	Consumer non-durables		Consumer durables		Industrial goods	
	1973	1983	1973	1983	1973	1983
Advertising	3.9	3.9	4.2	4.8	3.6	3.8
Branding	5.5	4.2	5.0	4.4	3.7	3.5

Note: 7 = total adaptation; 1 = total standardization.
Source: Boddewyn *et al*, op. cit.

decision on standardization is not a dichotomous one between complete standardization and customization; rather, there can be degrees of standardization;[59] (d) a variety of internal and external forces, of which product/industry characteristics are paramount, impinge on the standardization decision; and (e) generally standardization is most feasible in settings where marketing infrastructure is well developed.[60] Using the framework provided by Jain and shown in Figure 11.1, the issue of standardization in the international hospitality industry can be addressed.

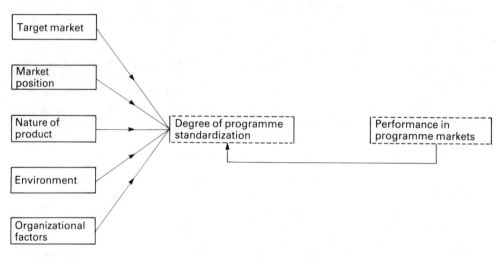

Figure 11.1   *A framework for determining marketing programme standardization.*
Source: Jain, S.C., 'Standardization of international marketing strategy: some research hypotheses', *Journal of Marketing*, vol. 53, Jan. 1989, pp. 70–9.

The standardization framework is concerned only with marketing programme standardization. The latter refers to the various aspects of the marketing mix which can be classified as product design, product positioning, brand name, packaging, price, basic advertising message, creative expression, sales promotion, media allocation, role of sales force, type of retail outlets and customer service.[61] Standardization of one or more parts of the marketing programme is a function of the five factors identified in Figure 11.1.

Target market

It is argued by several authors that standardization is almost a given for countries that are economically similar.[62] If one accepts this assumption, standardization should be rife across the USA, Western Europe and Japanese hospitality industries. This, however, is not the case.

For example, even with the fast-approaching 1992 in Europe whereby the goal is a uniform economic space across twelve European countries where people, goods and services can circulate unhampered by national frontiers, standardization, in the author's opinion, is unlikely to be practised to any significant degree. Despite the economic implications of one unified Europe, from an international marketing perspective there will not be a target market simply classified as 'Europeans'. The culture, traditions and history of the countries that make up the EC are far too diverse and unique ever to target members of those countries as one homogeneous mass.

This does not mean, however, that customers from different countries cannot be targeted with identical marketing strategies. The latter is possible if hospitality corporation identify segments across countries that are similar and represent a homogeneous market. Several scholars have explicitly endorsed this type of approach.[63] Indeed, Levitt states:

> The multinational corporation operates in a number of countries, and adjusts its products and practices in each at high relative costs . . . [companies should] know that success in a world of homogenized demand requires a search for sales opportunities in similar segments across the globe in order to achieve the economies of scale necessary to compete. Such a segment in one country is seldom unique – it has close cousins everywhere precisely because technology has homogenized the globe.[64]

It will still be possible for hospitality companies to adopt a degree of standardization if they are successful in developing and implementing the above inter-market segment concept. Attempts to do this have historically been confined to the business traveller.

Market conditions

There are three market conditions that influence the standardization decision in foreign markets. These are: (a) cultural differences;[65] (b) economic differences;[66] and (c) differences in customer perceptions.[67]

The globe is, and will remain, a culturally diverse place. Even within continents such as North America or Europe there remain as many cultures as there are states or countries. In Europe, for example, hospitality marketers would be foolish not to take different cultural backgrounds into account in the formulation and implementation of their marketing strategies, despite the current popularity of referring to Europe as if it were going to be one single, uniform entity. Lewis and Chambers state:

> Values that are important to one culture may mean little to another. These conflicts become more intense in an industry that sells very personal services to a very diversified clientele. Different cultures reflect different beliefs, attitudes, motivations, moralities, perceptions, and rituals. Although preconceived notions of what the hotel guest wants may be discrepant with the guest's own notions in

any country, they can result in disaster when marketing to different cultures. It thus goes without saying that cultural differences have a tremendous impact upon marketing mix decisions in international operations. Ignoring this impact has often resulted in expensive consequences for hotels operating in arenas outside their corporate homeland.[68]

Economic differences also need to be formulated into hospitality organizations marketing strategies. Each individual country will have its own unique economic characteristics that must be adapted and that defy standardization. For example, hotels in Singapore had to implement fiercer marketing strategies aimed at capturing travellers from Indonesia, Thailand and the Philippines when the respective governments of these countries effectively reduced the number of natives leaving by creating an expensive exit tax. The economic environment is in a constant state of flux and must be constantly monitored and adapted to; it is not uniform across countries.

Finally, differences in customer perceptions of the product also have implications for attempts to standardize international marketing strategies. In some parts of Indonesia black dog is considered a delicacy, yet imagine the reaction of customers if it were placed on the menu of an Indonesian restaurant operating in, say, Paris or London. In England 'lunch' (called 'dinner' by the English) is traditionally the main meal of the day, with 'tea' (called 'dinner' by everybody but the English) being more like an American 'lunch' in both form and content. Operators need to be aware of such traditions and implement marketing strategies accordingly.

Nature of the product

It is argued here that the degree of standardization of international marketing in the global hospitality industry is partly a function of the nature of the product. On a continuum of organic to mechanistic hospitality products, standardization of the international marketing strategy will be highest for those products at the mechanistic end of the continuum. Figure 11.2 offers examples of hospitality firms at each end of the continuum. Products offered by such companies as McDonald's, Motel 6, Formule

Figure 11.2   *The nature of the hospitality product and standardization.*
Source: Adapted from Nailon, P., 'Theory and art in hospitality management', *International Journal of Hospitality Management*, vol. 1, no. 3, 1982, pp. 135–43.

1 and Little Chef Lodges are primarily utilitarian in nature and more goods orientated than service oriented. It is thus easier to standardize the marketing strategy across countries. At the other end of the continuum are products offered by such organizations as THF with its Viscount chain, Hyatt and the Ritz-Carlton chain. These products are primarily hedonistic in nature and more service than goods oriented. This in turn means that standardization of marketing strategy is difficult to achieve due to the uniqueness of each service encounter.

Environment

The environment in which global marketing decisions are made is far more complex than the environment in which domestic marketing decisions are made. Differences in environment are undoubtedly an important concern affecting the feasibility of standardization.[69]

The hospitality environment can be viewed on two levels. First there is the general environment, which consists of the economic environment, the socio-cultural environment, the political environment, the technological environment and the ecological environment. Second there is the specific environment, which consists of the six organizational functions of marketing, finance, administration, human resources, R&D and operations. Several studies have contributed to our understanding of the hospitality environment and its unique characteristics.[70]

Hospitality environments differ in terms of three environmental states: (a) environmental variability, which is a function of the frequency of change in relevant commercial activities, the degree of difference involved at each change and the degree of irregularity in the overall pattern of change; (b) environmental complexity, which is defined as the heterogeneity and range of environmental activities; and (c) environmental illiberality, which is defined as the degree of threat from external factors which face organizational decision-makers in the achievement of their goals. Evidence from the aforementioned studies indicates that the hospitality environment is generally uncertain, unstable and highly volatile.

Given the diverse and uncertain nature of the hospitality environment both among and between countries, it would appear that there is little room for standardization. Where standardization has been attempted it has often led to confusion. For example, Lewis and Chambers recount several instances where standardization did not work but only led to confusion. An amusing example of an attempt at advertising standardization and its subsequent confusion is offered by these authors:

> In 1986 Ramada ran an advertising campaign in the United States headed 'What makes Madden mad' or 'What makes Madden glad'. John Madden is an American football figure, supposedly well known to all Americans, with a reputation for fierceness. Madden was featured in close-up describing what he liked and didn't like when staying in hotels. These things of course were properly taken care of by Ramada . . .
> However, when Madden showed up on the cover of Ramada's world wide directory in numerous lobby and front desk posters in European and Middle East hotels, you can be sure that even fewer people knew who he was. In fact, the following conversation was overheard at a Ramada front desk in Europe: 'What's that?' 'John Madden.' 'Who's John Madden?' 'A football coach.' 'What's football?'[71]

More operationally oriented examples of the problems created by standardization include the experience of the Holiday Inn, Marble Arch in London, which catered primarily to Arabs. After some confusion, seats were removed from the lobby area since the Middle Eastern clientele preferred to conduct business sitting cross-legged on the floor. The management also had to provide a sign in each room indicating the direction of Mecca in order that their customers could pray five times a day.

The rise in the demand for local hospitality discussed in the introduction indicates a dramatic increase in the growth of domestic travel by natives in many countries. This trend would suggests that local customs and traditions are beginning to play a more significant role in both the design and the implementation of marketing strategies by international hospitality firms. The situation that existed historically in the 1970s and early 1980s, whereby international hotel companies tended to target international travellers from their originating country, as in the case of Inter-Continental and Hilton International, is no longer a feasible strategy given the burst in domestic tourism in most countries. Catering to the local tourist market with its unique demands and patterns of consumption almost negates the use of standardized international marketing strategies. Mass marketing is a vestige of the past. Tomorrow's hospitality customer will need to be wooed through what is coming to be termed 'micro marketing' or 'niche marketing'.

There are six broad elements to micro marketing. First, know your customer. Hospitality firms will need to make use of existing high-tech techniques to find out who their customers are and are not. Second, customization is essential. Tailor the product to meet individual needs and tastes, or at least ensure that provision is equipped with adequate flexibility to be adapted to multiple market segments. Third, make use of targeted and new media. Hospitality companies aiming for micro markets should advertise using such media as cable TV and in magazines that reach specific audiences. Fourth, use of non-media is required. The most popular non-media advertising technique is through the sponsoring of sports events. We have yet to see major involvement by hospitality organizations in such events, despite their proven success with such giants as Procter & Gamble and Kraft. Fifth, reach customers on-site through the use of in-house promotions. Finally, work with middlemen such as travel agencies and tour operators. The hospitality industry is starting to move in this direction. An example, albeit somewhat ambitious, was Robert Maxwell's attempt to integrate hotel, airline and tour operator reservation systems throughout Europe with his 'UltraSwitch' concept.

Organizational factors

While the preceding four sections were primarily concerned with the external factors affecting standardization, this fifth section is concerned with those factors that are internal to the organization and affect the standardization issue. Three organizational factors influence the standardization issue.[72] These are corporate orientation, the headquarters–subsidiary relationship, and the delegation of authority.

The corporate orientation of hospitality firms has a significant influence on the standardization issue. In general it is possible to identify among hospitality organizations three primary orientations toward international operations: ethnocentric (home country oriented), polycentric (host country oriented) or geocentric (world oriented).[73] It is proposed that the more ethnocentric or geocentric the orientation, the greater the possibility for standardization of international marketing strategies.

The expansion of Hilton International and Sheraton into foreign markets was clearly dominated by an ethnocentric orientation, while the entry of Movenpick hotels into the Middle East will be characterized by a more polycentric orientation. Few hospitality firms, because of both the nature of the product itself and diverse environmental conditions, are allowed the luxury of adopting a truly geocentric corporate orientation.

The second organizational factor, the headquarters–subsidiary relationship and its implications for standardization, is very real in the hospitality industry. Because much international expansion in the industry is through franchising (around 20 per cent of all international expansion in 1982), there tends to be more loss of control over subsidiary activities and operations than would be the case with, say, foreign direct investment or management contracts. This lack of control over subsidiary operations and the need for even the most standardized hospitality organizations such as McDonalds and Burger King to adapt to the needs of local markets (e.g. McDonalds serves tea in England and wine in France) means that true standardization of the international marketing function is not only infeasible but inconceivable.

The final organizational factor affecting standardization is the extent to which decision-making authority is delegated to the foreign subsidiaries.[74] In general, it is posited that the greater the degree of decentralization of authority in hospitality organizations, the less favourable the conditions for the standardization of international marketing strategies. The last part of the 1980s saw the corporate level of hospitality organizations undergo often dramatic staff cuts and become leaner and meaner with decentralization and regionalization becoming the main modes of operation. This trend of decentralization does not favour standardization.

THE PRICING ISSUE

The pricing of international hospitality services is an exceedingly complex decision and one which has not yet been mastered by many corporations. One of the main factors contributing to the complexity of the international pricing decision is fluctuations in the exchange rate. An example of the types of problem faced by international hospitality organizations in their attempts to formulate and implement pricing decisions is found in the case of Mexico:

> Consider Mexico: Not long ago there were 50 pesos to the dollar. A hotel room at $80 to an American was 4,000 pesos to a Mexican. When, almost overnight, the pesos devalued to 150 to the dollar, the American price was still $80, but the Mexican price was now 12,000 pesos. In spring 1988, there were about 2,400 pesos to the dollar but, during the same periods, the Mexican's or Mexican company's earnings did not triple or increase 48-fold. Thus, Mexicans were shut out of their own market as well as the American market, where it took many more pesos to buy a hotel room. Americans, of course, flocked across the border to take advantage of the devalued pesos. Balancing exchange is a full-time occupation for any company that operates internationally.[75]

The pricing issue is a major problem for international operators in that they constantly have to monitor the economic conditions (inflation rates, devaluations, etc.) of the countries from which they draw business and in which they operate. The Mexican example described above had significant negative effects on the bottom line of American corporations operating in Mexico owing to the fact that, rather than pay an American travel agent $80 for a hotel room in Mexico, the American tourist could simply fly down to Mexico and buy the same room for only $40.

The pricing technique itself will, of course, have major implications in terms of how well the hospitality organization can adapt to changing environmental and economic conditions. Pricing techniques can be classified into one of four categories: (a) cost pricing techniques (cost-plus pricing, cost percentage or mark-up pricing, break-even pricing and contribution pricing); (b) competitive pricing techniques; (c) market demand pricing techniques; and (d) customer pricing techniques (price/value pricing, expectation pricing and psychological pricing).[76]

Unfortunately, the most popular form of pricing in the international hospitality industry tends to be cost oriented and myopic in nature. While relatively simple to follow, cost pricing techniques are not sophisticated or flexible enough to cater to the volatility of the international hospitality environment. Cost pricing techniques, by definition, set price levels independent of the broader hospitality environment. Such a luxury cannot be afforded in today's complex and ever-changing international economic environment.

Discounting

Much has been written on the subject of discounting in the hospitality industry.[77] Discounting has placed the hospitality industry in the midst of what can only be termed a profitless prosperity syndrome. In the USA discounting is rife in all segments of the industry. For example, resort locations averaged 28.1 per cent and 23.5 per cent discounts on advertised room rates in 1984 and 1985 respectively; centre city and airport properties respectively rented rooms at 20 per cent and 28 per cent below stated room rates in 1984, and 23 per cent and 24 per cent below stated rack rates in 1985. Discount methods include discount clubs for frequent travellers, corporate room sales, volume discounts, gimmicks involving putting more into a hotel package than just a room, use of outside agents, 'freebies' and upgraded rooms.[78]

Contrary to popular belief, a 10 per cent decrease in price is not made up for by a 10 per cent increase in volume. The equivalent volume increase required (equivalent volume = existing volume multiplied by existing contribution divided by discounted contribution) to make up for a 10 per cent decrease in price is 15 per cent. This is a basic cost truism. Discounting, which in the author's view has been primarily brought about by a lack of comprehensive and market-oriented segmentation and different-iation strategies, can only by detrimental to the industry as a whole in the long run. Discounting is no long-term solution to increasing business.

The long-term solution to increasing business lies in the differentiation of hospitality products along attributes other than price. Only by increasing the price/value perception of their products will hospitality operators overcome the problems faced in a market of oversupply and tap potentially lucrative market segments.

Yield management

This section on pricing would not be complete without mentioning what has been hailed one of the most revolutionary innovations to impact on the lodging industry.[79] That innovation is yield management. Yield management is defined as:

essentially an old concept, modified, enhanced, and integrated with sophisticated artificial intelligence knowledge acquired strategies. It focuses on revenue optimization, utilizing selling conditions manipulations across different market segments. It is simply a new generation tool used to enhance the present system's analytical methods for market condition analysis, and profit equation monitoring abilities.[80]

Simply stated, the yield management technique efficiently and speedily matches supply with demand by fluctuating price levels anything up to 80,000 times in a single day.[81] If, for example, demand is slack and there exists an oversupply of rooms for a given period, the yield management system will offer discounted room rates in an attempt to boost demand. Undoubtedly, the system has the potential to make the pricing decision far more market oriented than the largely cost-oriented techniques that are currently practised in the industry. On an international level, the large corporations will benefit tremendously because they already have massive reservation systems in operation. The smaller independent operations lack the existing technology to implement and take advantage of the yield management process. However, it is predicted that these smaller operators will eventually also be able to take advantage of the technique by joining forces in various forms of strategic alliance, such as consortia, representative firms and affiliations.

THE DISTRIBUTION ISSUE

There is a dearth of research on the subject of channels of distribution in services industries in general.[82] The hospitality industry is no exception to this paucity of research.

Distribution can be defined simply as the means through which the organization gets the product to the customer. The distribution channel in the hospitality industry can be classified into two main parts. First, there is the actual production of the product through some predetermined method (e.g. franchising, management contract or direct equity involvement). Second there is the distribution of the product by channel intermediaries (e.g. tour operators, consortia, reservation networks, incentive houses, affiliations and travel agents). The distinction between the two lies in the fact that the former both produces and distributes the product (a direct channel of distribution), usually simultaneously, while the latter only distributes the product (an indirect channel of distribution).

Direct channels of distribution in the hospitality industry are generally confined to one of four modes: (a) equity involvement (e.g. the ownership of the unit itself); (b)

Table 11.5 *Rooms of USA transnational hotels abroad by form of involvement 1982*

Form of involvement	Percentage
Management contracts	44.2
Leasing	20.0
Franchising	19.7
Direct equity involvement	16.3
Total	100.0

Table 11.6   *International restaurant franchising in 1984: location and number of establishments*

	Firms	Total	Canada	Mexico	Carib.	Europe		Australia	Asia		Other USA	South Africa	New Zealand	Central America
						UK	Other		Japan	Other				
Chicken	9	1,757	7	68	120	375	53	235	504	157	15	164	45	14
Hamburgers, franks and roast beef	16	3,117	1,233	0	100	196	428	205	667	183	47	0	19	39
Pizza	14	539	100	31	48	3	33	134	63	74	0	8	24	21
Mexican	7	90	64	0	20	0	0	2	0	2	1	0	0	1
Seafood	3	11	6	0	0	0	0	0	0	5	0	0	0	0
Pancakes, waffles	2	12	3	0	0	0	0	0	8	1	0	0	0	0
Steak, full menu	14	461	175	20	2	2	0	5	248	9	0	0	0	0
Sandwich, other	2	3	3	0	0	0	0	0	0	0	0	0	0	0
Total	67	5,990	1,591	119	290	576	514	581	1,490	431	63	172	88	75

Source: US Department of Commerce, *Franchising in the Economy 1984–1986*, US Government Printing Office, Washington DC, 1986.

leasing arrangements; (c) franchising; and (d) management contracts. Table 11.5 shows that in 1982 the most popular of these four modes of distribution for USA transnational hotels abroad was management contracts, followed by leasing, franchising and finally direct equity involvement. Since 1982 the picture has undoubtedly changed somewhat with franchising taking the lead. For example, in 1984, 67 restaurant franchisors operated 5,990 units in foreign countries (see Table 11.6), compared to only 64 restaurant franchisors and 5,516 units a year earlier. Sales of franchised restaurants of all types reached almost $48 billion in 1985, up about 11 per cent on a year earlier, and rose by another 12 per cent to $54 billion in 1986. The story is similar in the international lodging industry. Hotel and motel franchisors in 1985 represented 7,639 establishments, with receipts estimated at $14.3 billion. These rose by over 9 per cent in 1986, reaching $15.5 billion (see Table 11.7).[83]

The nature of the direct channel of distribution is to some degree a function of the risk structure of the host country in which the hotel is being operated. For example, Hilton International takes an equity position in a few limited cases, where there is political and economic stability and no problem with repatriating earnings. The nature of the channel of distribution chosen has been shown to be a risk-minimizing strategy on the part of the organization.[84] This is one of the reasons for the predominance of non-equity involvement by lodging corporations in less developed countries where unsystematic risk is often high.[85]

Table 11.7   *Franchised hotels, motels and campgrounds*

Item	1984	1985	1986	Percentage changes	
				1984–1985	1985–1986
Total number of establishments	6,984	7,639	8,393	9.4	9.9
Company owned	1,025	1,081	1,187	5.5	9.8
Franchisee owned	5,959	6,558	7,206	10.1	9.9
Total sales of products and services	13,159,020	14,261,153	15,511,833	8.4	8.8
Company owned	4,061,835	4,361,525	4,675,609	7.4	7.2
Franchisee owned	9,097,185	9,899,628	10,836,224	8.8	9.5

Source: US Department of Commerce, op. cit.

Indirect channels of distribution in the international hospitality industry are beginning to play an increasingly important role. The example of Sol Hotels (Spain), which rely on wholesalers for 95 per cent of their room sales in their resort properties, illustrates this point.[86] Perhaps the single most noticeable growth area in indirect channels of distribution is consortia. A consortium is usually, but not always, a group of independent hotels which join together to take advantage of economies of scale, usually marketing or purchasing. Examples are the Preferred Hotel Group and Best Western.

Affiliations have proven to be a popular indirect method of distribution for companies entering, or trying to capture customers from, a market with which they are not overly familiar. For example, Radisson Hotels, which has no hotels in Europe, affiliates with Movenpick Hotels International of Switzerland and SAS International Hotels of Oslo in an attempt to capture the customers of these respective groups when they travel to the USA.

Representative firms are also classified as indirect channels of distribution. They market a hotel to a customer base for a fee and are often hired to act as sales organizations for independent properties which do not have their own sales or reservation networks. An example would be Utell International, which represents 3,500 properties in 133 countries, and maintains 30 worldwide sales offices.[87]

Travel agents and tour operators act as indirect channels of distribution, although they are often confused with each other. They are not synonymous. A travel agent is an intermediary in a channel of distribution who makes reservations for a variety of hospitality needs and is compensated in the form of a commission. A tour operator, on the other hand, actually takes possession of the hotel inventory to sell it to the market. Travel agents are without doubt the most prominent form of indirect distribution in the hospitality industry. For example, in the USA alone there are currently over 200,000 individual travel agents.

Several discernible trends are likely to shape the future of indirect channels of distribution in the hospitality industry. The first is increasing horizontal economic concentration. By this is meant the increasingly large percentage of total hotel rooms that are coming to be owned by an increasingly small percentage of hotel operators. A second trend is increasing vertical economic concentration. This refers to the fact that many previously unconnected entities such as hotels and travel agents or hotels and airlines are joining forces to reap the benefits of large-scale, fully integrated, synergistic systems. Examples of this type of integration are TWA–Hilton International, American–Americana, Pan American–Intercontinental, and United–Western International. A third trend is increasing competition among the separate vertical marketing systems. There will be fiercer competition between 'one-stop' marketing systems. A 'one-stop' marketing system is simply a single location where a customer can buy everything, ranging from a hotel room to airline seats, to car rental, to travel insurance, to restaurant reservations.[88]

SUMMARY

International marketing is a sophisticated, complex and resource-consuming practice. With international expansion forming a substantial part of the strategic agendas of today's hospitality corporations, international marketing is an issue that has to be mastered at both a conceptual and a practical level.

This chapter, by no means exhaustive, has attempted to cover several issues that should be taken in account by hospitality corporations when they operate at an international level. Attention was directed toward the issues of market segmentation, product segmentation, product differentiation, standardization, pricing and distribution. Current limitations within each of these respective areas were discussed and recommendations made for the formulation, implementation and content of future international marketing strategies.

NOTES

1. Crawford-Welch, S., 'The internationalization of the US hospitality industry', unpublished monograph, Department of Hotel, Restaurant and Institutional Management, Virginia Polytechnic Institute and State University, Blacksburg, Va, 1988.
2. Slattery, P.V.O., in *Hotels*, Jan. 1990, p. 47.
3. Ibid.
4. Anon. '1990 industry forecast', *Hotels*, Jan. 1990, pp. 45–55.
5. Crawford-Welch, op. cit.
6. Slattery, P.V.O., 'International hospitality review', Kleinwort Benson Research, Kleinwort Benson Securities Limited/Paterson Printing Limited, Tunbridge Wells, 1988.
7. Kotler, P.K. and Levy, S.J., 'Broadening the concept of marketing', *Journal of Marketing*, Jan. 1969, pp. 10–15.
8. Levitt, T., 'Marketing myopia', *Harvard Business Review*, Jul./Aug. 1960, pp. 24–47.
9. Kotler, P.K., 'A generic concept of marketing', *Journal of Marketing*, vol. 36, Apr. 1972, pp. 46–54.
10. American Marketing Association, Board of Directors, 1985.
11. Lewis, R.C. and Chambers, R.E. *Marketing Leadership in Hospitality: Foundations and Practices*, Van Nostrand Reinhold, New York, 1989. Several of the industry examples included in this chapter draw heavily from this work, pp. 606–36.
12. Cateora, P.R., *International Marketing*, Irwin, Homewood, Ill., 1987, p. 8.
13. See, for example, Levitt, T., 'Marketing myopia 1975: retrospective commentary', *Harvard Business Review*, Sep./Oct. 1975, pp. 28–44.
14. See, for example, Sasser, E., Olsen, M. and Wyckoff, D.E., *Management of Service Operations*, Macmillan, New York, 1978.
15. See, for example, Mill, R.C., 'Upping the organization: enhancing employee performance through an improved work climate', *Cornell HRA Quarterly*, Feb. 1986, pp. 30–7.
16. Mills, P.K. and Moberg, D.J., 'Perspectives on the technology of service organizations', *Academy of Management Review*, vol. 7, no. 3, 1982, pp. 467–78; Hart, C.W., Spizizen, G. and Wyckoff, D.D., 'Scale economies and the experience curve: is bigger better for restaurant companies?', *Cornell HRA Quarterly*, May 1984, pp. 91–103; Tse, E.C.Y., 'An exploratory study of the impact of strategy and structure on the organizational performance in restaurant firms', unpublished doctoral dissertation, Department of Hotel, Restaurant and Institutional Management, Virginia Polytechnic Institute and State University, Blacksburg, Va, 1988.
17. Berry, L.L., 'Service marketing is different', *Business*, May/June 1980, pp. 24–9.
18. Chase, R.B., 'Where does the customer fit in a service operation?', *Harvard Business Review*, Nov./Dec. 1978, pp. 137–42; Mills, P.K., *Managing Service Industries: Organizational Practices in a Postindustrial Economy*, Ballinger, Cambridge, Mass., 1986; Albrecht, R. and Zemke, R., *Service America!*, Dow Jones–Irwin, Homewood, Ill., 1986.
19. Lewis and Chambers, op. cit.
20. Ibid.; Lewis, R.C., 'Benefit segmentation for restaurant advertising that works', *Cornell HRA Quarterly*, Nov. 1980, pp. 6–12; Lewis, R.C., 'The basis of hotel

selection', *Cornell HRA Quarterly*, May 1984, pp. 54–70; Lewis, R.C., 'Predicting hotel choice: the factors underlying perception', *Cornell HRA Quarterly*, Feb. 1985, pp. 82–96; Mazanec, J.A., 'How to detect travel market segments: a clustering approach', *Journal of Travel Research*, Summer 1984, pp. 17–21; Weaver, P.A. and McCleary, K.W., 'A market segmentation study to determine the appropriate ad/model format for travel advertising', *Journal of Travel Research*, vol. 12, May 1984, pp. 196–213; Witham, G., 'Hotel companies aim for multiple markets', *Cornell HRA Quarterly*, Nov. 1985, pp. 39–51; Mooney, S. and Penn, J.M., 'Market segmentation in hotels: a move up-market with the club concept', *International Journal of Hospitality Management*, vol. 4, no. 2, 1985, pp. 63–5; Swinyard, W.R. and Struman, K.D., 'Market segmentation: finding the heart of your restaurant's market', *Cornell HRA Quarterly*, May 1986, pp. 89–96; Pizam, A. and Calantone, R., 'Beyond psychographics: values as determinants of tourist behavior', *International Journal of Hospitality Management*, vol. 6, no. 3, 1987, pp. 203–10; Lepsito, L.R. and McCleary, K.W., 'The effects of multiple measures of age in segmenting hotel markets', *Hospitality Education and Research Journal*, vol. 12, no. 2, pp. 91–9; Snepenger, D.J., 'Segmenting the vacation market by novelty seeking role', *Journal of Travel Research*, Fall 1987, pp. 8–14.

21. Yesawich, P.C., 'A market-based approach to forecasting', *Cornell HRA Quarterly*, Nov. 1984, pp. 47–53; Wind, J., Green, P.E., Shiftle, D. and Scarbrough, M., 'Courtyard by Marriott: designing a hotel facility with consumer-based marketing models', *Interfaces*, vol. 19, no. 1, 1989, pp. 25–47; Laventhal & Horwath, *Lodging Industry Report*, Philadelphia, 1987; Laventhal & Horwath, *Lodging Industry Report*, Philadelphia, 1988.

22. Haley, R.I., 'Benefit segmentation: a decision oriented research tool', *Journal of Marketing*, vol.32, Jul. 1968, pp. 30–35; Johnson, R.M., 'Market segmentation: a strategic management tool', *Journal of Marketing Research*, vol. 8, Feb. 1971, pp. 13–18; Wind, Y., 'Issues and advances in segmentation research', *Journal of Marketing Research*, vol. 15, Aug. 1978, pp. 317–37; Winter, F.W., 'Market segmentation: a tactical approach', *Business Horizons*, Jan./Feb. 1984, pp. 57–63.

23. Green, P.E., 'A new approach to market segmentation', *Business Horizons*, vol. 20, Feb. 1977, pp. 61–3; Wind, op. cit.; Tynan, A.C. and Drayton, J., 'Market segmentation', *Journal of Marketing Management*, vol. 2, no. 3, 1987, pp. 301–35.

24. For further discussion of componential segmentation, see Green, op. cit.; Carroll, J.D. and Carmone, F.J., 'Superordinate factorial designs in the analysis of consumer judgements', Working Paper, University of Pennsylvania, 1975; Green, P.E. and Carmone, F.J., 'Segment congruence analysis: a method for analyzing association among alternative bases for market segmentation', *Journal of Marketing Research*, vol. 3, Mar. 1977, pp. 217–22.

25. Blattenberg, R.C. and Sen, S.K., 'Market segmentation using models of multidimensional purchasing behavior', *Journal of Marketing*, vol. 38, Oct. 1974, pp. 17–28; Grensch, D.H., 'Image measurement segmentation', *Journal of Marketing Research*, vol. 15, Aug. 1978, pp. 384–94.

26. Philips, L.W. and Sternthal, B., 'Age differences in information processing: a perspective on the aged consumer', *Journal of Marketing Research*, vol. 14, no. 4, 1977, pp. 444–57.

27. Dickens, J. and Chappell, B., 'Food for Freud? A study of the sexual polarization of food and food products', *Journal of the Market Research Society*, vol. 19, no. 2, 1977, pp. 76–92.
28. Allt, B., 'Money or class: new lights on household spending', *Advertising Quarterly*, vol. 44, Summer 1975, pp. 6–9.
29. Chisnall, B., *Marketing: A Behavioral Analysis* (2nd edn), McGraw-Hill, Maidenhead, 1985.
30. Packard, V., *The Status Seekers*, Penguin, Harmondsworth, 1969.
31. Lansing, J.B. and Kish, L., 'Family life cycle as an independent variable', *American Sociological Review*, vol. 22, no. 5, 1957, pp. 512–9.
32. Reynolds, F.D, and Wells, W.D., *Consumer Behavior*, McGraw-Hill, New York, 1977.
33. Twedt, D.W., 'How important to marketing strategy is the heavy user?', *Journal of Marketing*, vol. 28, no. 1, 1964, pp. 71–2.
34. Bass, F.M., Tigert, D.J. and Lonsdale, R.T., 'Market segmentation: group versus individual behaviour', *Journal of Marketing Research*, vol. 5, no. 3, 1968, pp. 264–70.
35. Dickson, P.R., 'Person-situation: segmentation's missing link', *Journal of Marketing*, vol. 46, no. 4, 1982, pp. 56–64.
36. Wells, W.D., 'Psychographics: a critical review', *Journal of Marketing Research*, vol. 12, no. 2, 1975, pp. 196–213.
37. Ajzen, I. and Fishbein, M., 'Attitudinal and normative variables as predictors of specific behavior', *Journal of Personality and Social Psychology*, vol. 21, no. 1, 1973, pp. 41–57.
38. Ziff, R., 'Closing the consumer–advertising gap through psychographic', *Combined Proceedings: Marketing Education and the Real World, and Dynamic Marketing in a Changing World*, American Marketing Association, Chicago, Ill., 1973, pp. 457–61.
39. Haire, M., 'Projective techniques in marketing research', *Journal of Marketing*, vol. 14, no. 5, 1950, pp. 649–56.
40. Olsen, M.D., Damonte, T. and Jackson, G.A., 'Segmentation in the lodging industry: is it doomed to failure?', *American Hotel and Motel Association Quarterly Newsletter*, Sep. 1989.
41. Lewis and Chambers, op. cit.
42. Winter, op. cit.
43. For a complete discussion of these statistical concepts and their applications to segmentation in the hospitality industry see Lewis, 'The basis of hotel selection', op. cit.; Lewis, 'Predicting hotel choice', op. cit.
44. For a detailed discussion of the statistical techniques used by the Marriott Corporation in the developments of its Courtyard concept, see Wind *et al.*, 'Courtyard by Marriott', op. cit.
45. Dickson, P.R. and Ginter, J.L., 'Market segmentation, product differentiation and marketing strategy', *Journal of Marketing*, vol. 51, Apr. 1987, pp. 1–10.
46. Evans, J.R. and Berman, B., *Marketing*, Macmillan, New York, 1982; Mandell, M.I. and Rosenberg, L.J., *Marketing*, Prentice-Hall, Englewood Cliffs, NJ, 1981; Neidell, L.A., *Strategic Marketing Management: An Integrated Approach*, Penn Well Books, Tulsa, Okla., 1983; Pride, W.M. and Ferrell, O.C., *Marketing*, Houghton Mifflin, Boston, Mass., 1985; Stanton, W.J., *Fundamentals of Marketing*, McGraw-Hill, New York, 1981.

47. Abell, D.F. and Hammond, J.S., *Strategic Marketing Planning*, Prentice-Hall, Englewood Cliffs, NJ, 1979; Buell, V.P., *Marketing Management: A Strategic Planning Approach*, McGraw-Hill, New York, 1984; Busch, P.S. and Houston, M.J., *Marketing: Strategic Foundations*, Irwin, Homewood, Ill., 1985; Cravens, D.W., *Strategic Marketing*, Irwin, Homewood, Ill., 1982; Dalrymple, D.J. and Parsons, L.J., *Marketing Management*, John Wiley, New York, 1983; DeLozier, M.W. and Woodside, A., *Marketing Management: Strategies and Cases*, Merrill, Columbus, Ohio, 1978; Enis, B.J., *Marketing Principles*, Goodyear, Santa Monica, Calif., 1981; Guiltinan, J.P. and Paul, G.W., *Marketing Management: Strategies and Programs*, McGraw-Hill, New York, 1985; Hughes, G.D., *Marketing Management: A Planning Approach*, Addison-Wesley, Reading, Mass., 1978; Kotler, P.K., *Marketing Management: A Planning Approach*, Prentice-Hall, Englewood Cliffs, NJ, 1984; Reibstein, D.J., *Marketing: Concepts, Strategies, and Decisions*, Prentice-Hall, Englewood Cliffs, NJ, 1985.
48. Lewis and Chambers, op. cit.
49. Yesawich, op. cit.
50. Withiam, op. cit.
51. This section draws heavily on the work of Jain, S.C., 'Standardization of international marketing strategy: some research hypotheses', *Journal of Marketing*, vol. 53, Jan. 1989, pp. 70–9.
52. Ibid.
53. Ibid.
54. Levitt, T., 'The globalization of markets', *Harvard Business Review*, May/June. 1983, pp. 92, 93, 96.
55. Boddewyn, J.J., Soehl, R. and Picard, J., 'Standardization in international marketing: is Ted Levitt in fact right?', *Business Horizons*, Nov./Dec. 1986, pp. 69–75.
56. Jain, op. cit.
57. See, for example, Sorenson, R.Z. and Wiechmann, U.E., 'How multinationals view marketing standardization', *Harvard Business Review*, May/Jun. 1975, p. 38.
58. See, for example, Killough, J., 'Improved payoffs from transnational advertising', *Harvard Business Review*, Jul./Aug. 1978, pp. 102–10.
59. See, for example, Quelch, J.A. and Hoff, E.J., 'Customizing global marketing', *Harvard Business Review*, May/Jun. 1986, pp. 59–68.
60. See, for example, Peebles, D.M., Jr, Ryans, J.K. and Vernon, I.R., 'A new perspective on advertising standardization', *European Journal of Marketing*, vol. 11, no. 8, 1977, pp. 569–76.
61. Quelch, op. cit.; Sorenson and Wiechmann, op. cit.; Wind, P.E. and Douglas, S.P., 'The myth of globalization', *Journal of Consumer Marketing*, vol.3, Spring 1986, pp. 23–6.
62. Elinder, E., 'How international can advertising be?', *International Advertiser*, Dec. 1961, pp. 12–16; Fatt, A.C., 'A multinational approach to international advertising', *International Advertiser*, Sep. 1964, pp. 17–20; Roostal, I., 'Standardization of advertising for Western Europe', *Journal of Marketing*, vol. 27, Oct. 1963, pp. 15–20; Ohmae, K., *Triad Power: The Coming Shape of Global Competition*, New Free Press, New York, 1985.
63. Kale, S.H. and Sudharshan, D., 'A strategic approach to international segmentation', *International Marketing Review*, vol. 4, Summer 1987, pp. 61–70; Levitt, op. cit; Sheth, J.N., 'Global markets or global competition?', *Journal of*

Consumer Marketing, vol. 3, Spring 1986, pp. 9–11; Simmonds, K., 'Global strategy: achieving the concentric ideal', *International Marketing Review*, vol. 2, Spring 1985, pp. 8–17.

64. Levitt, op. cit., pp. 92, 94.
65. Arndt, J. and Helgesen, T., 'Marketing and productivity: conceptual and measurement issues', in *Educators' Conference Proceedings*, Series 47, American Marketing Association, Chicago, Ill., 1981, pp. 81–4; Hall, E.T., *The Silent Language*, Garden City, New York, Doubleday, 1959; Lee, J.A., 'Cultural analysis in overseas operations', *Harvard Business Review*, Mar./Apr. 1966, pp. 108–16; Ricks, D.A., *Big Business Blunders: Mistakes in Multinational Marketing*, Dow Jones–Irwin, Homewood, Ill., 1983; Ricks, D.A., 'How to avoid business blunders abroad', in Jain, S.C. and Tucker, L.R. (eds), *International Marketing: Managerial Perspectives*, Kent Publishing Co., Boston, Mass., 1986; Terpstra, V. and David, K., *The Cultural Environment of International Business*, (2nd edn), South-Western Publishing Co., Cincinnati, Ohio, 1985.
66. Douglas, S.P., Craig, S.C. and Keegan, W.J., 'Approaches to assessing international marketing opportunities for small and medium sized companies', in Jain, S.C. and Tucker, L.R. (eds), *International Marketing: Managerial Perspectives*, Kent Publishing Co., Boston, Mass., 1986; Henzler, H., 'Shaping an international investment strategy', *McKinsey Quarterly*, Spring 1981, pp. 69–81; Luqmani, M., Quraeshi, Z.A. and Delene, L., 'Marketing in Islamic countries: a viewpoint', *MSU Business Topics*, vol. 28, Summer 1980, pp. 16–26; Terpstra, V., 'Critical mass and international marketing strategy', in Jain, S. C. and Tucker, L. R. (eds), *International Marketing: Managerial Perspectives*, Kent Publishing Co., Boston, Mass., 1986.
67. Bilkey, W.J. and Nes, E., 'Country of origin effects on product evaluations', *Journal of International Business Studies*, vol. 13, Spring/Summer 1982, pp. 89–99; Cattin, P., Jolibert, A. and Lohnes, C., 'A cross-cultural study of 'made in' concepts', *Journal of International Business Studies*, vol. 13, Winter 1982, pp. 131–41; Kaynak, E. and Cavusgil, S.T., 'Consumer attitudes towards products of foreign origin: do they vary across product classes?', *International Journal of Advertising*, vol. 2, no. 3, 1983, pp. 147–57; Nagashima, A., 'A comparative "made in" product image survey among Japanese businessmen', *Journal of Marketing*, vol. 41, Jul. 1977, pp. 95–100; Narayana, C.L., 'Aggregate images of American and Japanese products: implications on international marketing', *Columbia Journal of World Business*, vol. 16, Summer 1981, pp. 31–4.
68. Lewis and Chambers, op. cit., p. 614.
69. Ibid.; Jain, op. cit.; Britt, S.H., 'Standardizing marketing in the international market', *Columbia Journal of World Business*, vol. 9, Winter 1974, pp. 39–45; Buzzell, R., 'Can you standardize multinational marketing?', *Harvard Business Review*, Nov./Dec. 1968, pp. 102–13; Cavusgil, S.T. and Yavas, U., 'Transfer of management knowledge to developing countries: an empirical investigation', *Journal of Business Research*, vol. 12, Jan. 1984, pp. 35–50; Donnelly, J.H., Jr, 'Attitudes toward culture and approach to international advertising', *Journal of Marketing*, vol. 34, Jul. 1970, pp. 60–3; Donnelly, J.H., Jr and Ryans, J.K., Jr, 'Standardized global advertising: a call as yet unanswered', *Journal of Marketing*, vol. 33, Apr. 1969, pp. 57–60; Dunn, S.W., 'Effect of national identity on multinational promotional strategy in Europe', *Journal of Marketing*, vol. 40, Oct. 1976, pp. 50–7; Green, R.T., Cunningham, W.H. and Cunningham, I.C.,

'The effectiveness of standardized global advertising', *Journal of Advertising*, vol. 4, Summer 1975, pp. 25–30.

70. Olsen, M.D., 'The importance of the environment to the food service and lodging manager', *Journal of Hospitality Education*, Winter 1980, pp. 35–45; Slattery, P.V.O. and Olsen, M.D., 'Hospitality organizations and their environment', *International Journal of Hospitality Management*, vol. 3, 1984, pp. 55–61; DeNoble, A.F. and Olsen, M.D., 'The food service industry environment: a market volatility analysis', *Florida International Review*, vol. 4, no. 2, 1986, pp. 89–100; West, J.J., 'Environmental scanning, industry structure and strategy making: concepts and research in the hospitality industry', unpublished monograph, Department of Hotel, Restaurant and Institutional Management, Virginia Polytechnic Institute and State University, Blacksburg, Va, 1987; Dev, C., 'Environmental uncertainty, business strategy and financial performance: a study of the lodging industry', unpublished doctoral dissertation, Department of Hotel, Restaurant and Institutional Management, Virginia Polytechnic Institute and State University, Blacksburg, Va, 1988; Crawford-Welch, S., 'An empirical examination of mature service environments and high performance strategies within those environments: the case of the lodging and restaurant industries', unpublished doctoral dissertation, Department of Hotel, Restaurant and Institutional Management, Virginia Polytechnic Institute and State University, Blacksburg, Va, 1990.
71. Lewis and Chambers, op. cit., p. 612.
72. Jain, op. cit.
73. Perlmutter, H.V., 'The tortuous evolution of the multinational corporation', *Columbia Journal of World Business*, vol. 4, Jan./Feb. 1969, pp. 9–18.
74. D'Antin, P., 'The Nestlé product manager as demi-god', *European Business*, vol. 6, Spring 1971, pp. 41–9; Doz, Y.L., 'Strategic management in multinational companies', *Sloan Management Review*, vol. 22, Winter 1980, pp. 27–46.
75. Lewis and Chambers, op. cit., p. 625.
76. For a more comprehensive discussion of these various pricing techniques see Lewis and Chambers, op. cit., pp. 353–87.
77. Ibid., Summer, J.R., *Improve Your Marketing Techniques: A Guide for Hotel Managers and Caterers*, Northwood Publications, Sussex, 1982; Abbey, J., 'Is discounting the answer to declining occupancies?', *International Journal of Hospitality Management*, vol. 2, no. 2, 1983, pp. 77–82; Greenberg, C., 'Room rates and lodging demand', *Cornell HRA Quarterly*, Nov. 1985, pp. 10–11; Buttle, F., *Hotel and Food Service Marketing: A Managerial Approach*, Holt, Rinehart and Winston, London, 1986; Carroll, J.D., 'Focus on discounting hotel rack rates', *Cornell HRA Quarterly*, Aug. 1986, pp. 12–19.
78. Laventhal & Horwath, 1987, op. cit.
79. DeVeau, P.M., 'Yield management: paradigm for the nineties', notes from a tutorial delivered at the IAHA Technology Conference, Dallas, Tex., Jun. 1989; Orkin, E.B., 'Boosting your bottom line with yield management', *Cornell HRA Quarterly*, Feb. 1988, pp. 52–6.
80. DeVeaux, op. cit, p. 1.
81. Orkin, op. cit.
82. Donnelly, J.H., Jr., 'Marketing intermediaries in channels of distribution for services', *Journal of Marketing*, vol. 40, Jan. 1976, pp. 55–7.
83. US Department of Commerce, *Franchising in the Economy 1984–1986*, US

Government Printing Office, Washington DC, 1986.
84. Crawford-Welch, op. cit.
85. Arbel, A. and Grier, P., 'Risk structure of the hotel and catering industry', *Cornell HRA Quarterly*, Nov. 1975, pp. 15–22.
86. Lewis and Chambers, op. cit.
87. Ibid.
88. Kaven, 'Channels of distribution in the hotel industry', unpublished monograph, n.d.

12

Changes in international hotel companies' strategies

David Litteljohn and Angela Roper

HOTELS AND INTERNATIONALIZATION

In relation to the analysis which follows it may be helpful to relate strategic areas directly to the hotel industry. This is done in Table 12.1. For the purposes of the current analysis, the strategic factors are related mainly to marketing/customer aspects and organization aspects. It is recognized that this greatly simplifies the relationships which may exist in an organization. However, it provides a useful stepping-stone into further analysis in the area of international hotel operations.

Internationalization is the process by which firms become involved in serving markets outside their home country. As a company becomes more international, so corporate strategies will have to reflect the fact that the business operates in a more diverse set of conditions than was the case when it faced only its home business environment. This study examines some of the relevant strategic considerations in internationalization in the hotel industry. By taking an overview of trends in the industry over thirty years (1970–2000), it emphasizes the evolutionary nature of the industry and stresses the competitive challenges that will be faced in the 1990s.

Porter[1] identifies ten different elements of strategy that a company should take into account. To emphasize the fact that the elements must be integrated, Porter shows them as spokes of a wheel, with the hub being the business's overall objectives of growth, profitability, market share and so on. The elements are shown in Figure 12.1

The chapter starts with analysis of the situation in the 1970s. This is then used as a base for comparison of industry experience in the 1980s. Finally, a scenario for industry development in the 1990s is postulated.

THE DEVELOPMENT OF MULTINATIONAL HOTEL COMPANIES IN THE 1970s

As international travel has grown, and as the companies which serve these markets have become larger themselves, so the opportunities and the reasons for international growth have become more complex. A very useful view of the developments in the field in the 1970s is available from the United Nations Centre on Transnational Corporations[2] and the further analysis it engendered, including Dunning and McQueen,[3] Davé[4] and Litteljohn.[5] While it would be inappropriate to quote at length

Table 12.1 *Strategic variables related to hotels as internationalization is pursued*

Strategic variables	Market implications	Organizational implications
Product line	How many brands are offered? How is differentiation achieved?	Do specifications, particularly in building and equipping, require modification?
Target markets	Are local and/or international markets pursued?	Nature of marketing strategies
Marketing sales	Location of marketing/sales effort centralized at head office or at regional or hotel unit level	
Distribution	Locational policy, and relationship with other organizations (e.g. airlines)	Adoption to host countries; relationship with parent company (if any); mechanisms to liaise with suppliers, etc.
Manufacturing/ investment	N/A	Investment in hotels, and methods of provision (e.g. direct investment or licensing agreements)
Labour	N/A	International human resource management approaches, or delegation to local levels?
Purchasing	N/A	International sourcing?
Research and development	Future market and organization strategies	Extent of R & D and location within organization hierarchy
Finance and control	Future market and organization strategies	Nature of F & C systems and location within organization hierarchy

N/A = not applicable.

from these sources, some of the main observations and conclusions may usefully be summarized.

The United Nations analysis was limited to enterprises which had associations with two or more foreign hotels at the end of 1978. It covered some 81 organizations, from 22 countries. These organizations represented a total of 1,025 foreign hotels and 270,646 rooms.

The North American influence

The development of hotels internationally can be seen to have started in the late 1940s and early 1950s. This was a time when the United States was the dominant world economic power. In the Dunning and McQueen survey[6] the United States accounted

Figure 12.1   *Dimensions in competitive strategy.*
Source: Based on Porter, M., *Competitive Strategy*, Free Press, New York, 1980.

for 22 companies, controlling 151,118 rooms – 56 per cent of the total operated by transnationals. By comparison French companies represented 13 per cent of the room capacity, and British ones 12 per cent.

In 1978, eight of the top ten international hotel companies, as judged by their room holdings, were owned by US-domiciled companies. Thus Inter-Continental, Hilton and Sheraton were all in the vanguard of international trends in the industry. Later, companies like Holiday Inns (i.e. The Holiday Corporation) – the largest international hotel company at the time – and Hyatt were to become influential in the field. This is not to say that the international operations were the exclusive domain of the North American corporation – there were important exceptions – but until the early 1980s US companies as a group represented a driving force in the phenomenon of international hotel operations.

Of the ten largest hotel companies in the late 1970s, those not controlled from the USA were Club Méditerranée and Novotel (France), and Trusthouse Forte and Travelodge, a THF subsidiary (UK). The full list of companies, with their hotel holdings, is included later in the chapter (see Table 12.3).

The types of company involved in hotel internationalization

According to the UN report there were four distinct types of international hotel operator. For 1978 the involvement of companies in their different categories were as shown in Table 12.2.

Thus, out of a total of 81 corporations in this sphere, 69 per cent were associated purely with hotel chain operations. This, to some extent, shows that the importance of the airline-associated international chain was becoming less of a feature of the industry. Pan-American later sold its Inter-Continental holding, Transworld, its Hilton International chain. Even when ownership did remain in the hands of an airline, the immediacy between the location of units and the routes flown by the airline became less strong.

Table 12.2   *Types of hotel multinational 1978*

Types of company/parent	Number of companies
Hotel chains associated with airlines: trans/multinational companies	16
Hotel chains independent of airlines	56
Hotel development and management consultants	3
Tour operators and travel agents	6

Source: UN Centre on Transnationals, *Transnationals in the Tourism Industry*, United Nations, New York, 1982.

The location/distribution of multinational hotel operations

From a total of 1,025 hotel units located outside the home country of the various hotel companies covered in the UN survey, there were a large number located in developing (as opposed to developed) economies: 486 units, representing 47 per cent of the sample, were sited in these less advanced economies. This represents a major feature of the industry at the time and indicates a high investment in the transferring of skills and expertise to these less developed countries.

Considering the size of the hotel industry in developed economies, the role of multinational-owned units was relatively unimportant. The only exception of any significance was Canada, which was host to many chains from the United States. However, bearing in mind the proximity of the two countries in terms of geography and culture, it is not surprising that there should be significant penetration by the more powerful US chains into Canada. What is perhaps more surprising is the fact that the UN report saw international hotel operations as being insignificant within the European context at the time.

The mechanisms of multinational hotel development

A remarkable feature at this stage of progress in the industry was the use of licensing arrangements. Essentially licensing provides a means of separating the ownership and control elements of the business. Franchising and management contracts were used extensively during the 1970s. Davé[7] notes that by the early 1980s 57.6 per cent of rooms in multinational hotel chains were covered by either franchising or management contracts, and that these forms of arrangement accounted for just over 90 per cent of capacity growth in the sector in the period from 1975 to the end of the decade. The propensity for these arrangements was at its highest in the developing, rather than the advanced, economies.

The trend was remarkable because it ran counter to the situation in most other industries, where it was considered necessary to ensure that the parent owned the assets located abroad, in order that the operation could be easily controlled.

In summary, therefore, the situation by the end of the 1970s could be seen as one where the North American chains played a commanding role. They did this mainly through the provision of a narrow product chain, in that companies invariably operated single brands. Their success in these operations no doubt derived from their ability to appeal to high-spending international travellers, in particular the international business traveller. This does not mean that they targeted only business travellers, but the exceptions underline this general marketing strategy. Club Méditerranée is a holiday-oriented operation, while Novotel and Travelodge cater for more medium-spend business and leisure markets.

This distribution/location policy meant that companies would, in the main, target sites and cities with good international communications and good business and commercial networks. For instance, until 1980 Holiday Inn and Novotel were the only foreign-controlled international hotel companies in the UK to have hotels outside London (a Sheraton unit at Aberdeen being short lived).

In their investment policies, these international companies showed a predisposition to enter into licensing (whether franchise or management contract agreements). Thus, they became expert at attracting investors to finance their expansion in this industry.

The reasons for early hotel internationalization

The fact that different types of hotel organization were identified means that there can be no single reason which accounts for hotel internationalization in the 1960s and 1970s. However, several reasons were put forward at the time to help explain the trend.

In the first place, there is what may be termed the *demand explanation*. This concentrates on the notion that, from a customer purchaser's perspective, the hotel service is an experience good rather than a search good; it is the type of good that does not easily lend itself to quantification and testing, as the characteristics of hotel consumption involve a high degree of intangibility. Also, even if information on the whole range of hotel facilities and services were available, it could be difficult for an individual consumer to obtain, particularly on an international basis. Under these conditions, therefore, the hotel which can give the customer some trademark or guarantee of quality and dependability will have a competitive advantage over its rivals.

Secondly, there is the *supply explanation*. This simply states that those firms that are international operate more efficiently (in the countries into which they expand) than firms which operate only on a national basis. The achievement of a superior production function can come about for a variety of reasons, including better purchasing, organization, training and other management factors.

There are other factors, such as the provision of sophisticated advance reservation and referral systems, which clearly fall in both demand and supply camps. In fact, all these factors may be seen to be very closely connected, and it is often difficult to find out which were the most influential factors for all firms. It is likely that all these factors will play some part in explaining any particular case.

The case of the airline- and the travel-operator-owned chains are more straightforward. In both cases it was seen that there were advantages to the parent in a degree of vertical integration. However, the case is not absolute as not all airlines spawned hotel chains and not all tour operators owned their own hotels. Even in cases where operation of hotels did become a feature, it is worth noting that the organizations embarked on fairly modest operations: the total of 22 chains associated with airlines and operators shown in Table 12.2 accounted for 20 per cent of internationally owned hotel units in 1978.[8]

The nature of hotel internationalization: an explanation of the popularity of licensing

The fact that licensing arrangements were so prevalent in the industry requires some explanation. This is important because the conventional approach to internationalization strategy as applied to other industries states that a firm will prefer to own its assets directly, rather than to license its expertise to another party. In other words, the conventional approach would hold that the hotel parent would stand to gain greater success and face less risk if it were to fund and manage operations directly.

The pedigree of this approach draws heavily from economic theory. It assumes that the company will wish to create internal markets – which it can control – rather than rely on external market forces. Thus, for instance, a company which relies on the extraction of certain raw materials for use in its manufacturing process will feel that it can plan with a greater degree of certainty if it controls the sourcing of the materials itself. Therefore, it will prefer to own a foreign supplier, rather than rely on the external/world market mechanism to provide it, with the uncertainties this may imply in terms of price, quantity and quality.

From a hotel perspective, many of the advantages of internal markets spring from economies of scale, the supply factors mentioned above, but could also include the ability to organize functions which relate specifically to the international nature of its operations. For instance, a hotel chain may have more control of management and labour if it owns all its units; it may have more discretion in pricing, investment policies and so on.

Problems, it is argued, could be greater if a company follows a route other than foreign direct investment. For instance, a management contract may involve start-up problems such as finding a suitable financial investor, and negotiating costs in arriving at a favourable package of financial and operational conditions. Franchising, another non-equity route, could also present problems. There may be an initial difficulty in finding suitable franchisees. Then there are the inherent troubles of franchising, which include quality control and, in the longer term, the possibility of creating new competitors by inducting new operators into an established hotel system and providing training for their members.

These types of problem are also likely to be involved if a company, in going international, chooses to become involved in a joint venture. The actual risks in this type of operation will depend greatly on the characteristics of the firms involved, and the reasons for the venture, so it is unwise to generalize about them.

Commenting on the popularity of licensing as a vehicle for international expansion at the time of their survey, Dunning and McQueen[9] stated that the hotel industry had important characteristics which distinguished it from other forms of commercial activity. In the hotel industry, licensing did not necessarily mean that the parent's control was significantly lessened. Both management contractors and franchisors have a significant influence on the operational conditions of their respective units. More importantly, they claimed, each unit within an international hotel framework is relatively independent of the other members of the chain – for instance, the success of a hotel in Paris is not directly affected by the operation of a fellow chain member in Cairo, although they may both share the benefits of a trade or brand name; in addition, there is no advantage for one unit to specialize in one particular function and supply members of the group with this (as may be the case in a manufacturing company) – hotels simply do not operate on this basis.

Examining the situation from an ecomomic perspective, Litteljohn[10] stated two possible reasons for the popularity of licensing. In the first place, there is the relatively capital-intensive nature of hotel investment. The fact that the amounts of capital required to develop in the industry were large relative to the size of companies undertaking expansion internationally in the 1970s could have constrained their ability to grow unless they had resorted to this strategy. Secondly, there was the possibility that the markets pursued by the hotel multinationals at the time were essentially small ones, and therefore that the economies of scale generated at the time were not great enough to create sufficient competitive advantages. Thus companies found it more convenient and profitable to use licensing mechanisms, which were readily available and in demand.

It is possible that there were other important factors which favoured the use of licensing. Firstly, economies of operation in certain locations might have been suspect. Thus licensing would have been a strategy to maximize the company's exposure but minimize its financial risks. This would be particularly true if a management contract which guaranteed a fixed management fee, or gave some percentage on turnover (rather than looking at the profitability as well), were employed. Secondly, it could also be the case that some locations which are prone to political instability would be more suited to a policy of low capital involvement. This would be particularly true where economies were less developed. Bearing in mind the relatively low penetration of foreign-owned hotels in areas such as Europe and the higher number of developments in less developed or developing countries, which tended to be the ones more prone to economic instability, it is likely that this factor did have some influence.

One additional factor evident during the mid-1970s was the expansion of international hotels in areas such as the oil-rich Middle East. At a time when their presence was often related to the desire to have a well-known hotel brand in oil-rich countries, rather than to the pure economics of the situation, there was a definite preference from the companies involved to minimize their potential exposure to commercial failure. Thus, a company like Hyatt would enter into contract arrangements on the basis of a fee, independent of the performance of a unit.

It is unlikely that any of these reasons operated on their own, but rather that the licensing policy emerged as a consequence of a combination of these factors. As has been shown above, the prevalence of these arrangements reflected more than the intrinsic characteristics of management contracts and franchising, but were also related to more general factors affecting the industry.

IMPORTANT TRENDS IN THE 1980s

One of the first important points to make is that there has been a significant growth in the international nature of the hotel industry. No study comparable to that sponsored by the United Nations has been undertaken, but some indication of growth can be seen from Table 12.3. This lists the top ten international hotel companies identified by Dunning and McQueen,[11] the number of hotels each operated outside its home country in 1978, and the comparable figure for 1989.

To ensure that the hotels comparison over the period remains constant, the domicile of the hotel company is taken to be that obtaining in 1978, even though this may have changed during the period (e.g. Holiday Inns are no longer owned by Holiday Corporation of the USA, but by the UK's Bass plc, and the number of international hotels in 1989 has been calculated on the basis of those units operating as Holiday Inns outside the USA). If this action had not been taken, the international-

19 88 - 199 2

Table 12.3   *A comparison of the top ten hotel groups in 1978 by international hotel holdings 1978–1989*

Company	Foreign-operated hotels		Growth over period (%)
	1978 (units)	1989 (units)	
Holiday Inns	114	177[1]	55
Inter-Continental	74	95[2]	30
Hilton International	72	102	42
Sheraton	72	99	38
Club Méditerranée	56	102	82
Trusthouse Forte	53	56	6
Novotel/Accor	45	263[3]	484
TraveLodge International	34	506–61[4]	79
Ramada	33	100[5]	203
Hyatt	26	63	142
Total	579	1,118	93

[1]   Figures from 1988 directory.
[2]   Includes hotels branded as Forum. The company is now (1990) owned by Saison International (60 per cent) and SAS (40 per cent); international holdings taken as those outside the USA.
[3]   1990 figure, including those under construction.
[4]   TraveLodge is owned by the British-based THF and much of the international growth stems from its development in the UK (where it has 61 units).
[5]   Ramada Hotels are now owned by New World, a Hong Kong-based company; for comparative reasons, however, international holdings are taken as those outside the USA.

Sources: Dunning, J. and McQueen, M., 'Multinational corporations in the international hotel industry', *Annals of Tourism Research*, vol. 9, 1982, pp. 69–90; 1989 directories; unless otherwise stated.

ization trends would have appeared much stronger. This type of analysis is therefore not ideal for all comparisons, but is the best to show the organic rather than the acquired growth in the industry.

In addition to the overall growth rate of 93 per cent in international hotel holdings operated by these companies, there were other significant trends in the 1980s.

The dilution of US ownership

During the period some of the major companies, which had been American, changed hands. Thus, the Holiday Corporation sold out its interests in Holiday Inns to Bass of the UK. Inter-Continental was sold to Grand Metropolitan of the UK, which in turn sold out the hotels to Seibu Saison of Japan (which now operates the hotels jointly with SAS). Hilton International is now controlled by Ladbroke, the British-based leisure and property group, while Ramada is owned by the Hong Kong-based New World group. The British acquisitions were a result of both strategic decisions by firms to enter and expand holdings in international hotels and British accounting conventions which allow asset appreciation of property. This convention is at variance with regulations in many other countries.

Growth by acquisition

A chosen medium for expansion has been through the acquisition of existing companies, rather than the pursuit of an organic growth strategy. This is not to say that growth through other routes has been less important (see, for instance, Sheraton and Novotel/Accor above); but it does indicate that a hitherto relatively unused route was now coming into prominence. No clearer example can be given than that of the British brewing company Bass. By the mid-1980s Bass already had a substantial domestic hotel chain in Crest. In addition to this UK base, the hotel group had representation in continental Europe. However, Bass decided that Holiday Inns presented a stronger vehicle for international expansion, and in due course acquired sole rights to the operation and disposed of Crest Hotels.

More varied forms of internationalization

The growth of hotel consortia was a significant phenomenon during the period. Its extent has been well documented for Britain by Slattery and Roper,[12] and other indications show that the growth of consortia was not purely a UK event. This form of organization allowed airlines, most notably British Airways, to offer passengers recommended hotels, together with convenient reservation services, without the airline actually operating the hotels. Golden Tulip Hotels, a part of KLM airlines, also operated a chain with owned, managed and consortia units in its portfolio.

A greater focus on financial management

Probably as response to the greater levels of competition emerging in the industry, a greater emphasis was placed on the revenue-earning capacity of assets. Hilton International, for instance, was able to increase the profitability of its chain substantially.

Market segmentation

A common feature of the 1980s was the fashion for hotel groups to develop a portfolio of different operations, targeted to appeal to different markets (see Table 12.4). This meant that groups now had a more complex choice of internationalization strategy than had been the case previously, when most of the operators had single brands/ operations. If the group decided that it would internationalize with several operations, it is evident not only that the strategic choice process would become more complex, but that the management of the international network would become more complicated.

A greater emphasis on developed markets

While the swing towards the developing countries continued in the early part of the

Table 12.4   *Market segmentation of international hotel groups*

Hotel company	Hotel brands
Accor	Sofitel
	Novotel
	Mercure
	Ibis/Urbis
	Formule 1
Hilton International	Hilton International Resorts
	Hilton International Airports
Holiday Inns	Crowne Plaza
	Holiday Inns
	Garden Courts
Hyatt	Hyatt Regency
	Hyatt Hotels & Resorts
Inter-Continental	Inter-Continental
	Forum
Ramada	Ramada Renaissance
	Ramada Hotels & Resorts
	Ramada Inns
Trusthouse Forte	Exclusive
	Forte
	Travelodges
	Thrift Inns

1980s, with new areas such as China becoming available for expansion, by the end of the period more emphasis was being placed on the more developed market areas, such as the USA and Europe. The focus on the USA can partly be explained by its affluent population base and acquisition candidates, while the attraction of Europe is better explained by the fragmented nature of the industry and the opportunities this offered for corporate expansion, together with the implied benefits of the 1992 harmonization moves in the European Community.

The trends in the 1980s can be compared to those of the previous decade. The growth achieved during the period was significant. However, while the vehicles for achieving this growth remained relatively unchanged, the ownership and expansion methods used showed important differences. There were significant changes in ownership, and companies attempted a more market-segmented approach to their operations. Attention paid to locations reflected interest in major cities and, more innovatively, some secondary locations in developed countries.

Companies became more involved in direct investment, although management contracting and franchising still played an integral part in expansion strategies. In relation to financial matters there appears to have been more attention paid to operational considerations (e.g. financial control and planning). The greater involvement in direct investment also created a requirement for capital sourcing. Perhaps it was some over-ambitious growth by US companies that precipitated the takeovers:

Ramada's aggressive growth through non-equity means has, for instance, been cited as a contributing factor in its financial problems and subsequent sale in the late 1980s.

From a strategic perspective, it is now important to establish what important trends will affect the nature of international expansion in the 1990s.

TRENDS IN THE 1990s: A LOOK TOWARDS THE FUTURE

While not offering any detailed review here, we would judge that global trends in economic, social, political and technological factors will all favour the further growth of international holdings by hotel companies. Their plans at the moment (1990) certainly point towards this conclusion. For instance:

- **Sheraton** aims to double the number of its hotels in Europe in the next five years.
- **Holiday Inns** aims to place its brand into an unassailable position among its international competitors.
- **Accor** plans to open another 120 hotels in 1990 in Italy, Britain, France, Spain and the Pacific Rim. Currently the fourth largest hotel operator in the world in terms of rooms, the company is striving to be number 1 by the end of the decade.
- **Hilton International Hotels** is embarking on a substantial development programme in key areas of the world. This involves providing hotels in new locations and expanding and improving existing hotels.
- **Hyatt Hotels** is starting a major expansion in Europe, and is becoming more global in its organization by centralizing its reservations office in London.
- **Marriott** has announced plans to commit $5 billion to expansion over the next five years, aiming to double the company's size. A particular focus on European expansion is planned.

One consequence of such international development will be the realignment of hotel companies' portfolios domestically. Such portfolio restructuring can be seen presently among particularly the European players: Holiday Inns' disposal of Crest Hotels; Hilton International's relaunching of the International and National hotel brands; and Trusthouse Forte with the restructuring and launching of new national and international brands. All these attend to the implications of gearing up to international operations.

Hotel groups and ownership

The interesting point to note is that what since the 1970s have been the major hotel groups will remain a force in the worldwide hotel industry. However, this continuity belies the fact that there have been major ownership changes among such companies. Future takeover and merger activity among international players cannot therefore be discounted. Table 12.3 reiterates this point: of the ten largest international organizations listed in the 1978 study, 42 per cent of the current international holdings are now owned by groups which changed their ownership during the period 1978–89.

The advent of 'new' international hotel groups

Over the past few years a number of entrants to the international hotel scene have provided a new emphasis.

The increasing importance of Pacific Rim developers

Reflecting changes in the world economic scene, the influence of hotel competitors from the Pacific Rim will increasingly impact on the industry. Table 12.5 serves as a reminder of the recent acquisitions by such new international players. Entrants include World International (purchase of Omni Hotels from Aer Lingus); Saison International (acquisition of Inter-Continental Hotels from Grand Metropolitan); and New World International (takeover of Ramada Hotels in 1989). In the longer term, these groups will further impact as they rationalize, restructure and increase their portfolios. Although, as they are new entrants, it is difficult to predict their influence on the industry, they will undoubtedly provide an important impetus.

Significant are the Pan-Pacific air travel carriers who have used hotels as part of their growth strategy. Japan Airlines and All Nippon Airlines are committed to a continuing international expansion of hotels in the future through their subsidiaries, Nikko International Hotels and ANA Hotels respectively. Although of less importance on a total market share basis, hotel companies such as Mandarin International, Regent International and Peninsula Hotels have ambitious plans to expand from their Pacific base, and thus are likely to have an important influence on the 'de luxe' end of the international hotel market.

Japanese companies have now gained a reputation for being powerful investors in hotels – with the exception of Hong Kong-based New World International, the organizations featured in Table 12.5 are all Japanese in parentage. In 1988, Japanese investment in the industry worldwide totalled approximately $2 billion. Of this, 75 per cent was invested in hotels in the USA; further acquisitions by this sector have substantially increased this amount. The extent of Japanese involvement in the USA is such that 60 per cent of hotel rooms in Hawaii are under their ownership. While investors were first concerned with the ownership of 'trophy' hotels (i.e. up-market prestige units), they are now involved in the budget sector of the market. Thus, they are likely to become further entrenched as powerful investors with the potential to take equity stakes in hotel properties and/or hotel companies.

The future growth of such groups depends on the strength of their specific currency markets domestically, on the state of their customer base internationally and on their earnings and international exchange rate valuation, as this will affect their ability to raise capital and finance expansion.

Table 12.5   *Acquisition of international hotel chains by Pacific Rim companies*

Hotel company	Acquired by	Date	Cost (m)
Ramada Hotels	New World International	Aug. 1988	$540.00
Inter-Continental	Saison International	Dec. 1988	$1,000.20
Westin Hotels	Aoki[1]	Apr. 1988	$1,000.53
Omni Hotels	World International	Jun. 1988	$135.00
Swissotel	Aoki	Mar. 1990	$200.00

Total number of hotels involved: 1,033

[1]   Represents an 85 per cent interest in Westin; 15 per cent held by Robert M. Bass family of Fort Worth, Texas.

Additional new entrants to the global hotel scene

Further growth will come from conventional hotel companies which are extending their operations internationally and also from less traditional entrants.

In the first group, there will be room for companies expanding out of their home countries or regions. Two examples are Scandic Hotels (from Sweden) and the USA company Conrad Hilton Hotels. Thus, Scandic has as a stated aim the desire to be the most attractive hotel company in Western Europe for business travel and conferences. Conrad Hilton (a separate entity from Hilton International) will concentrate on the provision of suite hotels.

Among the less traditional entrants Center Parcs is the best example. It is similar to Club Méditerranée in that it offers a specific leisure and recreational experience rather than appealing to a wider range of markets. However, newer Center Parcs are designed to offer conference facilities and services, thus introducing a new competitive element into the industry.

In contrast to the Pacific Rim companies with their strong financial footing, it is likely that these entrants will grow more through marketing orientation. Market segmentation and location/distribution will be the key to their success, together with the need to adopt appropriate capital-financing policies.

Marketing: product development and branding

Past explanations of internationalization trends in the industry held that branding was axiomatic with gaining competitive advantage (the notion that hotel good is an expensive good and its purchase is a search activity, as previously discussed). However, it seems naive to assume that the ideas which may have been appropriate to international hotels markets when these were only on a small scale will be those that drive the industry in the 1990s.

The debate of the 1970s and early 1980s was based upon the premiss that the market was mainly composed of a frequent international business traveller. This traveller was presumed to require some degree of certainty and 'quality' when he travelled to new locations (commentators of the time did not recognize the growing importance of the female traveller, hence the omission of the other gender here). The acceptable brand would give him just that, particularly if it were tailored in some way to what he was used to when travelling on business at home, so the presumption went.

Boorstin,[13] in the mid-1950s, anticipated this analysis when he suggested that Hilton International Corporation's attraction to American travellers abroad rested in brand identity and image among Americans. (Dunning and McQueen,[14] Casson[15] and Davé[16] developed this approach within a more rigorous framework.) However, such an analysis of branding must be taken in the context of its time and must be updated.

Single or multiple branding strategies

Taking the debate on the importance of brand recognition as not yet conclusive, it remains the case that many hotel companies will be growing internationally through marketing strategies which embrace wider segments than the traditional international 'de luxe' sector. Two internationalization patterns may thus be witnessed in the future:

- Path 1: Focusing upon 'global' expansion, but only targeting a minimum of locations in any particular country.

- Path 2: Penetrating specific countries with a range of hotel brands, internationalization is therefore a more focused geographical strategy.

The first path is presently being taken by mainly 'de luxe' hotel brands, such as Hilton International Hotels. These groups will continue to gain representation in gateway cities and selected resort locations where they presently lack a hotel property. Thus, this line of expansion follows the pattern of that internationalization witnessed by Dunning, McQueen and Davé back in the 1970s. The main difference will be the need to ensure that the brands evolve with market requirements maintaining competitive edge, and that their geographical distribution is appropriate; that new opportunities are identified and that locations no longer suitable are dropped.

Companies following the second internationalization path may well have a sizeable portfolio of properties outside their home market, but these will be contained within a smaller dispersion of countries. The important point here is that expansion internationally may be with a range of hotel brands covering a wide set of market levels. An example is the organization Accor SpA, which is the umbrella holding group for six hotel brands. The company seeks international expansion not only with its 'de luxe' Sofitel hotel brand but also with the other five types, targeted at a variety of customer groupings. In the UK, for example, the company hopes to operate 371 hotels by the year 2000 (see Table 12.6).

Table 12.6   *Accor, projected brands and units in the UK*

Hotel type	Brand description	No. of hotels by year 2000
Sofitel	International 'de luxe' hotel in gateway or resort locations	6
Novotel	Mid-market business hotel, located in strategic business/communications sites	60
Mercure	Mid-market business hotel, located in city centres	40
Ibis/Urbis	Economy business and leisure hotel	65
Formule 1	Budget hotel	170
Hotelia	Serviced hotel accommodation for the elderly	30
Total hotels		371

Source: Company information.

International expansion by Accor is not only planned for the United Kingdom; other European countries, in particular, will be penetrated with a range of Accor hotel products/services. The important aspect to consider here is that the clientele for the middle and lower market products/services will in the main come from the host country. Thus, the international hotel company must be competitively able to penetrate markets by appealing to domestic markets which may not be international in orientation.

This point is further emphasized by internationalization of middle and lower market hotel brands. Marriott Hotels with the Courtyard by Marriott brand; Holiday Inns with Garden Court Hotels; Quality Inns with Sleep Inns; and Société du Louvre with Campanile Hotels – all must be translated and integrated into domestic markets which differ from each other and from the home country of the hotel chain. It is not only in broad marketing philosophies that companies have to consider adapting to local circumstances. For example, Accor debated long and hard on whether to add tea- and coffee-making facilities to its Novotel and Ibis rooms in the UK. It is not customary to provide these facilities in continental Europe and their provision will add to the fixture and fittings cost per bedroom. On the other hand, not to provide them could mean losing some appeal to competitors in Britain.

International marketing is currently addressing the issue of global and local brands to assess their relative benefits. If local hotel brands are seen to present significant benefits then it is possible that the two paths identified will be complemented by a web of partnerships and alliances between different hotel companies, where co-operation is seen to be mutually beneficial but where takeovers or acquisitions could be counterproductive.

Thus, the Pacific Rim area is particularly targeted by Accor for extensive development in this decade. The company's recent acquisition of 10 per cent of Mandarin Oriental, the Hong Kong-listed hotel arm of the Jardine Matheson empire for HK $370m (£31.6m) is evidence of such a commitment. The French company states that it is not interested in acquiring the hotel chain outright, but that there are lucrative elements of worldwide expansion that the two organizations can achieve together. Mandarin has wanted to expand into Europe, while Accor is expanding in Asia.

The European context

Europe seems likely to be a focus of hotel chain development. The industry is fragmented in continental Europe (in comparison to the UK and the USA); Kleinwort Benson[17] consider that this offers substantial scope for the expansion of existing brands. This may occur through acquisition and new build strategies.

Additional market forces within Europe which will impact on the hotel industry include the effects of the 1992 single market initiative of the European Community; for Britain and France, in particular, the Channel Tunnel, timed to open in 1993; and the Euro-Disney development near Paris. Undoubtedly, the opening of Eastern Europe and the USSR will present further opportunities for expansion. Many hotel chains would appear to agree with Trusthouse Forte's view that existing hotels in the former Communist countries have been inadequate in number and standard to attract foreign visitors. Potential demand is reflected in research carried out by Marriott in Poland, where considerable increases in demand are expected: for instance, in the late 1980s only 33,000 Britons and 51,000 US citizens visited the country. With only one de luxe and eight other four-star hotels in the capital, and only one hotel of international appeal in Poland's second city, there would appear to be scope for considerable expansion. The rate of expansion will be affected both by the stability of the changes begun in 1989–90 and, specifically, by measures which are implemented relating to inward investment and repatriation of profits.

Many current initiatives involve joint ventures between Western companies and state-owned organizations. Sheraton announced the first USA–USSR joint venture in late 1989. The project is to own and operate two hotels in the heart of Moscow. Other partners are Pan-American Airways, Mossoviet (City of Moscow) and the Soviet state airline Aeroflot. Hilton International, Inter-Continental, Marriott and Trusthouse Forte all plan further development in the Soviet Union and Poland.

The Mediterranean regions of Italy and Spain are forecast to be areas which will in the future account for a higher percentage of European manufacturing output. Thus, these countries as a whole are set to be influenced by a shift in the balance of trade and commerce within the continent.

In predicting such changes, and assuming the increased demand particularly for business travel throughout such regions, Trusthouse Forte stands as an example. The UK company has recently entered into a partnership deal with Repsol, the state-owned Spanish petrol retail chain, to build one hundred of its Travelodge and Little Chef outlets in Spain over the next five years. Meanwhile, the UK company is still negotiating a joint venture with ENI, the Italian state energy corporation which runs the AGIP chain of hotels. Thus, Trusthouse Forte is an example of a hotel conglomerate which is well positioned to provide a range of different hotel types to match differing customer groups in locations worldwide. The following section discusses further innovative modes of development.

Organizational and financial factors

In the future, hotel companies will examine more intently those development modes which they choose to employ. As discussed previously, the rapid global expansion of some companies in the past ultimately led to their failure to achieve adequate financial returns. This is not to say that all growth was necessarily achieved by means of costly equity involvement, but that even management contract and franchising arrangements had their own strain administratively on the organization, as well as providing less substantial financial returns.

Joint-venture agreements have been mentioned in previous sections. Further innovative deals will follow throughout the 1990s, as trade links become stronger between different types of organization. Examples given previously concerning Trusthouse Forte are indicative of such developments, particularly in the growth of middle and lower market hotel concepts. Meanwhile, a hotel company which was airline owned in the past is returning to such a business association. Inter-Continental is obviously linked with part-owner Scandinavian Air Systems, but in addition the chain's majority owner Saison International has recently paid £36 million for a 10 per cent stake in Virgin Airways (announced in May 1990). The move came at a time when Virgin was increasing its London–Tokyo service substantially. Such allowances show symbiotic business associations, and for the future ownership of international hotel chains indicate the importance of linkages between different nationalities of airlines.

At the same time the new owners of global hotel chains will continue to reassess their involvement in hotel units as a consequence of changing capital and asset markets. Inter-Continental, which previously created many management contracts, is increasing its ownership of hotels, reflecting perhaps the longer-term priorities placed on equity investment by the Japanese parent. The company recently purchased outright units in Chicago and Miami and increased equity holdings in a number of hotels worldwide, such as in Frankfurt, Hamburg, Toronto and Montreal. On the other hand, Hilton International is looking in the future to sell shares in 82 of its 140 hotels. Such 'selling down' of the equity in hotels follows Ladbroke's desired strategy to improve return on capital by realizing the added value of the group's hotel assets. This release of capital is intended to allow the expansion programme to continue at the current rapid rate.

The emphasis on growth through ownership of hotel properties is also due to change. For example, franchising of their hotel brands will be Holiday Inns' desired method of expansion in many European locations in the future, whereas growth in such a region was previously more equity related. Thus, what was an expansion strategy mainly used in the USA will now be pursued aggressively in other regions. Such changes are due to a number of factors, many specific to the mission and projected returns of the companies in questions. The important point to note in this example, however, is that a change in ownership (to Bass) has led to different orientations and financial aims, though generally these changes are perhaps symptomatic of a maturity of certain hotel concepts where movement along the experience curve has enabled more management and franchise arrangements to be viable.

Indeed, purchase of hotel brands may be seen to have been a successful strategy during the 1980s. Its adoption is not limited to the major players. Queens Moat House, a successful if not internationally large UK company, took over Bilderberg Hotels in the Netherlands. While retaining the Bilderberg organization and image, Queens Moat was able to become, overnight, the largest hotel company in the country. This form of international organization runs counter to the demand-led view that international branding is the driving force in the field.

Other areas of potential – and risk

Many geographical regions have not been highlighted in the analysis. This is not because they will not participate in international hotel development. India, South America and Africa will create both leisure and business demand for hotels as their economies develop. Their hotel industries, too, are fragmented enough to ensure that they appear attractive to the large chains. Thus, it is more than likely that they will be the recipients of international investment, government regulations allowing. It is less likely that they will be generators in the field, as will be the case with the Pacific Rim countries.

The problem here is not to generalize about the high levels of potential demand in certain locations, but to remember that developments will also carry risks. Most relevant here is the case of China. During the 1980s many up-market hotels were provided by international chains, with Chinese government involvement, to attract affluent tourists. The 1989 Tiananmen Square massacre of students and civilians by army troops caused a sharp downswing in tourism. It was estimated that over £2.4 billion was lost in tourism revenue. Companies such as Sheraton and Hilton International were at times recording room occupancies as low as 20–30 per cent. Political, economic and religious/social factors, if not stable, may considerably impair the potential rate of international hotel development within a country.

CONCLUDING REMARKS

The past 30 years have been a dynamic period in the internationalization of the hotel industry. This internationalization has been characterized by a growth of American-type brands, albeit that there has often been a change in the ownership of the parent company. These changes in ownership have given the industry a more truly international flavour, with Japanese, British, Scandinavian, Hong Kong and French operators all among the major players in the industry.

In the future brand diffusion will be greater. The early phase of growth was dominated by up-market/de luxe hotel brands, often aimed primarily at business travel markets. Saturation in this segment will ensure a wide range of concepts aiming at both business and pleasure markets.

- Methods of expansion will be more diverse and complex in the future. While management contracting and franchising will remain, there will be more involvement in mergers and acquisitions, joint ventures and direct ownership. Direct ownership in particular will be given a boost through the expansion of hotels aimed at middle and budget sector segments, whose investment requirements will be significantly lower than for those in de luxe sectors.
- Hotel companies with various brands in their portfolio will have a choice in their market penetration strategies – whether to strive for growth of a selected brand or number of brands in many different locations, or to concentrate on portfolio growth in particular locations/countries. Important organizational and management implications flow from these different approaches.
- Less certain is the development of truly global brands. Much development of hotel brands relates to a view driven more by product differentiation than by a real appreciation of marketing related to the hotel industry. Expansion strategies which pay too much attention to competition trends in the industry without a solid marketing base may lead to over-capacity and attendant programmes of rationalization.

Further supply issues

This analysis has dealt mainly with industry-level developments in the internationalization of hotel companies. Other supply issues included in the competitive wheel will require close attention. In particular, attention will be given to the following:

- The importance of information technology. This has potential in marketing (central reservation systems) and in finance and control aspects (through management information systems). Bearing in mind that international management will create its own problems in reporting, liaising, currency fluctuations and units of accounting, investment in information systems should reap significant rewards.
- Labour issues. As always in a service industry, these will be critical to success. As the organizations grow significantly, more attention will be given to management training and development.

In conclusion, the competitive dimensions by which strategy in the international hotel industry will be judged will encompass a wider set of conditions than was previously the case.

NOTES

1. Porter, M., *Competitive Strategy*, Free Press, New York, 1980.
2. United Nations Centre on Transnationals, *Transnationals in the Tourism Industry*, United Nations, New York, 1982.
3. Dunning, J. and McQueen, M., 'Multinational corporations in the international hotel industry', *Annals of Tourism Research*, vol. 9, 1982, pp. 69–90.
4. Davé, U., 'US multinational involvement in the international hotel sector', *Service Industries Journal*, no. 4, 1984, pp. 48–63.

5. Litteljohn, D., 'Towards an economic analysis of trans/multinational hotel companies', *International Journal of Hospitality Management*, vol. 4, no. 4, 1985, pp. 157–65.
6. Dunning and McQueen, op. cit.
7. Davé, op. cit.
8. Litteljohn, op. cit.
9. Dunning and McQueen, op. cit.
10. Litteljohn, op. cit.
11. Dunning and McQueen, op. cit.
12. Slattery, P. and Roper, A., *UK Hotel Groups Directory*, Hotel and Catering Research Centre, Cassell, London, 1988.
13. Boorstin, D. J., *The Image: A Guide to Pseudo Events in America*, Peter Smith, Magnolia, Mass., 1984.
14. Dunning and McQueen, op. cit.
15. Quoted by Dunning, J., 'The electric theory of the multinational enterprise in the hotel industry', in Rugman, A. (ed.), *New Theories of Multinational Enterprises*, Croom Helm, London, 1982.
16. Davé, op. cit.
17. Kleinwort Benson Securities, *UK Hotels plc: The Decade Review*, 1990.

13

The global hospitality industry of the 1990s

Michael Olsen, Simon Crawford-Welch and Eliza Tse

INTRODUCTION

The importance of monitoring and analysing the hospitality environment has been documented by several authors.[1] These authors argue that corporate decision-makers should be familiar with evolving, continuing and declining trends in the hospitality environment in order that they may steer their respective organizations along the optimum path. It was with this logic in mind that members of the Center for Hospitality Research and Service located in Blacksburg, Virginia, USA, began to create in 1981 a system for identifying, categorizing and analysing major trends facing the hospitality industry.

This system, known as the Trends Data Base, has now been in existence for over seven years and has evolved into the most sophisticated and extensive computerized information system of its kind in the world. The data base is modelled around dBase III and AskSam computer programs and contains over 25,000 bits of information concerning trends in the hospitality industry for the period 1983–90. It is this data base which acts as a foundation for the positions adopted by the authors throughout this chapter.

The chapter is divided into two main parts. The first part outlines and discusses major trends in the worldwide hospitality industry. We have termed this section of the chapter 'Seven new directions for the hospitality industry of the 1990s'. The second part outlines and discusses major strategies that hospitality corporations have adopted as a direct result of these trends. We have termed this section of the chapter 'Strategies for global hospitality firms of the 1990s'.

SEVEN NEW DIRECTIONS FOR THE HOSPITALITY INDUSTRY OF THE 1990s

While the following seven trends are by no means exhaustive, we believe that they represent the most important and pressing issues facing the global hospitality industry of the 1990s.

(1) The asset evolution phenomenon

The US hospitality industry of the early 1980s was characterized as a heavily asset-based industry with a large part of world hospitality assets being concentrated in the hands of a few powerful US hospitality firms. The second half of the 1980s, however, witnessed what we term the 'asset evolution phenomenon' (see Figure 13.1). By this we refer to the situation whereby US hospitality firms have all but relinquished their assets. The US hospitality industry is no longer an asset-based industry; rather it is a management contract-based industry. In order to meet unrealistic pressure from the capital markets for continued bottom-line growth, US hospitality organizations have been forced to pursue a strategy of asset liquidation. The buyers of those assets have predominantly been the Japanese and British.

- Japan: long-term asset appreciation and concentration

- Europe: asset accumulation; more difficult to get adequate return

- USA: asset liquidation; growth in management contracts

- Asia: asset acquisition

Figure 13.1   *The asset evolution phenomenon.*

The entry of the Japanese into the US industry has been well documented.[2] What has not been discussed at any length is the underlying philosophy that we believe fuels this Japanese investment. The Japanese are clearly pursuing a strategy of asset appreciation. They are investing strategically: that is, on a long-term basis. When first entering the US real estate market, the Japanese tended to buy quietly and moderately. However, we have recently witnessed Japanese investors paying well above market price for individual hotel properties. An example of this is the purchase of the Hotel Bel-Air in Los Angeles for $110 million in 1988 by Tokyo's Sekitei Kaihatsu Co. Ltd. Conventional financial wisdom views such an acquisition as being detrimental to the long-term financial stability of both the industry and the individual firm paying the premium. We disagree with conventional wisdom in this instance. We believe that there is a sound logic in this strategy of paying above market price. The logic is this: by suddenly purchasing a property above market price Japanese investors are consciously raising the value of all other properties in their portfolio, which significantly raises the value of their total asset holdings and in turn provides them with much greater leverage in the marketplace. This leverage permits further acquisition of properties.

It should be noted, however, that the Japanese are not the only major Far Eastern investors with interests in the hospitality industry. Many other Asian corporations, especially those originating from the newly industrialized nations (NICs), have actively been pursuing strategies of asset acquisition in the industry.

(2) The technological flood

We predict that the 1990s will see the hospitality industry, which has traditionally been a craft-oriented industry, being transformed into a more technology-oriented industry (see Figure 13.2). One only has to look at the evolution of the 'smart hotel room' with its use of fibre optics in video checkout facilities for evidence of the emerging emphasis on technology. The Japanese have even gone as far as to develop a 'litmus paper toilet', which allows a guest, by observing the colour of the litmus paper automatically injected into the toilet basin that he or she has just used, to determine his or her biomedical status.

- The smart hotel room

- Decision support systems and management expertise

- Marketing the industry

- Transportation

Figure 13.2 *The technological flood.*

On a more serious note, we predict an increase in the development and use of decision support systems. A forerunner of this explosion in decision support technology is the yield management pricing system currently receiving so much attention throughout the industry. Once the euphoria over yield management has subsided we will see additional sophistication in such areas as inventory control and in the gathering of current and detailed data for market research purposes.

We predict that the technological flood will have a most pervasive and radical impact in the functional area of marketing, especially where channels of distribution are concerned. A primary consideration will be the linkage between reservation systems as we know them now and the evolution of an interactive video system whereby it will be possible to select a hotel room through use of a video disk. The video disk will enable the potential guest to view the room/restaurant/bar before actually making the purchase. In other words, we will progress from the use of a simple toll-free number to the use of a sophisticated video-disk-based system which we will ultimately be able to access from our homes and offices. On a more strategic level, we are already seeing many previously unconnected entities, such as hotels and travel agents or hotels and airlines, joining forces to reap the benefits of large-scale, fully integrated, synergistic systems. In addition, we predict an increase in the use of, and in the competition between, 'one-stop' marketing systems. A 'one-stop' marketing system is simply a single location where a customer can buy everything ranging from a hotel room to an airline seat, to car rental, to travel insurance, to restaurant reservations.

The transportation industry, specifically the airline industry, will also need to make use of the developments in technology if it is to overcome the key problems associated with capacity shortage. If the airline industry is to keep up with demand, we estimate that it needs to increase capacity by approximately 50 per cent by the mid-1990s.[3] Most of this growth will be American, with only a small part going to long-range travel, the rest into medium and short range. We currently see all too few companies developing systems for airline capacity handling, and all this in the face of pioneering developments in high-speed aircraft.

Current developments in the designs and engines of aircraft incorporating ceramic technology will ultimately make the supersonic transport (SST) a profitable plane. Developments in this area will enable supersonic aircraft to have increased distance capacities and to fly non-stop from the USA to Australia at a profit, an achievement even Concorde has yet to attain.

While the evolution of high-speed travel, both on the ground and in the air, creates excitement, it also poses considerable problems because of the inability of destinations to handle the increase in traffic volume. There are few plans to build new airports in the 1990s, with the major emphasis being placed on the enlargement of existing ones. Congestion will increase, leading local governments to levy higher landing fees and to insist on tighter scheduling. All this is going to be expensive, and who will ultimately pay has yet to be determined.

(3) Non-conventional marketing on the rise

We believe that in the hospitality industry of the 1990s conventional marketing wisdom will lead to a conventional marketing result – failure. As an example of the failure of conventional marketing wisdom we offer the attempts of lodging organizations to pursue branding strategies.

Attempts at branding to date in the lodging industry are indicative of the product orientation of many organizations as well as of their use of descriptive criteria for segmentation purposes. Branding, as currently practised, is not, as practitioners would have us believe, a result of market segmentation. Rather, it is a result of product segmentation. Many of the attempts at branding in the lodging industry were developed to create brand awareness, recognition and ultimately brand loyalty by maximizing brand-switching costs. Unfortunately, the product orientation driving the whole branding issue has led to customer confusion. Differentiation through the use of brands in the lodging industry has become all but meaningless, for it does not clarify customer confusion but only serves to enhance it. We predict a greater emphasis on a truly market orientation to branding, which will involve the development and implementation of strong positioning statements, the creation of well-defined images, the determination of benefits sought by the consumer, and the differentiation of those benefits. This in turn will only come about when lodging organizations employ more sophisticated methods of segmentation: that is, when they move beyond purely descriptive methods of segmentation to behavioural, psychographic and psychological methods of segmentation.

In connection with the proliferation of brands, we predict an increase in the use of focus or concentrated growth strategies (see Figure 13.3). By this we mean that growth for growth's sake is no longer feasible – as demonstrated by the case of Holiday Corporation. Rather, organizations will focus on what they do best. Marriott's recent divesture of its restaurant division is evidence of this trend. There will be a focus approach to global brand proliferation.

- Brand proliferation to core businesses

- Focus strategies

- Closer to the customer

- Service

- Product design and the smart hotel room

- Industry capacity control

- Business and pleasure travel

- Mature in the West, growth in the East

Figure 13.3   *Non-conventional marketing.*

The 1990s will see a continuous stream of attempts by major hospitality corporations to become 'closer to the customer'. Examples of trends can be found in such publications as *Service America!*,[4] *Managing in the Service Economy*[5] and *Managing Service Industries*.[6] Customer expectations of service will rise. We suggest that service, not price, will be the differentiating factor of the 1990s.

In an attempt to provide more effective and efficient service we predict an increase in expenditures by hospitality corporations on product design. Product innovation will result in the introduction of new products ranging from the smart hotel room already mentioned to the use of the computerized touch-screen systems currently being tested by Burger King. Such touch-screens effectively eliminate all contact with any service personnel by allowing the customer to select his or her choice of items by simply touching the appropriate selection displayed on the VDU screen.

Technology will also impact on the control of industry capacity. We will see the growth of what we term 'megasystems', consisting of several interchange systems between various components of the hospitality industry. An excellent example of an attempt to introduce such a system is Rupert Murdoch's venture with 'UltraSwitch', which is an international network linking travel agencies and hotel and airline reservation systems through a satellite communication network. The major issue arising out of this growth in megasystems is, who will control industry capacity? Unless closely supervised, such systems will effectively take the control of industry capacity out of the hands of the organizations that actually provide the capacity.

Penultimately, we believe that there will be an increase in emphasis on catering to the needs of pleasure travellers, not least because of the changing demographic structure in the USA and several European nations. Differentiation of the pleasure traveller will follow much the same path as the differentiation of the business traveller has followed over the past few years.

Finally, we will become increasingly aware of the maturing of the industry in the West and the development of appropriate marketing strategies designed to prolong the life-cycle. In the East, however, the industry is still in the growth stage of its life-cycle. This dichotomy of different stages of the life-cycle will demand the pursuit of several different strategies by the global hospitality organization. What works in the European market may not necessarily work in the Pacific Rim, and vice versa.

(4) Think green!

There will be a continued increase in environmental awareness by major hospitality corporations (see Figure 13.4). In developed nations, the premier problem of the 1990s will be waste water. In the USA, for example, the cost of water will be rising faster than the cost of living, and in some areas will be rising at double the rate of inflation. This will result in higher water rates being passed on to the consumer, with the possibility of each bathroom facility in a hotel room being equipped with a meter to enable the establishment in question to charge guests for the exact amount of water usage during their stay.

● Developed nations:
□ Waste water
□ Solid waste

● Developing nations:
□ Waste water
□ Energy

Figure 13.4 *Think green!*

The disposal of solid waste is another issue with which hospitality organizations must become familiar in the 1990s. We will see an increase in cogeneration.

Cogeneration simply means using waste to produce electricity. Just now, this process is most common in such lines as pulp and paper, refining, food processing and chemicals, where large-scale operations require a lot of heat. However, it is also beginning to appear on a smaller scale as more efficient equipment is developed – in fast-food outlets, for example, and hospitals.

In developing nations, the need for a consistent source of energy supply is not always met. This has some impact on travellers using high-tech items that might need to plug into the local power supply. As hospitality corporations become truly global in their focus they will need to develop techniques to overcome these seemingly trivial, but in reality important issues. The issue of waste water is also important in developing countries, which often do not possess the necessary infrastructure to rid hotels of sewage in an effective and sanitary way. Developing countries depend on groundwater reserves for a high percentage of their drinking water, and as these countries gear more and more toward catering to the international tourist and business traveller, these water supplies are in turn becoming more and more polluted by insufficiently treated waste, chemical run-off, seepage of oil and gasoline, and chemicals in waste dumps.

(5) Political heavy-weights are out for the count!

We believe that it is economic power, and not political power, that will shape the world of the 1990s. In the global economy, economic considerations will almost always transcend political considerations (see Figure 13.5). Heads of state will become less and less important as CEOs take over the leading role in the global marketplace.

- Global economics versus politics

- Economic power centres:
  China
  Europe 1992
  Japan
  USA
  USSR

Figure 13.5   *Political heavyweights are for the count!*

We can already see examples of this trend. Taking Sweden, for instance, who is more important and well known, Jan Carlzon, head of SAS, and Pehr Gyllenhammer, head of Volvo, or the top political figures whose names are not even known outside Sweden?

The changing political structure brings with it a whole host of evolutionary changes the impact of which has yet to be determined. The effect of all this on the hospitality industry is also yet to be determined, but be sure it will be no minor matter.

Paul Kennedy in his book *The Rise and Fall of the Great Powers*[7] argues for the existence of what is essentially a life-cycle of nations. He convincingly demonstrates that the evolution of power of every nation to date has been determined not by military might, but by a sophisticated and healthy industrial structure supporting that military might. It is, in his view, economic power which determines the ability, or inability, of a power to compete and dominate globally. The point we are making is that military might has been transcended by economic might – by economic power centres. In the case of many newly developing countries much of that economic might will be made up of revenues brought about through tourism. Thus, as an industry, we have a crucial role to play in the development of many currently underdeveloped countries. This brings with it responsibilities that, as an industry, we ought not to ignore.

(6) The labour issue

Management culture in the hospitality industry is rooted in the 'how-to' side of the business, as opposed to the behavioural side (see Figure 13.6). Traditionally, hospitality managers have been very task oriented and have practised reactive, as opposed to proactive, management styles. If hospitality management is truly to come of age, we need to pay increasing attention to developing a more behaviourally oriented manager. It is only through the development of such an individual that corporations will be able successfully to pursue a strategy of differentiation through service. As hospitality managers and educators, we still have an abundance of needs to address in the area of multicultural management.

- Management culture worldwide is technically rooted: the wrong culture for tomorrow

- Not enough labour in the West

- Competition for labour in the East

- No behavioural perspective

- No multicultural perspective

- A demanding workforce

- Education is too technical

Figure 13.6   *The labour issue.*

In terms of labour supply, we see a growing similarity between the situation of the Western and Eastern worlds. In the West, changing demographics have led to a labour shortage. In the USA, for example, on any given working day, we estimate that just over 20 per cent of positions go unfilled, or are filled unsatisfactorily, due to a lack of available labour. The East has traditionally had an abundance of labour and has, as a direct result of labour supply outstripping labour demand, been able to produce the levels of service for which Far Eastern hotels have become famous. We predict, however, that the 1990s will see the beginning of some intense competition for labour in several Far Eastern countries, with a resulting lowering of the service level offered by hospitality organizations in these countries.

As the hospitality industry becomes more and more global in its focus, we need to devote increasing attention and resources to educating (not training) individuals to be aware of, and adapt to, the multicultural nature of the industry. The USA and UK are especially guilty of viewing the situation in terms of their own culture. They are guilty of hegemony. This 'imprinting' of one's own culture will no longer be acceptable either to host countries in which a hospitality organization operates or to customers of varied nationalities and beliefs. Multicultural education and training is a major issue that we need to address in the 1990s.

The workforce of the 1990s will be more demanding. By this we mean that employees will expect more of their employers. Employees will no longer accept what can often be considered the capricious and whimsical nature of management.

Finally, we believe that hospitality education is far too technically oriented. There exist too many 'diploma mills' in hospitality education today. We refer to this, with all due respect, as the 'MBA mentality'. By this we mean that too many hospitality programmes today emphasize rote learning of lists, methods and formulas without ever fostering the ability in students to question what they learn. We believe that the role of institutions of higher learning in the hospitality field should be to furnish students with an ability to analyse critically what they read and see: in short, to furnish them with thinking skills, not technical skills.

(7) Global wild cards

Finally, we have listed several 'global wild cards' (see Figure 13.7). These are factors which we predict will have a major impact on the hospitality industry of the 1990s, but unlike the above six issues we are not able, for one reason or another, to predict their exact impact with any degree of confidence.

- Eastern bloc

- NICs

- Regulation

- Multinational financial power

Figure 13.7   *Global wild cards.*

The recent events in the Eastern bloc bode well for the hospitality industry of the 1990s – probably initially in the form of joint ventures. However, the vast market potential that exists for the hospitality industry in the Eastern bloc is somewhat tainted by poor infrastructrue and poor, if existent, tourism organizations.

The impact of the NICs also has yet to be determined. Recent events seem to indicate that these countries will experiment with service industries far earlier in their economic development than did Japan. Hospitality organizations need to be poised to take advantage of this trend, should it emerge with force.

We predict that government regulation will continue to be an aspect of the hospitality industry for several reasons. Perhaps the two most important reasons are pollution and industry capacity control. Both these issues will become volatile areas of debate and legislation in the 1990s.

Finally, evidence clearly suggests that money is becoming multinational in nature. Since the early 1970s, the industrialized nations of the world have steadily lifted regulatory restrictions on international capital flows and on foreign participation in domestic financial markets. At the same time that governments have been liberalizing their trade and foreign investment policies, telecommunications have provided instantaneous transmission and processing of information around the globe. Capital now moves swiftly across borders because technological changes have reduced transaction costs associated with global arbitrage. This recent globalization of capital markets has radically altered the way lodging and other real estate properties are funded. Traditionally, financing came from local lending institutions. Today the global integration of capital markets has widened the gap between real properties and their financing sources. The globalization of finance may represent the final outcome in the gradual development of funding sources for hospitality properties.[8] Today, debt and equity capital for hotel investments emanates principally from six geographical regions: Asia (Hong Kong, Taiwan, Korea and Australia), Europe, Canada, the Middle East, Japan and India.

STRATEGIES FOR GLOBAL HOSPITALITY FIRMS OF THE 1990s

In an attempt to adjust to, and take advantage of, these trends in the global hospitality industry, major hospitality firms appear to have followed an overall strategy of concentrated growth. A concentrated growth strategy implies that a firm will direct its resources to the profitable growth of a single product, in a single market, with a single dominant technology.[9] In the hospitality industry there appear to be several forms of concentrated growth as practised by the major corporations. These forms are strategic alliances, franchising, management contracts, joint ventures and acquisition. All five of these strategic forms reflect the unique nature of the hospitality industry's almost pure competitive status. Each will now be discussed in turn.

(1) Strategic alliances

Strategic alliances or inter-company co-operative link-ups can, in our view, be categorized into two types. The first type of alliance occurs at the strategic level of organizations and is exemplified by the growth of consortia-type organizations such as Best Western and Consort. In the simplest form of this strategy, firms are tied together by a common reservation and marketing system. While the physical product may not be standardized, attempts are made by participating organizations to standardize quality. The mainstay of this type of strategic alliance has been the small independent operator. A more complex type of strategic alliance is best exemplified by the Russian Hotel Company affiliating with Movenpick (Swiss), SAS (Scandanavian), Park Lane (Hong Kong), Commonwealth Hospitality of Canada, and Pacific Rim Leisure (Australia) in order to better promote its product worldwide.

The second type of alliance takes place at an operational level and is best exemplified by the concept of cross-franchising, which is defined as the process of two organizations with different products but similar management styles or philosophies joining forces under one roof with the intention of reducing overheads and increasing profits. Three versions of cross-franchising can be seen: (a) where one franchisee becomes a franchisee of another concept; (b) where there is a combination of units offering signature items of units within the same company; and (c) where there is a combination of units featuring signature items of companies not in the same organization.[10]

The strength of strategic alliances as a form of concentrated growth lies in the fact that they can rapidly take advantage of the brand recognition of several multinational firms. This is especially important in today's operating environment, where it is becoming increasingly difficult to harness the capital for international expansion. Entering into an alliance of the type described here requires little capital but produces substantial benefits such as: (a) the spreading of marketing costs over a larger base; (b) a reduction in the potential problem of acquiring labour and management expertise; and (c) a minimization of the problems associated with any multicultural difference that might be encountered by an organization when seeking to expand into a new region of the world.

Strategic alliances as a form of concentrated growth are a direct response to some of the issues raised under the heading of non-conventional marketing in the first part of this chapter. In what is becoming an increasingly fierce, saturated and competitive operating environment, hospitality organizations are having to join forces to ensure they harness the necessary resources, both financial and non-financial, to penetrate the marketplace. We believe that the 1990s will see an increase in both the number and the type of strategic alliances in the hospitality industry. Alliances will no longer be confined to companies operating in the same industry, as in the case of Radisson. Rather, we will see an increase in strategic alliances between synergistically related organizations such as car rental organizations, life insurance companies, airlines and lodging corporations.

(2) Franchising

This is one of the most popular methods of growth for international hospitality organizations. In 1984, 67 restaurant franchisors operated 5,990 units in foreign countries, compared to 64 restaurant franchisors and 5,516 units a year earlier. Sales of franchised restaurants of all types reached almost $48 billion in 1985, up about 11 per cent on a year earlier, and rose by another 12 per cent to $54 billion in 1986. The story is similar in the international lodging industry. Hotel and motel franchisors represented 7,639 establishments in 1985, with receipts estimated to be around $14.3 billion. In 1986 these receipts rose by over 9 per cent, reaching almost $15.5 billion.[11]

The reasons for the popularity of franchising are numerous: (a) the franchisor seldom has to provide the capital; (b) the franchisor does not have to endure alone the various problems associated with regulations and licensing activities required by many nations; and (c) the franchisor does not have to engage in extensive site selection activities in relatively unknown territories. Despite these advantages of franchising as a form of growth, there are several concerns which the franchisor ought not to ignore. These include: (a) the selection and structure of organization of the franchise; (b) the nature of the relationship between the franchisor and the host government; and (c) the ability to control standards and operational procedures of the franchisee.

The franchise method implemented can be as simple as one firm with one unit licensed from a franchisor or as complex as master regional franchises. This is where one firm has the rights to expand the brand throughout an area or region of the world. Quality International has used the master regional franchise extensively in order to expand internationally, while Days Inns in India have used the concept in conjunction with the establishment of partnerships, thus necessitating little or no equity on their part.

We believe that the growth in franchising as a form of international expansion is directly related to the brand proliferation evident in the international hospitality industry. Many organizations believe that brand awareness, recognition and loyalty is the key to maintaining and increasing market share in this industry. By franchising, organizations are able effectively to implant their brand into any given location with few, if any, changes to the general concept. We are sceptical of this logic of brand proliferation for two reasons. First, it has yet to be empirically proven that brand loyalty exists in the context of the hospitality industry. Certainly, the current emphasis on discounting throughout the industry does little, in our view, to lend any weight to the argument that brand loyalty is an important issue in the hospitality industry. Second, we do not believe that the market share game is applicable to the hospitality industry. It was the Profit Impact on Market Strategy (PIMS) school which suggested that a 10 per cent increase in market share resulted in a 5 per cent increase in profit. When one considers that the five largest hospitality companies by turnover (Marriott, McDonald's, Trusthouse Forte, TW Services and Accor) hold only 1.01 per cent of world hospitality market share,[12] it is difficult to see how the PIMS market share law 'holds water' in the context of this industry.

According to J. Pearce (1990)

(3) Management contracts

Another popular form of international growth for hospitality organizations is the management contract method. A management contract is an agreement between a hotel owner and a hotel operating company, by which the owner employs the operator as an agent to assume full responsibility for the management of the property in a professional manner. As an agent, the operator pays, in the name of the owners, all property and operating expenses from the cash flow generated through operations, retains its management fees and remits cash flows, if any, to the owner. The owner provides the hotel land, building, furniture, furnishings, equipment and working capital, while assuming full legal and financial responsibility for the hotel. Hyatt International, Hilton International, Marriott, SARA, Nikko and Holiday are perhaps the best-known examples of management contract companies. Management contracts are also one of the common methods of expansion used by large multinational food service companies such as Marriott, Trusthouse Forte and ARA.

The greatest advantage of the management contract is that it allows rapid expansion and easy market penetration with little or no capital from the investor or developer of the asset itself. Occasionally the management firm will adopt an equity interest in the business. Some management firms have also engaged in the development of a property only to sell that property once it has been fully developed.

(4) Joint ventures

The joint venture has proved to be a popular growth vehicle for those firms with substantial financial resources. The development of both local and global partners has brought together such firms as SAS and Saison of Japan as they plan to spread their Intercontinental chain worldwide. Additional joint ventures include World International and Wharf Holding with their purchase of the Omni chain, and the Pritzker family of Chicago and William Hunt Holdings of Hong Kong with their purchase of the Southern Pacific Hotel Corporation of Australia.

The joint venture strategy has usually taken the form of a large real estate developer/holder and a hospitality/travel-related firm joining forces. Investors are usually global in nature and oriented to holding assets which can provide them with long-term appreciation. The joint venture differs from the other three strategies discussed, in that it concentrates upon low capital investment with most of the capital risk being shouldered by independent businesses which come together primarily for marketing purposes. J. Pearce (1990), p. 19.

(5) Acquisition

J. Pearce (1990) Points out that

The recent years have seen a tremendous growth in the number of acquisitions in the international hospitality industry.[13] The fact that the five largest hospitality organizations in the world control just over 1 per cent of hospitality market demand,[14] in conjunction with other market factors, has led to an increase in the number of acquisitions in the global hospitality industry. ~~In the period 1981–8 there were 325 merger and acquisition transactions in the hospitality industry with a total value of approximately $19,877 million. Of these 325, 74 per cent occurred in eating and drinking places, with the remaining 26 per cent occurring in the lodging sector of the industry.~~[15] Examples of the recent increase in acquisitions are Ladbroke Ltd's acquisition of Hilton International Co. from the Allegis Corporation in 1987 for $1.07 billion, and Grand Metropolitan's acquisition of Pillsbury and its Burger King subsidiary in 1989.

On the basis of historic and current trends in acquisition activity worldwide, and current and projected market conditions, we predict a continued growth in horizontal integration, geographical diversification and forward integration. In addition, we predict a decline in acquisition involving backward integration and conglomerate diversification. *(J. Pearce 1990, p-24)*

SUMMARY

With international expansion forming a substantial part of the strategic agenda of today's hospitality corporations, scanning the environment for trends that dictate strategic postures is a necessary and vital part of strategic hospitality management. This chapter has attempted to cover several trends that we believe should be taken into account by hospitality corporations when they are formulating and implementing their global strategies.

NOTES

1. Olsen, M.D., 'The importance of the environment to the food service and lodging manager', *Journal of Hospitality Education*, Winter 1980, pp. 35–45; Slattery, P.V.O., 'Hospitality organizations and their environment', *International Journal of Hospitality Management*, vol. 3, 1984, pp. 55–61; DeNoble, A.F. and Olsen, M.D., 'The food service industry environment: a market volatility analysis', *Florida International Review*, vol. 4, no. 2, 1984, pp. 89–100; West, J.J., 'Environmental scanning, industry structure and strategy making: concepts and research in the hospitality industry', unpublished monograph, Department of Hotel, Restaurant and Institutional Management, Virginia Polytechnic Institute and State University, Blacksburg, Va, 1987; Dev, C., 'Environmental uncertainty, business strategy and financial performance: a study of the lodging industry', doctoral dissertation, Department of Hotel, Restaurant and Institutional Management, Virginia Polytechnic Institute and State University, Blacksburg, Va, 1988; Crawford-Welch, S., 'An empirical examination of mature service environments and high performance strategies within those environments: the case of the lodging and restaurant industries', doctoral dissertation, Department of Hotel, Restaurant and Institutional Management, Virginia

Polytechnic Institute and State University, Blacksburg, Va, 1990.
2. Burnstein, D., *Yen! Japan's New Financial Empire and Its Threat to America*, Fawcett Columbine, New York, 1990.
3. Kiplinger, A.H., *The New American Boom*, Kiplinger Washington Editors, Washington DC, 1986.
4. Albrecht, K. and Zemke, R., *Service America! Doing Business in the New York Economy*, Dow Jones-Irwin, New York, 1987.
5. Heskett, J.L., *Managing in the Service Economy*, Harvard Business School Press, Boston, Mass., 1986.
6. Mills, P.K., *Managing Service Industries: Organizational Practices in a Postindustrial Economy*, Ballinger, Cambridge, Mass., 1986.
7. Kennedy, P., *The Rise and Fall of the Great Powers: Economic Change and Military Conflict from 1500 to 2000*, Vintage Books/Random House, New York, 1989.
8. Tsui, J.F., 'Lodging finance goes global', *Lodging Hospitality*, July 1989, p. 78.
9. Pearce, J.A. and Harvey, J.W., 'Concentrated growth strategies', *Academy of Management Executive*, vol. 4, no. 1, 1990, pp. 61–8.
10. Dee, S., 'The future of franchising', *Restaurant Business*, Jun. 1988, p. 24.
11. US Department of Commerce, *Franchising in the Economy 1984–1986*, US Government Printing Office, Washington DC, 1986.
12. Slattery, P.V.O., *International Hospitality Review*, Kleinwort Benson Securities, London, 1988.
13. Crawford-Welch, S. and Tse, E.C.Y., 'Mergers, acquisitions and alliances in the European hospitality industry', *International Journal of Contemporary Hospitality Management*, vol. 2, no. 1, 1990, pp. 10–16.
14. Slattery, op. cit.
15. Tse, E.C.Y., Olsen, M.D. and Crawford-Welch, S., 'An analysis of merger and acquisition activity in the hospitality industry for the period 1970–1988', *Hospitality Education and Research Journal*, vol. 13, no. 3, 1989, pp. 1–15.

Index